RADIO AND TELEVISION

A Selected, Annotated Bibliography

compiled by
William E. McCavitt

The Scarecrow Press, Inc.
Metuchen, N.J. & London
1978

Ref
Z
7221
.M23

Library of Congress Cataloging in Publication Data

McCavitt, William E., 1932-
  Radio and television.

  Includes index.
  1. Broadcasting—Bibliography. I. Title.
Z7221.M23 [PN1990.8]   016.38454   77-28665
ISBN 0-8108-1113-8

TABLE OF CONTENTS

269966

21. REFERENCES

PREFACE

This selected bibliography contains 1100 listings of books and other printed materials associated with all aspects of broadcasting. The listings include books spanning a time period from 1920 to 1976.

Various books and other materials provided or made available to me by publishers and other professional groups were very useful in the compilation of this book. The list of organizations that assisted in any way with the research included in this project is too long to include here; however, I do want to thank them for their assistance and encouragement.

The facilities of the Pattee Library at The Pennsylvania State University, located at University Park, and the Carlson Library at Clarion State College, Clarion, Pennsylvania, have been essential in pursuing this work.

Personal thanks are extended to Mr. Paul Redfern, my graduate assistant, who helped in the literature search, and to the Clarion State College Foundation for the financial support it gave to this undertaking.

I am grateful especially to Ms. Beverly Brooks who served as my research assistant, typist, and proofreader, as well as the motivating force behind this bibliography.

A special thanks to Dr. Christopher Sterling who saw the need for such a bibliography and provided the author with some of the material found in this book.

INTRODUCTION

The literature on radio and television broadcasting is larger than most people realize. From the beginning of radio broadcasting in the 1920s, an impressive number of solid studies as well as lighter materials has filled library bookshelves.

This volume is intended as a guide to over a half-century of broadcasting literature; it is a selection from the total literature available. Its major purpose is two-fold: 1) to guide institutional and personal collectors in the purchase of broadcasting books, and 2) to suggest what is still needed by showing what exists now.

This is not, of course, the first such effort although to the best of my knowledge it is the most recent. For earlier efforts, readers are directed to the bibliographies listed under Section 18.

To list virtually everything written on radio and television including all books and periodical articles, would take a multi-volume work even without any form of annotation. The most important limitation, then, is that this is a guide only to selected books on broadcasting.

The bibliography is subject-divided since it was felt that most readers, casual or research-minded, would prefer to have like titles grouped together for more ready comparison. Within the major categories are numerous sub-categories, but each listing of books is in alphabetical order by the author's last name. The major sections are:

1. Surveys: Broad reviews of most aspects of broadcasting. This is probably the best starting point for a casual reader interested in broadcasting today or in the past.

2. History: Included here are only those general volumes which intend to tell radio and/or television history in broad terms.

3. Regulation: Includes government and self-regulation studies.

4. Organization: Volumes that deal with or stress advertising, management, and other business-oriented features of radio-TV are found here.

5. Programming: Includes general reviews and histories as well as the many volumes devoted to specific types of radio/TV content.

6. Production: Most how-to-do-it books are found here.

7. Minorities: A small but growing area with new volumes coming out more in recent years.

8. Responsibility: Volumes that deal with the responsibility of broadcasting in broad terms.

9. Society: Studies with a point of view. Emphasis on studies of broadcast impact and how to improve the system and its parts.

10. Criticism: Studies of a generally critical nature are included here.

11. Public Broadcasting: Includes histories, criticisms, reviews, and how-to-do-it studies for public and instructional television.

12. Audience: Descriptions, preferences, studies on the audience, and impact of broadcasting on the audience are found here.

13. Cable Television: Studies of both general and specific natures on this type of broadcasting are found in this section.

14. Research: Research studies dealing with all aspects of broadcasting.

15. Broadcasting Careers: Includes career encouraging books.

16. International: Selective review of English-language works on other countries: system of broadcasting, international broadcasting, propaganda, and satellites.

17. Technical: Brief selection of technical and technical-related books.

18. Bibliographies: Includes previously printed broadcasting bibliographies.

19. Annuals: Listing of annual publications relating

to the broadcast field.

  20. <u>Periodicals</u>: An alphabetical listing of broadcast periodicals.

  21. <u>References</u>: Includes available broadcast references.

  Each entry has a reference number, full indicia on author(s), title, city and place of publication, date of last edition, reprint publisher if any, and number of pages. The annotation is intended to briefly describe the book's contents. The last thing in each entry is a listing of supplementary items (such as photographs, illustrations, bibliography, index) if they are provided.

  Below most sub-headings there is a listing of cross-reference numbers which also pertain to the topic. Essential bibliographic details are given in full for most entries. Others which could not be obtained but were felt to be significant enough to be included in this volume were used even though the bibliographic details are incomplete.

  This being a selected bibliography means that certain judgments had to be made by the compiler. Books that have been omitted were either not found during the literature search or were omitted deliberately.

  This book is out of date. Any bibliography is, by the nature of its production process. It is suggested that the book review sections of several periodicals are the best means of keeping this reference up to date until such time as a supplement and/or revision may appear.

1. SURVEYS

A. Radio

See also nos. 234, 736.

1 Aly, Bower and Gerald D. Shively, eds. A Debate Handbook on Radio Control and Operation, and Supplement. Norman: University of Oklahoma Press, 1933. 448 pp.

A two-volume compendium of articles, bibliography, views, and arguments for the year's college debate topic comparing U.S. and British methods of radio control. The 21 articles in the first volume are nearly all reprints, and are half devoted to the British system. The Supplement divides its 54 selections (all reprints) into international, American, and British sections. Articles and views on all sides of the question are included and virtually all topics in radio are touched upon. Bibliography and charts.

2 Arnheim, Rudolf (translated by Margaret Ludwig and Herbert Read). Radio. London: Faber & Faber, 1937 (reprinted by Arno Press, 1971). 296 pp.

Author deals with radio as sound and explores words and music as kinds of sound. He discusses direction and distance as an influencing factor in sound and refers in separate chapters to spatial resonance and sequence and juxtaposition in creating sound images. Other topics included in this 12 chapter review are comparison of radio and film techniques and effects, the art of announcing, the role of author and producer, the psychology of listening, a review of radio around the world, and a discussion of the prospects for television. Index and photographs.

3 Codel, Martin, ed. Radio and Its Future. New York: Harper & Bros., 1930 (reprinted by Arno Press, 1971). 349 pp.

1

Some 29 articles by prominent radio industry leaders explore all areas of radio (not just broadcasting),
including domestic and international broadcasting, maritime radio, radio and flying, radio amateurs, radio
and the military, the receiver market and set manufacture, radio regulation, a proposal for a communications commission, how radio works, short wave
radio, early television, etc. Valuable for its broad
scope showing development of broadcasting as part of
larger radio field. Index and photographs.

4   Federal Council of the Churches of Christ in America,
    Department of Research and Education. Broadcasting
    and the Public: A Case Study in Social Ethics. New
    York: Abingdon Press, 1938. 220 pp.
        A 13-chapter review of radio's role in American
    society, this book has discussions of radio's develop-
    ment, federal regulation (and comparison to control
    in other countries), organization of broadcasting, mo-
    nopoly in radio, advertising, entertainment, education-
    al radio, a long chapter on religious radio, broadcast-
    ing of controversial issues, and an international over-
    view of broadcasting. Bibliography, charts, glossary,
    and index.

5   Frost, S. E., Jr. Is American Radio Democratic?
    Chicago: University of Chicago Press, 1937. 234 pp.
        Discussion of the technology of radio, the four per-
    iods of federal radio regulation, the station owner and
    the structure of broadcasting, role of the advertiser,
    education on the air, the public role as audience, and
    a concluding chapter suggesting possible changes in
    broadcasting. Compares U.S. and foreign approaches
    to radio. Charts and index.

6   Gernsback, Hugo. Radio for All. Philadelphia: J. B.
    Lippincott Co., 1922. 292 pp.
        Not intended as a technical reference; written for
    the public at large who were not acquainted with radio.
    It mentions possible uses of radio in the future;
    makes interesting reading now that the future is here.
    Illustrations, index, and photographs.

7   Goldsmith, Alfred N. and Austin C. Lescarboura. This
    Thing Called Broadcasting: A Simple Tale of an Idea,
    an Experiment, a Mighty Industry, a Daily Habit, and
    a Basic Influence in Our Modern Civilization. New

York: Henry Holt, 1930.   362 pp.
A broad survey of the entire scope of radio.   The
25 chapters cover the rise of radio, technical basics,
role of announcer, networks, musical programs, radio
and politics, radio and women-farmers-churches, business of broadcasting, receivers as hobby and business,
breaking down social barriers, etc.   Charts and photographs.

8   Hayes, John S. and Horace J. Gardner.   Both Sides of
the Microphone: Training for the Radio.   Philadelphia: J. B. Lippincott Co. , 1938.   180 pp.
The first half discusses station operations, while
the second part consists of 14 short articles by as
many well-known radio personalities on radio programs
as perceived by listeners.   Aim of second part is to
show what listener should expect from radio.

9   Hettinger, Herman S. , ed.   "New Horizons in Radio,"
Annals of the American Academy of Political and
Social Science, Volume 213, January 1941 (reprinted
by Arno Press, 1971).   189 pp.
Directly descendent from the following Annals, this
compilation of 24 articles considers broadcasting as
a social force, current problems in radio, and coming
developments.   As with the Annals below, these
are of value as historical reference.   Charts and index.

10   Hettinger, Herman S. , ed.   "Radio: The Fifth Estate,"
Annals of the American Academy of Political and Social Science, Volume 177, January 1935 (reprinted by
Arno Press, 1971).   219 pp.
The second of the three Annals devoted to radio,
this volume concentrates on broadcasting.   A narrow-
er focus than the 1929 collection but directly compar-
able to the 1941 volume.   The first of three parts
considers broadcasting systems; the second, the service of broadcasting; and the third, some current
questions in radio.   Charts and index.

11   Hilliard, Robert L. , ed.   Radio Broadcasting: An Introduction to the Sound Medium.   2nd edition.   New
York: Hastings House Publishers, 1974.   312 pp.
This book is a basic text on principles and techniques of modern radio broadcasting.   In developing
this book on the "what" and "how-to" of radio, it was

4

decided to approximate the kind of information the
reader might receive if enrolled as a student at a
good university. Bibliography.

12 Landry, Robert J. This Fascinating Radio Business.
    Indianapolis: Bobbs-Merrill, 1946. 343 pp.
        An overview of radio as it stood just prior to the
    inception of network television. Coverage of history,
    organization, economics, technology, all types of
    program content, with some review of audience re-
    search and government regulation. Author was long-
    time radio editor and later general editor of Variety.
    Index and photographs.

13 Rose, Cornelia B. National Policy for Radio Broadcast-
    ing. New York: Harper & Bros., 1940 (reprinted
    by Arno Press, 1971). 289 pp.
        An examination of the technical structure of broad-
    casting, commercial structure, program content,
    freedom of the air, and a final three chapters at-
    tempting to rough out suggestions for a national policy.
    Bibliography, charts, glossary, and index.

14 Rothafel, Samuel L. and Raymond Francis Yates.
    Broadcasting: Its New Day. New York: Century
    Co., 1925 (reprinted by Arno Press, 1971). 316 pp.
        Probably the first popular discussion of radio's
    role and impact on American society. Covers drama,
    politics, education, international aspects, sports,
    religion, advertising, radio receivers, TV, jobs in
    radio, technical problems, and radio's likely future.
    Illustrations and photographs.

15 Siepmann, Charles. Radio's Second Chance. Boston:
    Atlantic-Little, Brown, 1946.
        A critical analysis of radio's strength and its
    weakness in the United States with a "plan for the
    future."

16 Stewart, Irwin, ed. "Radio," Annals of the American
    Academy of Political and Social Science, Supplement
    to Volume CXLII, March 1929 (reprinted by Arno
    Press, 1971). 107 pp.
        A collection of 16 articles surveying the use of
    radio in the broadest terms. This volume includes
    discussion of radio's development, broadcasting
    around the world, two discussions of federal radio

regulation, four articles on radio uses other than
broadcasting, and five articles on international radio
regulation and radio in the First World War.   Charts
and index.

17   Waller, Judith C.   Radio: The Fifth Estate.   2nd edition.   Boston: Houghton-Mifflin, 1950.   482 pp.
A director of public affairs for NBC wrote this
long-used college text covering structure of broadcasting, programming, public service shows, sales,
audience, publicity and program traffic, engineering,
and educational radio.   Little on impact of television.
Bibliography, charts, glossary, index, and photographs.

B.   Television

18   Brown, Les.   Televi$ion: The Business Behind the
Box.   New York: Harcourt, Brace, Jovanovich,
1971.   374 pp.
The dollar sign is really part of the title and a
major part of this network-oriented book which reviews events of television in 1970 to demonstrate
what a typical (or perhaps atypical) year is like.
The 15 chapters by the radio-TV editor of Variety
cover in an entertaining fashion such topics as network program development, specials, use of films,
ratings battles, advertising, summer replacement
shows, public service programs, etc., all the time
focusing on selected key individuals in decision-mak-
ing positions.   Index.

19   Bussell, Jan.   The Art of Television.   London: Faber
& Faber, 1952.   163 pp.
This book is written from personal experience as
a television producer, performer, and keen viewer.
The author's aim was to give a general picture to the
reader and to provide newcomers to the medium with
food for basic thought.   Charts, illustrations, index,
and photographs.

20   Cole, Barry G., ed.   Television: A Selection of Readings from TV Guide Magazine.   New York: Free
Press, 1970.   605 pp.
A collection of 79 articles from TV Guide in the
1960s, coverage here concentrates on programming,

censorship and control, the audience, effects, and a
review of coming changes in the medium, including
CATV and cassettes. Annotations to each main section bring the coverage up to date of publication. Index.

21 Dizard, Wilson P. Television: A World View. Syracuse, N. Y.: Syracuse University Press, 1966. 349
pp.
    The author's purpose in this work is to survey the
present condition and the future implications of the
development of television, with particular emphasis
on its effect on American world leadership. Bibliography, charts, index, and photographs.

22 Donner, Stanley, ed. The Future of Commercial Television, 1965-1975. Stanford, Calif.: Department of
Communications, Stanford University, 1965. 150 pp.
    A report of the Stanford TV Seminar sponsored by
TV Guide in which television industry leaders, advertising executives, and television advertisers met
to discuss problems of mutual interest and explore
problems of the future.

23 Dunlap, Orrin E., Jr. The Future of Television. 2nd
edition. New York: Harper & Bros., 1947. 194 pp.
    Though revised from the 1942 edition, this still
concentrates heavily on the potential of TV. The 12
chapters cover such topics as the technical and legal
development of TV, the role of TV in the home,
types of programs, effects on the motion picture industry and theaters, likely effect on radio, sports,
educational television, backstage data on TV production, and a brief technical review of the medium.
Index and photographs.

24 Floherty, John J. Television Story. 2nd edition.
Philadelphia: J. B. Lippincott Co., 1957. 160 pp.
    Aimed at high school readers, this is a basic re-
view of TV including comment on TV history, TV
news, the studio and its operation, business of TV,
advertising, color TV, etc. Glossary and photographs.

25 Friendly, Fred W. Due to Circumstances Beyond Our
Control. New York: Vintage Books, 1968. 339 pp.
    A first-person account of the television industry
by the former president of CBS News. Index.

26 Gable, Luther S. H.   The Miracle of Television.   Chi-
    cago: Wilcox & Follett Co. , 1948.
    This is a general overview of TV just as its post-
    war commercial growth was underway. Chapters deal
    with studio operations, programming, some technical
    background, and some coverage of fluorescent rocks
    on TV! Illustrations, index, and photographs.

27 Glick, Ira O. and Sidney J. Levy.   Living with Tele-
    vision.   Chicago: Aldine Publishing Co. , 1962.
    262 pp.
    This volume gives the reader an objective picture
    of what TV is today and what it is in the process of
    becoming. It is an exciting contribution to our body
    of knowledge about the meanings and functions of the
    symbol systems commonly shared by most Americans.
    Charts and index.

28 Hilliard, Robert L. , ed.   Understanding Television.
    New York: Hastings House Publishers, 1964. 254 pp.
    Six well-known educators present a basic under-
    standing of the major areas of television broadcasting.
    Bibliography, illustrations, index, and photography.

29 Hubbell, Richard.   Television Programming and Produc-
    tion.   3rd edition.   New York: Rinehart & Co. ,
    1956.   272 pp.
    The purposes of this book in text, photo, picture
    story, and diagram are to: 1) analyze and define the
    nature of television, 2) formulate basic theory for its
    development as an art, 3) demonstrate practical tech-
    niques for program production, 4) show how programs
    are created and produced, 5) show what is happening
    in television around the world, and 6) show some of
    the far-reaching effects of economics on programming
    and television growth.   Charts, illustrations, index,
    photographs.

30 Hutchinson, Thomas.   Here Is Television: Your Win-
    dow to the World.   3rd edition.   New York: Hastings
    House Publishers, 1950.   366 pp.
    An extensive review of television just as network
    operations were beginning to expand.   The 32 chapters
    include discussion of the tools of television, programs,
    and TV as a business.   Much of the book is stated as
    potential and is thus an interesting view of perspec-
    tives on the medium at the time.   Glossary, illustra-
    tions, photographs.

31 Kerby, Philip. The Victory of Television. New York:
      Harper & Bros., 1939. 120 pp.
         This 10-chapter review of TV in the late 1930s is
      a status report with discussions of the modern TV
      studio, lighting-music-accessories for production, the
      problem of TV's likely effect on movies, theater and
      the radio, the many kinds of programs, and two
      chapters on how the costs will be met. Brief review
      by NBC employee stresses the future. Glossary, in-
      dex, photographs.

32 Lee, Robert E. Television: The Revolutionary Industry.
      New York: Essential Books, 1944. 230 pp.
         A war-time examination of likely TV industry de-
      velopment in the post-war years, Lee examines the
      rise of television, asks who will pay the predicted
      high costs, reviews likely program types, looks at
      the relationship of TV to movies, discusses TV com-
      mercials, and problems in the way of TV develop-
      ment. Interesting to compare his predictions with
      what subsequently happened.

33 Lohr, Lenox R. Television Broadcasting: Production-
      Economics-Technique. New York: McGraw-Hill,
      1940. 274 pp.
         One of the earliest detailed views of television,
      this concentrates almost totally on the experience of
      NBC (of which the author was then president). Dis-
      cussion of early studio and remote operations and
      various types of programs aired in the late 1930s
      gives good viewpoint of TV status when approved for
      full-time commercial operation. Other chapters re-
      view role of the sponsor, legal aspects of TV, the
      problems of establishing networks, and basic econom-
      ic factors of operation. Charts, index, and photo-
      graphs.

34 Mayer, Martin. About Television. New York: Harper
      & Row, 1972. 434 pp.
         A well-researched 14-chapter review of television
      in the early seventies, Mayer's coverage includes a
      brief review of TV's development, audience research,
      time-selling, prime-time and daytime commercial
      programs and stars, children's programs, sports,
      network news, politics and TV, documentaries, local
      TV outlets and their programming, public television,
      the role of cable TV, etc. Index.

35 Opotowsky, Stan. TV: The Big Picture. New York:
   Collier Books, 1961. 285 pp.
   This is a broad-based overview of television reviewing industry development, package agency role, advertising, role of FCC and other government agencies,
   westerns, unions, TV journalism, public service programs, sports, pay television, TV around the world,
   a brief review of the quiz scandals, effects on radio,
   etc. Index.

36 Paul, Eugene. The Hungry Eye: An Inside Look at TV.
   New York: Ballantine Books, 1962. 285 pp.
   An informal but data-packed review of TV in the
   early sixties with two major parts: the first discusses the ways and means and the second concentrates on programs and personalities. Emphasis
   throughout is on organization of industry and its related parts, and the costs of television on the network level.

37 Porterfield, John and Kay Reynolds, eds. We Present
   Television. New York: W. W. Norton, 1940.
   298 pp.
   Eleven articles by as many contributors cover the
   techniques of TV, role of engineers, programming,
   the director, the actor, TV newsreels, TV on the
   West Coast, relationship of facsimile and FM to television, and how to finance the expected high costs.
   Interesting for its broad spectrum of viewpoints by
   different writers. Charts, glossary, and photographs.

38 Roe, Yale. The Television Dilemma: Search for a So-
   lution. New York: Hastings House Publishers, 1962.
   184 pp.
   A general discussion of the problems facing TV in
   America. Includes chapters on financing, educational
   TV, advertising and several sections concerning the
   author's views on responsibility and government regulation. Index.

39 Sharps, Wallace S. Commercial Television. London:
   Fountain Press, 1958. 496 pp.
   Treats both form and content of television. Discusses thoroughly the differences and similarities between television and motion picture production.
   Charts, glossary, illustrations, index, and photographs.

40   Shulman, Arthur and Roger Youman. The Television
        Years. New York: Popular Library, 1973. 322 pp.
           Essentially the same material as How Sweet It
        Was: Television, a Pictorial Commentary by the
        same authors, with some updating and rearranged by
        year rather than program type. Mainly pictures.
        Photographs.

41   Wilk, Max. The Golden Age of Television: Notes from
        the Survivors. New York: Delacorte Press, 1976.
        274 pp.
           A long-time television writer has combined a kind
        of professional memoir with interviews with early
        television stars and not-so-stars, to provide a feel-
        ing for the milieu of network-level live production
        values. Index and photographs.

42   Williams, Raymond. Television: Technology and Cul-
        tural Form. London: Fontana, 1974. 160 pp.
           Useful structural analysis of what television is and
        does, focusing on the effects of technology on content
        and impact.

43   Wylie, Max. Clear Channels: Television and the
        American People. New York: Funk & Wagnalls,
        1955. 408 pp.
           A program and effects-oriented review of the TV
        industry in the midst of its decade of growth, the
        book contains chapters on television and Congress,
        baseball, radio versus TV, cultural programs, ef-
        fects on children, three chapters on educational tele-
        vision, and three on the foibles of TV advertising.
        Index and photographs.

C.   General

See also nos. 203, 270, 813.

44   Abbot, Waldo and Richard L. Rider. Handbook of
        Broadcasting: The Fundamentals of Radio and Tele-
        vision. 4th edition. New York: McGraw-Hill, 1957.
        531 pp.
           This book has 29 chapters discussing technology
        of radio-TV, programming, announcing and speaking
        on the air, news programs, sports, talks and ad-
        dresses, public service, music, children's shows,

educational broadcasting, writing for broadcast, directing, sound effects, TV production and direction,
recording, advertising, radio-TV law, broadcasting
careers, etc. The list suggests the breadth of
coverage with emphasis on practical over theoretical
and critical. Bibliography, glossary, illustrations,
index, and photographs.

45 Chester, Giraud; Garnet R. Garrison; and Edgar E.
    Willis. Television and Radio. 4th edition. New
    York: Appleton-Century-Crofts, 1971. 613 pp.
    First 250 pages offer 15 chapters tracing growth
of broadcasting, programming, the FCC, networks,
stations and cable TV, advertisers and agencies,
audience, politics on the air, self-regulation, comparative systems and international broadcasting, educational radio-TV, and criticism. Second part of 15
chapters offers about 300 pages on all aspects of TV
and radio in the studio. Bibliography, charts, glossary, index, and photographs.

46 Crosby, John. Out of the Blue: A Book About Radio
    and Television. New York: Simon & Schuster,
    1952. 301 pp.
    Selections from the author's syndicated column,
"Radio and Television." Index.

47 Davison, W. Phillips; James Boylan; and Frederick T.
    C. Yu. Mass Media Systems and Effects. New
    York: Praeger, 1976. 245 pp.
    Has chapters on the age of media, contrasting
media systems, media sociology, and communication
channels. Bibliography, illustrations, and index.

48 DeFleur, Melvin L. and Sandra Ball-Rokeach. Theories
    of Mass Communication. 3rd edition. New York:
    David McKay, 1975. 185 pp.
    This work attempts to pull together a number of
theoretical ideas, some widely studied already and
some not well investigated, so as to give an organized indication of about where we are at present
in the development of theories of mass communication. Bibliography, charts, illustrations, and index.

49 Dexter, Lewis A. and David Manning White, eds.
    People, Society, and Mass Communications. New
    York: Free Press, 1964. 595 pp.

Twenty-eight articles combining the new and old
and concentrating on audience and effects with a
lengthy section on research methods and trends.
Bibliography and index.

50   Emery, Edwin; Phillip Ault; and Warren K. Agee. In-
     troduction to Mass Communications.   5th edition.
     New York: Harper & Row, 1976.   469 pp.
        Reviews each of the media separately. Good refe-
     rence book with an annotated bibliography which in-
     cludes books, periodicals, reports, and organizations.
     Bibliography, charts, and photographs.

51   Emery, Michael C. and Ted Curtis Smythe, eds.
     Readings in Mass Communication: Concepts and Is-
     sues in the Mass Media. 2nd edition. Dubuque,
     Iowa: William C. Brown, 1974.   562 pp.
        Offers an alternative, media-arranged table of
     contents to supplement regular organization: chang-
     ing concepts of media, revolution in media, and mul-
     tiplying media debates. Bibliography.

52   Ewbank, Henry L. and Sherman P. Lawton.   Broad-
     casting: Radio and Television. New York: Harper
     & Bros., 1952.   528 pp.
        One of the raft of college texts written for the
     post-war expansion of curricula in this area, this
     volume begins with several chapters of overview of
     broadcasting, then delves deeply into program types,
     directing the program, and evaluating it with audi-
     ence research.   Emphasis throughout is heavily on
     radio rather than TV. Bibliography, charts, index,
     and photographs.

53   Hammel, William M., ed.   The Popular Arts in Ameri-
     ca.   New York: Harcourt, Brace, Jovanovich, 1972.
     436 pp.
        A general media anthology which covers popular
     music as well as the major media.

54   Head, Sydney W.   Broadcasting in America: A Survey
     of Television and Radio.   3rd edition.   Boston:
     Houghton-Mifflin, 1976.   629 pp.
        Best single volume explaining American broadcast-
     ing, how it works, and how it got that way.   Up-
     dates the second edition which was released just four
     years ago. Bibliography.

55   Hellman, Hal.   Communications in the World of the Fu-
     ture.   New York: M. Evans & Co. , 1969.   201 pp.
        Story of communications from the distant past to
     the near future.   Everything is either actual or pos-
     sible.   Bibliography, index, and photographs.

56   Hixon, Richard F. , ed.   Mass Media: A Casebook.
     New York: Crowell, 1973.   285 pp.
        Twenty-three previously published essays dealing
     with the whole media spectrum.   Bibliography.

57   Holmgren, Rod and William Norton, eds.   The Mass
     Media Book.   Englewood Cliffs, N. J. : Prentice-Hall,
     1972.   421 pp.
        A general media anthology which is divided into
     sections on news and entertainment media.

58   Kingson, Walter K. ; Rome Cowgill; and Ralph Levy.
     Broadcasting Television and Radio.   New York:
     Prentice-Hall, 1955.   274 pp.
        A college text in three parts: radio-TV per-
     formance, writing and directing, and just over 100
     pages on broadcasting in general.   Bibliography, in-
     dex, photographs.

59   Lawton, Sherman P.   Introduction to Modern Broadcast-
     ing: A Manual for Students.   New York: Harper &
     Row, 1963.   157 pp.
        A workbook offering over 30 group and individual
     work projects.   Quite useful for those needing ideas
     and/or ready-made assignments.

60   Lawton, Sherman P.   The Modern Broadcaster: The
     Station Book.   New York: Harper & Bros. , 1961.
     351 pp.
        Designed for station employees and potential em-
     ployees, this volume is divided into two parts: your
     station, and jobs at broadcast stations.   Radio and
     TV are treated together and evenly throughout in this
     basic book.   Charts, glossary, index, and photo-
     graphs.

61   Lichty, Lawrence W. and Joseph M. Ripley, II, eds.
     American Broadcasting: Introduction and Analysis--
     Readings.   Madison, Wisc. : College Printing &
     Typing Co. , 1969.   778 pp.
        A massive collection of reprinted articles,

documents, trade publications, statistics, and tables
on the broadcasting industry. Some 25 pages on
world and international broadcasting, 158 on broadcasters and stations, programs, audience and audience
research, regulation, and goals-effects. Charts.

62   Lindsley, Charles Frederick. Radio and Television
      Communication. New York: McGraw-Hill, 1952.
      492 pp.
      A heavily radio-oriented text with the first 180
      pages covering an overview of the industry, a second
      part of 140 pages discussing principles and types of
      performance, about 60 pages on the probable effects
      and role of television, and some 60 pages of a "per-
      formance manual." Bibliography, charts, glossary,
      index, and photographs.

63   Lineberry, William P. , ed. Mass Communications.
      New York: H. W. Wilson Co. , 1969. 206 pp.
      Twenty-two articles from the 1960s generally ex-
      ploring media's role. Bibliography.

64   Lutz, William D. , ed. The Age of Communication.
      Pacific Palisades, Calif.: Goodyear Publishing Co. ,
      1974. 431 pp.
      This book has three parts: advertising, news
      media, and current culture. Illustrations.

65   Machlup, Fritz. The Production and Distribution of
      Knowledge in the United States. Princeton, N.J.:
      Princeton University Press, 1962. 416 pp.
      Includes chapters on historical and statistical sur-
      veys of printing and publishing, the stage and cinema,
      and radio and television. Charts and index.

66   Maddox, Brenda. Beyond Babel: New Directions in
      Communications. New York: Simon & Schuster,
      1972. 288 pp.
      Offers a highly literate discussion of satellites,
      cable television, and the changing role for telephones.

67   Martin, James. Future Developments in Telecommuni-
      cations. Englewood Cliffs, N.J.: Prentice-Hall,
      1971. 413 pp.
      Focuses on the next 30 years of telecommunica-
      tions developments and looks at picturephones, com-
      puters, cable television, lasers, home terminals,

satellites, and miniturization. Analyzes the public
policy aspects of all of these in a fascinating well-
illustrated view of where we are likely to be in the
next several decades. Illustrations.

68 Michaelis, Anthony R. From Semaphore to Satellite.
Geneva: International Telecommunications Union,
1965. 343 pp.
An excellent historical survey of the development
of international telecommunications (radio, telephone,
telegraph, and television) technology and law built
around a core discussion of the International Telecommunication Union's first century.

69 Newman, Joseph, ed. Wiring the World: The Explo-
sion in Communications. Washington, D.C.: U.S.
News and World Reports, 1971. 207 pp.
Discusses modern communications media including
pay television. Makes heavy use of maps and diagrams. Illustrations.

70 Phillips, David C.; John M. Grogan; and Earl H. Ryan.
Introduction to Radio and Television. New York:
Ronald Press Co., 1954. 423 pp.
As an introductory survey, this book is written for
those who want a general understanding of radio and
television, as well as for those who plan careers in
the two media. The book combines practical information on the production of broadcasts with background material on the development of the industry,
its organization, operations, and special problems.
Bibliography, charts, glossary, illustrations, index,
and photographs.

71 Pool, Ithiel de Sola and Wilbur Schramm, eds. Handbook of Communication. Chicago: Rand McNally,
1973. 1011 pp.
A review of the entire field of communications (including mass media) in 31 sections, each of which is
essentially an analysis of research and other literature to about 1970. Each article has a supplementary
bibliography, and items listed are discussed in the
article. Bibliography and index.

72 Rissover, Frederick and David G. Birch, eds. Mass
Media and the Popular Arts. New York: McGraw-
Hill, 1971. 348 pp.

Good illustrations including a color section. Offers readings on advertising, journalism, cartoons,
radio-television, photography and motion pictures,
pop literature and music, public education, etc. Illustrations.

73   Rosenberg, Bernard and David Manning White, eds.
     Mass Culture Revisited. New York: Van Nostrand/
     Reinhold, 1971. 473 pp.
         A collection of 29 articles with Rosenberg taking
     the elitist point of view and White countering with a
     defense of media's role.

74   Sandman, Peter; David Rubin; and David Sachsman.
     Media: An Introductory Analysis of American Mass
     Communications. 2nd edition. Englewood Cliffs,
     N.J.: Prentice-Hall, 1976. 483 pp.
         Coverage of wire services, books, film, and mi-
     norities and women in media have all been expanded
     in this edition.

75   Sandman, Peter M.; David M. Rubin; and David B.
     Sachsman, eds. Media Casebook: An Introductory
     Reader in American Mass Communications. Engle-
     wood Cliffs, N.J.: Prentice-Hall, 1972. 184 pp.
         A journalistically oriented review of the develop-
     ment, responsibility, structure, and news reporting
     of American media.

76   Schiller, Herbert I. Mass Communications and Ameri-
     can Empire. Boston: Beacon Press, 1971. 170 pp.
         The first comprehensive examination of domestic
     and international mass communications structure and
     policy in the United States. Index.

77   Schramm, Wilbur, ed. Mass Communications: A Book
     of Readings. Urbana: University of Illinois Press,
     1960. 695 pp.
         Though now dated, still offers one of the clearest
     selections of data for beginning students. Bibliogra-
     phy and charts.

78   Schramm, Wilbur and Donald F. Roberts, eds. The
     Process and Effects of Mass Communication. 2nd
     edition. Urbana: University of Illinois Press, 1971.
     997 pp.
         This edition of Process and Effects is a combination

of old classics, new classics, and reports on "state of the art" in important areas of communication study. It also looks at some of the new media that lie just over the horizon. Bibliography, charts, illustrations, and index.

79 Siepmann, Charles A. Radio, Television, and Society. New York: Oxford University Press, 1950. 410 pp.
A well-written analysis divided into two parts: systems of broadcasting, and social implications of radio and television. Bibliography, charts, and index.

80 Smythe, Ted C. and George A. Mastroianni, eds. Issues in Broadcasting: Radio, Television, and Cable. Palo Alto, Calif.: Mayfield Publishing, 1975. 430 pp.
Provides 38 previously published selections examining broadcasting, cable, public broadcasting, international and foreign systems, and new technology.

81 Stanley, Robert H., ed. The Broadcast Industry: An Examination of Major Issues. New York: Hastings House Publishers, 1975. 256 pp.
Presents the views of prominent broadcasting practitioners and teachers on the problems facing broadcasters today. Major issues included are: news management, license renewal, regulation, program content, public television, and economic questions. Index and photographs.

82 Steinberg, Charles S. The Communicative Arts: An Introduction to Mass Media. New York: Hastings House Publishers, 1970. 371 pp.
This is a concise historical and critical survey of every area of mass communication, from newspapers to magazines to comics to movies. Bibliography, charts, and index.

83 Stevens, John D. and William E. Porter, eds. The Rest of the Elephant: Perspectives on the Mass Media. Englewood Cliffs, N.J.: Prentice-Hall, 1973. 186 pp.
Sixteen previously published writings on mass media audiences, business aspects, behind-the-scenes views, and journalism. Bibliography and index.

84 Summers, Robert E. and Harrison B. Summers. Broad-
    casting and the Public. Belmont, Calif.: Wadsworth,
    1966. 402 pp.
        A solid 13-chapter overview of American broad-
    casting with chapters on comparative systems, broad-
    cast history, business of broadcasting, stations and
    networks, regulation, programs, audience measure-
    ment, criticism, news and education, etc. Charts,
    index, and photographs.

85 Tyler, Poyntz, ed. Television and Radio. New York:
    H. W. Wilson Co., 1961. 192 pp.
        A small collection of 24 articles and excerpts from
    the late 1950s dealing heavily with issues in television
    broadcasting. Emphasis is on role of broadcasting
    and its problems. Bibliography.

86 Valdes, Joan and Jeanne Crow, eds. The Media Reader.
    (Teacher's guide available.) Dayton, Ohio: Pflaum,
    1975. 390 pp.
        Contains more than 50 readings on all aspects of
    media, stressing content trends and including popular
    music and still photography subjects.

87 Willis, Edgar E. Foundations in Broadcasting: Radio
    and Television. New York: Oxford University Press,
    1951. 439 pp.
        A well-organized review of practical and theoreti-
    cal concepts, the first half covers broadcast history,
    station-network role, advertising, regulation, measur-
    ing audience and program, programs, educational
    radio, etc. The next two parts cover radio tech-
    niques and TV production. Bibliography, charts,
    glossary, index and photographs.

88 Wilmotte, Raymond M. Technological Boundaries of
    Television, 3 volumes, document number PB-241 599.
    Washington, D.C.: National Technical Information
    Service, U.S. Department of Commerce, 1975. Ap-
    proximately 100 pp.
        In this report to the FCC the author presents a
    carefully researched and reasoned set of predictions
    about what we can expect television to be and do dur-
    ing the next ten years and beyond. Illustrations and
    photographs.

2. HISTORY

A. Radio

See also nos. 287, 389, 1066, 1067.

89 Archer, Gleason L. Big Business and Radio. New
   York: American Historical Society, 1939 (reprinted
   by Arno Press, 1971). 503 pp.
       Though ostensibly a continuation of History of
   Radio, this volume's first half is devoted to new findings and restatements of the AT&T versus RCA liti-
   gation of the 1922-1926 period. The second half is
   essentially a history of RCA and especially NBC, with
   information on CBS and some individual stations.
   The story is taken to 1938 with emphasis on the major business organizations and their economic-political
   doings, rather than on radio as a social and entertaining force. Illustrations and index.

90 Archer, Gleason L. History of Radio to 1926. New
   York: American Historical Society, 1938 (reprinted
   by Arno Press, 1971). 421 pp.
       The most detailed history of wireless and radio
   developments to the mid-1920s, this volume was written primarily from the files of RCA and NBC. Emphasis is on economics and organization for international and domestic radio uses. Index and photographs.

91 Banning, William Peck. Commercial Broadcasting Pio-
   neer: The WEAF Experiment--1922-1926. Cambridge, Mass.: Harvard University Press, 1946.
   308 pp.
       The formative years of one of the most important
   stations in the country (now WNBC in New York),
   this detailed history relates the founding of then

19

WEAF by AT&T and early decisions on acceptance of
advertising by this, the first station to do so. Important for the key role WEAF played in early program and network trends, and as it led to first na-
tionwide NBC network. Charts, index, and photographs.

92 Barnouw, Erik. A Tower in Babel: A History of Broadcasting in the United States to 1933. Volume I. New
York: Oxford University Press, 1966. 344 pp.
The first of what is presently the definitive three-
volume history of American radio-TV, this concentrates on the pre-1920 development of radio, role of
radio in World War I, the growth of radio in the
1920s, details early growth of networks and regulation, and concludes with radio in the depression.
Bibliography, index, and photographs.

93 Chase, Francis, Jr. Sound and Fury: An Informal
History of Broadcasting. New York: Harper & Bros.,
1942. 303 pp.
The 16 chapters concentrate on program types
(talk shows, political radio, early news programs,
soap operas, drama, comedy shows, dance bands,
international propaganda) with a stress on personalities. First three chapters offer brief history of the
industry as a whole.

94 Dalton, W. M. The Story of Radio, 8 volumes. London: Adam Hilger Ltd., 1975-1976.

95 Dunlap, Orrin E., Jr. Radio Advertising. New York:
Harper & Bros., 1931. 383 pp.
A 27-chapter review of radio advertising practices,
this is a reorganized and expanded treatment of an
earlier (1929) book by the same author. Useful for
its information on radio versus print media, the radio
audience, research as to radio advertising effects,
advertising and the law, and a chapter on television
advertising prospects. Charts and index.

96 Evans, James F. Prairie Farmer and WLS: The Bur-
ridge D. Butler Years. Urbana: University of Illinois Press, 1969. 329 pp.
History of the pre-1948 development of a key midwestern (Chicago) clear-channel station and its agri-
cultural programming. View of a typical large station

operation with insight on radio's effects on farmers
and rural areas in the thirties and forties. Bibliography, index, and photographs.

97 Frost, S. E. , Jr. Education's Own Stations: The
    History of Broadcast Licenses Issued to Educational
    Institutions. Chicago: University of Chicago Press,
    1937 (reprinted by Arno Press, 1971). 500 pp.
    Short descriptions of all known attempts to es-
    tablish educational radio in the U.S. and brief his-
    tories of educational broadcasting in individual com-
    munities across the country are given by Frost who
    details as well the problems faced by such stations.

98 Gordon, George N. and Irving A. Falk. On-the-Spot
    Reporting: Radio Records History. New York:
    Julian Messner, 1967. 191 pp.
    The author covers the growth of broadcasting,
    its increasing impact on America's daily life, and
    its importance in times of war, national and inter-
    national crises, and political struggles. Photo-
    graphs.

99 Gray, G. J. Bits of Wireless History. Cincinnati:
    The Author, 1969. 60 pp.
    A very brief description of the collection of old
    radio apparatus in the author's museum in Ohio,
    this is a useful guide to the intricacies of early
    radio apparatus and its manufacture. Photographs.

100 Greenwood, Harold S. A Pictorial Album of Wireless
     and Radio: 1905-1928. Los Angeles: Floyd Cly-
     mer, 1961 (reissued as Vintage Radio with some
     revisions in 1972). 222 pp.
     A virtual picture encyclopedia of old radio re-
     ceivers, apparatus, and equipment from radio's first
     decades, interspersed with information on early
     radio manufacturing companies and some of their
     advertisements. Most items illustrated are labeled
     with manufacturer, date made, and original price.
     Good reference for old radio collectors, and of inte-
     rest for the general historian. Photographs.

101 Haslett, A. W. Radio Round the World. London:
     Cambridge University Press, 1934. 196 pp.
     A brief but solid analysis of radio's development
     and role in the early 1930s, seen from essentially

a technical point of view.   Chapters include the development of radio, the effect of sun and sky on
radio waves, future of radio and short-wave, television, radio and medicine, radio and safety at sea,
radio at war, and radio and weather forecasting.
Charts, illustrations, index, and photographs.

102   Herron, Edward A.   Miracle of the Air Waves: A
      History of Radio.   New York: Julian Messner,
      1969.   191 pp.
         This is the story of radio's amazing growth, the
      scientific pioneers who fostered it, and the trans-
      formation it has worked on the twentieth-century
      world.   Index and photographs.

103   Koch, Howard.   The Panic Broadcast: Portrait of an
      Event.   Boston: Little, Brown, 1970.   163 pp.
         The author, who wrote the radio script of H. G.
      Wells' The War of the Worlds has, through re-
      search, interviews, and personal recollections, re-
      created the terror and excitement of that night when
      America lost its wits.   Illustrations and photographs.

104   Low, A. M.   Wireless Possibilities.   New York:
      Dutton, 1924.   77 pp.
         Short, technical view of coming trends in and
      uses of radio, including television and radio at war.
      Illustrations.

105   Maclaurin, W. Rupert.   Invention and Innovation in the
      Radio Industry.   New York: Macmillan, 1949 (re-
      printed by Arno Press, 1971).   304 pp.
         Essentially a technical/business history of the
      radio manufacturing industry and key inventor/inno-
      vators in the 1900-1945 period.   There are lengthy
      discussions of the role of Marconi, Fessenden,
      DeForest; major electrical firms' role in radio; the
      struggle over radio-TV patents; industrial research
      into radio; government regulation and industrial re-
      search as factors in the rise of FM and television;
      etc.   Bibliography, charts, illustrations, index, and
      photographs.

106   McNicol, Donald.   Radio's Conquest of Space.   New
      York: Murray Hill Books, 1946 (reprinted by Arno
      Press, 1974).   374 pp.
         A solid technical history of radio from the late

1900s to the end of World War II, with a focus on
key inventions. Chapters trace the rise of key types
of equipment and discuss key inventors at some
length. An understanding of the basics of radio is
useful in approaching this work, written by a long-
time radio engineer. Illustrations, index, photographs.

107 The Radio Industry: The Story of Its Development.
Chicago: A. W. Shaw, 1928 (reprinted by Arno
Press, 1974). 330 pp.
Collection of 11 lectures given to a 1927-1928
graduate seminar by prominent radio leaders.
Topics covered include pre-World War I development, radio in the war, development of radio and
broadcasting since 1920, research and manufactur-
ing of radio equipment, radio law, early radio stations, first year of NBC, distribution and selling of
radio receivers, advertising on the air, etc. Valuable for contemporary view by then-leaders of the
industry. Charts, illustrations, index, and photographs.

108 Sanger, Elliott M. Rebel in Radio: The Story of
WQXR. New York: Hastings House Publishers,
1973. 190 pp.
In 1936 Elliott Sanger and his associate, John V.
L. Hogan, had the unique idea of combining the
science of radio with the ancient art of music, and
started what eight years later became the now-
famous WQXR, "The Radio Station of the New York
Times." Illustrations, index, and photographs.

109 Schubert, Paul. The Electric Word: The Rise of
Radio. New York: Macmillan, 1928 (reprinted by
Arno Press, 1971). 311 pp.
One of the best histories of the development of
radio covering the first three decades of this century. Part 1 details the era of maritime adoption
(from Marconi up to the war), part 2 examines
radio's role in World War I, and part 3 looks into
the rise of broadcasting.

110 Settel, Irving. A Pictorial History of Radio. 2nd edition. New York: Grosset & Dunlap, 1967. 192 pp.
A fairly solid text and picture review from
radio's technical pre-history (twenties through

sixties). Stress is on programs and personalities,
but there is good information on other aspects of
radio development (regulation, the audience, stations
and networks, etc.) in the text. Index and photographs.

111 Shurick, Edward P. J. The First Quarter-Century of
American Broadcasting. Kansas City, Mo.: Mid-
land Publishing Co., 1946. 374 pp.
Basically a collection of 16 annotated chronologies
reviewing various aspects of radio broadcasting history, this volume concentrates on local stations'
"firsts" in programming types. Index and photographs.

112 Slate, Sam J. and Joe Cook. It Sounds Impossible.
New York: Macmillan, 1963. 270 pp.
Written by two CBS executives, this is a very informal, light, and people-oriented review of radio
history. The stress is on specific programs and
stars in a readable episodic treatment of radio nos-
talgia. Index and photographs.

113 Summers, Harrison B., ed. A Thirty Year History of
Programs Carried on National Radio Networks in
the United States: 1926-56. Columbus: Ohio State
University Press, 1958 (reprinted by Arno Press,
1971). 218 pp.
An invaluable reference source, this book lists
by program type every known radio network show on
the air in January of each year from 1927 to 1956.
This book is the only reference of its kind in existence.

114 White, Llewellyn. The American Radio: A Report on
the Broadcasting Industry in the United States From
the Commission on Freedom of the Press. Chicago:
University of Chicago Press, 1947 (reprinted by
Arno Press, 1971). 255 pp.
One of the Hutchins Commission studies, this
volume is a good review of radio's first quarter
century with a stress on problems of regulation and
responsibility. Volume seeks out major trouble
spots for analysis, and suggests several methods of
improving radio.

B.   Television

See also nos. 342, 529, 1074.

115 Abramson, Albert. Electronic Motion Pictures: A
       History of the Television Camera. Berkeley: Uni-
       versity of California Press, 1955 (reprinted by Arno
       Press, 1974). 212 pp.
         An important and detailed technological history of
       the development of television from experiments with
       mechanical systems to introduction and development
       of the electronic system. Solid information pre-
       sented in a well-illustrated fashion ends up with the
       first decade of commercial operation (1946-1955),
       details changing methods of showing film on tele-
       vision, and describes the rise of color TV. Glos-
       sary, illustrations, index, and photographs.

116 Barnouw, Erik. Tube of Plenty: The Evolution of
       American Television. New York: Oxford University-
       sity Press, 1975. 518 pp.
         A single volume summation of the television ma-
       terial contained in Barnouw's three-volume history.
       Charts, illustrations, index, and photographs.

117 Blum, Daniel. A Pictorial History of Television.
       New York: Chilton, 1959 (reprinted by Bonanza,
       1965). 288 pp.
         The first such TV book, it is nearly all pictures
       with little or no text. Of interest for its informa-
       tion on specific episodes of programs in the first
       decade of TV networks. Index and photographs.

118 Dinsdale, A. A. First Principles of Television. New
       York: John Wiley, 1932 (reprinted by Arno Press,
       1971). 241 pp.
         One of the best early descriptions of the status
       of television in the early 1930s, this volume explains
       in illustrated detail the existing mechanical and elec-
       tronic systems of television in the U.S. and Europe.
       Extensive coverage is given to the systems of Baird,
       Jenkins, AT&T's work, then-current developments
       in Germany, England and America, and the many
       basic considerations in any TV system. Valuable
       for its detailed look at TV in its earliest years.
       Illustrations, index, and photographs.

119 Dunlap, Orrin E., Jr. The Outlook for Television.
     New York: Harper & Bros., 1932 (reprinted by
     Arno Press, 1971). 297 pp.
          Essentially a collection of the author's reporting
     in the New York Times in the 1920s and early 1930s
     on the developments taking place in experimental
     television. Good contemporary views on important
     experiments, announcements, developments, and
     trends. Each article is dated, thus showing when
     it was written and originally published. Illustra-
     tions, index, and photographs.

120 Everson, George. The Story of Television: The Life
     of Philo T. Farnsworth. New York: W. W. Nor-
     ton, 1949 (reprinted by Arno Press, 1974).

121 Felix, Edgar Herbert. Television: Its Methods and
     Uses. New York: McGraw-Hill, 1931. 272 pp.
          Book outlines development of existing television
     systems, the standards of performance essential for
     a commercial service, the limitations of existing
     methods, and the nature of the developments neces-
     sary to bring performance of public service quality.
     Illustrations, index, and photographs.

122 Fielding, Raymond, ed. A Technological History of
     Motion Pictures and Television. Berkeley: Univer-
     sity of California Press, 1967. 255 pp.
          A collection of disconnected articles of varying
     authoritativeness and varying dependability.

123 Hubbell, Richard. 4000 Years of Television. New
     York: Putnam, 1942. 256 pp.
          A light and informal history of television. Es-
     sentially its technical development but with business
     highlights as well, up to the start of World War II.
     Most of the work is devoted to the developments of
     CBS and RCA in the 1925-1940 period. Glossary,
     illustrations, and index.

124 Metz, Robert. CBS: Reflections in a Bloodshot Eye.
     Chicago: Playboy Press, 1975. 428 pp.
          Offers a somewhat episodic history of CBS.
     Stresses people and programming; also offers fas-
     cinating behind-the-scenes content.

125 Settel, Irving and William Laas. A Pictorial History

of Television. New York: Grosset & Dunlap, 1969.
209 pp.
Though stressing programs and personalities like
the matching volume on radio, this volume contains
good material on TV's development technologically
and refers to important non-program events as well.
Index and photographs.

126 Waldrop, Frank and Joseph Borkin. Television: A
Struggle for Power. New York: Morrow, 1938
(reprinted by Arno Press, 1971). 299 pp.
A critical study of the attempt of big business to
monopolize the development and exploitation of then-
new television broadcasting. Detailed discussion of
the patent problem, corporate contracts, the role
of government regulation, etc. Provides a good
business history of TV to 1938. Bibliography and
index.

127 Yates, Raymond F. New Television: The Magic
Screen. New York: Didier, 1948. 175 pp.
An informal technical history of television from
the earliest forebears to commercial operations.
Illustrations and photographs.

C.   Biographies and Autobiographies

See also nos. 373, 392.

128 de Forest, Lee. Father of Radio. Chicago: Wilcox
& Follett Co. , 1950. 502 pp.
The autobiography of the inventor of the three-
element tube or triode (audion) in 1906-1907 which
allowed for amplification and better detection of
radio signals than ever before. After 1930, and a
series of disastrous business deals, de Forest
worked almost full time on film sound projects.
Illustrations, index, and photographs.

129 Dunlap, Orrin E. , Jr. Marconi: The Man and His
Wireless. Revised edition. New York: Macmillan,
1938 (reprinted by Arno Press, 1971). 362 pp.
This is the story of Marconi--of his ingenuity.
The emphasis is on the man's work and on his per-
sonality. Index and photographs.

130   Dunlap, Orrin E. , Jr.   Radio's 100 Men of Science.
      New York: Harper, 1944.   294 pp.
         A useful reference collection of short two-three
      page biographies of technical pioneers in the devel-
      opment of radio and television, gathered by the
      former radio editor of the New York Times.   The
      biographies are arranged chronologically by birth
      date from key people of the 1600s and 1700s up to
      contemporaries of the 1930s and 1940s.   Index and
      photographs.

131   Field, Charles K.   The Story of Cheerio by Himself.
      Garden City, N. Y. :   Garden City Publishing Co. ,
      1936.   382 pp.
         Autobiography of the host of a long-running net-
      work inspirational program, mainly devoted to the
      program and its effect.   Photographs.

132   Husing, Ted.   Ten Years Before the Mike.   New York:
      Farrar & Rinehart, 1935.

133   Jolly, W. P.   Marconi.   New York: Stein & Day,
      1972.   292 pp.
         The latest full-length biography of the early in-
      ventor-innovator, this is perhaps the most objective
      view of the man now available in English.   Written
      essentially from primary sources, Jolly reviews the
      man and his invention, giving much attention to the
      rise and role of radio and the Marconi Company.
      Bibliography, index, and photographs.

134   Kaltenborn, H. V.   Fifty Fabulous Years.   New York:
      Putnam, 1950.

135   Kendrick, Alexander.   Prime Time: The Life of Ed-
      ward R. Murrow.   Boston: Little, Brown, 1969.
      548 pp.
         Traces the life of one of America's outstanding
      newsmen.   Intriguing chronicle of one man's influ-
      ence on the development of broadcast news.   Bibli-
      ography, index, and photographs.

136   Lessing, Lawrence.   Man of High Fidelity: Edwin
      Howard Armstrong.   Philadelphia: J. B. Lippin-
      cott Co. , 1956 (reissued in a somewhat expanded
      form by Bantam Books, 1969).   320 pp.
         A sympathetic biography of the inventor of the

regenerative, superheterodyne, and frequency modulation radio circuits, with major emphasis on the inventor's all-consuming passion--the frustrating early development of FM radio which eventually drove Armstrong to his suicide in 1954. The paperback revision contains valuable added information on the end of the patent wars fought by the Armstrong estate against RCA and other firms, and describes the eventual rebirth of FM broadcasting in the 1960s. Bibliography, illustrations, index, and photographs.

137   Lyons, Eugene. David Sarnoff: A Biography. New York: Harper & Row, 1966. 372 pp.
    The only book-length treatment of the long-time guiding light of RCA, this is an admiring book which tends to overlook low points and faults. Provides fascinating reading on the rise of Sarnoff from immigrant to early wireless operator, to initial work with American Marconi, to his rise within RCA. Much of the volume is a history of both RCA and the radio-television media as well, with a stress on the technological developments Sarnoff championed. Index and photographs.

138   Marconi, Degna. My Father, Marconi. New York: McGraw-Hill, 1962. 320 pp.
    An interesting look into the life of one of the pioneers in mass communications. Discusses the man as a father and a scientist. Index and photographs.

139   Mugglebee, Ruth. Father Coughlin, the Radio Priest. New York: Garden City Publishing Co., 1933.
    A very sympathetic biography of Michigan's radio preacher.

140   Spivak, John L. Shrine of the Silver Dollar. New York: Modern Age Books, 1940. 180 pp.
    A critical polemic against Father Charles Coughlin, this book is heavily based on documents showing his financial manipulations made possible by large donations to his radio speeches. There is a good deal of information on the administration and operation of the "Shrine of the Little Flower," as well as excerpts and information on the radio programs themselves.

141   Stern, Bill. The Taste of Ashes: An Autobiography.
      New York: Holt, 1959.

D.   General

See also nos. 160, 194, 269, 295, 349, 352, 568, 671, 746,
750, 803, 840, 844, 863, 1087, 1090.

142   Barber, Red. The Broadcasters. New York: Dial
      Press, 1970. 271 pp.
          Good historical report on sports in broadcasting,
      baseball in particular. Humorous account of early
      days of sportscasting of which the author was a
      part. Illustrations.

143   Barnouw, Erik. The Golden Web: A History of Broad-
      casting in the United States 1933-1953. Volume 2.
      New York: Oxford University Press, 1968. 391 pp.
          Second of three volumes, this book concentrates
      on the major broadcasting networks and includes de-
      tailed discussion of the coming of the New Deal and
      the 1934 Act, news and politics on the air, the
      "golden age of radio" in the late 1930s and war
      years, radio in the second war, post-war confusion
      as TV and FM grew with AM, blacklisting, and the
      early growth of TV stations and programs. Bibli-
      ography, index, and photographs.

144   Barnouw, Erik. The Image Empire: A History of
      Broadcasting in the United States from 1953.
      Volume III. New York: Oxford University Press,
      1970. 396 pp.
          One of three volumes on the history of broadcast-
      ing. The Image Empire begins when television was
      just becoming a dominant force in our nation. A
      chronicle of events in the field of broadcasting from
      1953 to 1969. Bibliography, index, and photo-
      graphs.

145   Barnouw, Erik. Mass Communication: Television,
      Radio, Film, Press; The Media and Their Practice
      in the United States of America. New York: Rine-
      hart & Co., 1956. 280 pp.
          Good reference on the history of mass communi-
      cations up to publishing date. Offers sections on
      psychology of mass communications and the sponsors

of mass communications.   Bibliography, illustrations, and index.

146 Codding, George A.   The International Telecommunication Union: An Experiment in International Coopera-
tion.   Leiden: Brill, 1952 (reprinted by Arno Press,
1972).   505 pp.
    This volume is a standard and definitive history
of the International Telecommunication Union from
its formation in 1865.   The volume covers world
regulation of telegraph, telephone, cable, radio, and
television communications.   Bibliography and index.

147 Dunlap, Orrin E. , Jr.   Communications in Space:
From Marconi to Man on the Moon.   3rd edition.
New York: Harper & Row, 1970.   338 pp.
    The book begins with the discovery of electro-
magnetic waves and the electron, advancing with
radio, television, and radar through unmanned
probes and the earliest space flights of Alan Shepard
and Yuri Gegarin, to the very latest in manned and
unmanned space exploration and research.   Illustrations, index, and photographs.

148 Dunlap, Orrin E. , Jr.   Dunlap's Radio & Television
Almanac: Men, Events, Inventions and Dates That
Made History in Electronics from the Dawn of Elec-
tricity to Radar and Television.   New York: Harper & Bros. , 1951.   211 pp.
    The title pretty well sums up this chronology as-
sembled by long-time New York Times radio writer
who later worked for RCA.   Chronology is divided
into eight major periods and is supplemented by
lists of FRC and FCC members and presidents of
major trade organizations.   Index and photographs.

149 Fabre, Maurice.   A History of Communications.   New
York: Hawthorn Books, 1963.   112 pp.
    Traces human communications from drawings on
the walls of caves to modern satellite communication systems.   Illustrations and photographs.

150 Farrar, Ronald T. and John D. Stevens, eds.   Mass
Media and the National Experience: Essays in Communications History.   New York: Harper & Row,
1971.   196 pp.
    Offers 11 original essays on problems in commu-
nications history.

151 Galloway, Jonathan F. The Politics and Technology of
     Satellite Communications. Lexington, Mass.: Lex-
     ington/Heath, 1972. 247 pp.
         Provides a detailed history of space communica-
     tion and the organizations built up around that pro-
     cess. The author analyzes Comsat and Intelsat,
     their organizational problems, and their likely pros-
     pects.

152 Green, Abel and Joe Laurie, Jr. Show Biz: "Variety"
     from Vaude to Video. New York: Holt, 1951 (re-
     printed by Kennikat Press, 1971).

153 Gross, Ben. I Looked and I Listened: Informal Recol-
     lections of Radio and TV. New York: Random
     House, 1954 (reprinted with additional 24 pages by
     Arlington House, 1970). 373 pp.
         A personal view of highlights by the long-time
     radio-TV editor of the New York Daily News.
     Heavy concentration on radio era, and main empha-
     sis is on people and programs. Index and photo-
     graphs.

154 Mitchell, Curtis. Cavalcade of Broadcasting. Chicago:
     Follett Publishing Co., 1970. 254 pp.
         Official NAB-backed picture history of radio and
     television is aimed at high school and junior college
     level. While suffering from oversimplification and
     numerous errors of fact, book still offers adequate
     overview of first half-century of radio-TV with
     emphasis on people, programs, and events rather
     than trends and analysis. Photographs.

155 Sarnoff, David. Looking Ahead: The Papers of David
     Sarnoff. New York: McGraw-Hill, 1968. 313 pp.
         Selections from the public and private writings
     of the long-time head of RCA are collected under
     headings of wireless communications (1914-1947),
     radio broadcasting (1915-1947), black and white TV
     (1923-1954), color TV (1930-1965), the communica-
     tions revolution (1948-1965), and a final general sec-
     tion on science and technology in human affairs
     (1926-1967). All are based on (and carefully anno-
     tated from) the extensive collection at the Sarnoff
     Library at Princeton, N. J. Index and photographs.

156 Schmeckebier, Laurence F. The Federal Radio

Commission: Its History, Activities and Organization. Washington, D. C. : Brookings Institute, 1932
(reprinted by Arno Press, 1976).

157   Sobel, Robert. The Manipulators: America in the
      Media Age. New York: Doubleday, 1976. 458 pp.
      Traces the rise and development of American
newspapers, motion pictures, radio, and television
and their effects on American life in general.

158   Tebbel, John. The Media in America. New York:
      Crowell, 1975. 422 pp.
      Covers a vast amount of data in limited space.
The book deals with broadcasting in only 20 pages
and does not cover film at all. As a history of
books, magazines, and newspapers the study is of
value.

159   Thomas, Lowell. Magic Dials: The Story of Radio
      and TV. New York: Polygraphic Co. , 1939.
      142 pp.
      One of radio's oldest newsmen tells the story of
broadcasting from Franklin's kite to the start of
World War II. Illustrations.

3. REGULATION

A. FCC

See also nos. 182, 192, 196, 207, 228, 266, 365, 372, 512, 671, 884, 913, 1021, 1022, 1023, 1024, 1025, 1035, 1083, 1087.

160   Bunce, Richard. Television in the Corporate Interest. New York: Praeger, 1976. 160 pp.
      Examines the history of FCC policy making, the regulatory doctrine of business pluralism, the political economy of the corporations which control most of American broadcasting, expansion and diversification among broadcasting corporations, and the effect of all of these upon actual programming and freedom of expression in broadcasting.

161   Emery, Walter B. Broadcasting and Government: Responsibilities and Regulations. East Lansing: Michigan State University Press, 1961. 482 pp.
      This book is mainly concerned with the FCC and its control of broadcasting. The work is divided into sections covering creation of the American system of broadcasting, powers of the FCC, the broadcast spectrum, regulation, and current problems of regulation. Bibliography, charts, and index.

162   Erickson, Don V. Armstrong's Fight for FM Broadcasting: One Man vs. Big Business and Bureaucracy. University: University of Alabama Press, 1974. 226 pp.
      A hardhitting expose of collaboration between the FCC and the broadcasting lobby. The author charges, and documents the charges, that the FCC has protected the industry instead of regulating it. Erickson fully details circumstances that involved RCA

34

and that implicated the FCC.   Bibliography, charts,
and index.

163   Federal Communications Commission.   Report on
      Chain Broadcasting.   Washington, D. C. :   Govern-
      ment Printing Office, 1941 (reprinted by Arno Press,
      1974).
           This is the report of a two-year investigation of
      the role, history, and operations of CBS, NBC, and
      Mutual up to 1940.

164   Grundfest, Joseph A.   Citizen Participation in Broad-
      cast Licensing Before the FCC.   Santa Monica,
      Calif. :   Rand Corp. , 1976.   129 pp.
           Explains developments in the past and suggests
      improvements for the future role of the public in
      the often complicated legal proceedings in Washing-
      ton.

165   Jennings, Ralph M.   Guide to Understanding Broadcast
      License Applications and Other FCC Forms.   New
      York: Office of Communications, United Church of
      Christ, 1972.   130 pp.
           Offers a step-by-step guide to the intricacies of
      FCC forms in a fashion useful for management stu-
      dents and managers alike.   There is careful explana-
      tion of all the things requested in the major broad-
      cast application forms.

166   Jennings, Ralph M. and Veronica M. Jefferson.   Tele-
      vision Station Employment Practices, 1975:   The
      Status of Minorities and Women.   New York: Of-
      fice of Communications, United Church of Christ,
      1976.
           This is the fourth in an annual series of statisti-
      cal reports based on FCC-gathered data.   The bot-
      tom line conclusion of the authors is that concern
      about, and therefore action on hiring of minorities
      and women is decreasing, especially compared to
      the gains of the early 1970s.

167   Jones, William K.   Cases and Materials on Electronic
      Mass Media: Radio, Television and Cable.   Mine-
      ola, N. Y. :   Foundation Press, 1976.   474 pp.
           Focuses on the regulation of radio, television
      and cable by the FCC in accordance with enabling
      federal legislation and subject to judicial review in
      the federal courts.   Charts.

168   Minow, Newton N.   Equal Time: The Private Broad-
      caster and the Public Interest.   New York: Athen-
      eum, 1964.   316 pp.
         A personal account of Mr. Minow's activities as
      chairman of the FCC during the administration of
      President John Kennedy.   Written to explain and
      justify his ideas.   Index.

169   Office of Telecommunications Policy.   The Radio Fre-
      quency Spectrum: United States Use and Manage-
      ment.   Washington, D. C. :   O. T. P. , 1973.   Ap-
      proximately 200 pp.
         Gives clear illustrated discussion of the technol-
      ogy, economics, and politics (national and interna-
      tional) behind regulation of the radio frequency spec-
      trum, the basis for nearly all broadcast regulation.
      Illustrations.

170   Rivkin, Steven R.   Cable Television: A Guide to Fede-
      ral Regulation.   New York: Crane, Russak, 1974.
      343 pp.
         Last of the key 1973 Rand Corporation cable re-
      ports.

171   Vainowski, Robert.   In Our View.   Belmont, Calif. :
      Tresgatos Enterprises, 1976.   174 pp.
         A practical manual stressing the latest version
      of the FCC's ascertainment rules and primer.
      Index.

B.   Self-Regulation

See also nos. 344, 509, 1040.

172   Linton, Bruce A.   Self-Regulation in Broadcasting: A
      Three-Part College-Level Study Guide.   Washington,
      D. C. : National Association of Broadcasters, 1967.

173   National Association of Broadcasters.   Radio Code.
      Washington, D. C. : NAB, 1976.   31 pp.
         Code set up by NAB supposedly to guide member
      stations in self-regulation.   See also The Television
      Code.   Index.

174   National Association of Broadcasters.   The Television
      Code.   Washington, D. C. : NAB, 1976.   38 pp.

Code set up by NAB supposedly to guide member stations in self-regulation.   See also Radio Code. Index.

C.   Censorship

See also nos. 202, 285, 335, 515, 521, 551.

175 Brindze, Ruth.   Not to Be Broadcast: The Truth About the Radio.   New York: Vanguard Press, 1937.   310 pp.
A study of censorship on the air which focuses on the program control of networks and major broad-casters.   The 13 chapters include discussion of the broadcast system, role of advertisers as means of support and occasional suppression of programs, program control by the FCC, Henry Ford's program of commentary, the press-radio war, and many ex-amples of specific censorship by all of these parties.

176 Phelan, John, ed.   Communications Control: Readings in the Motives and Structures of Censorship.   New York: Sheed & Ward, 1969.   238 pp.
A Jesuit priest's considered viewpoint on the role of censorship, providing ten interesting articles on a theoretical plane.

177 Summers, Harrison B. , ed.   Radio Censorship.   New York: Arno Press, 1971.   302 pp.
A collection of excerpts reprinted from both articles and books dealing with all aspects of radio broadcasting content control and including a brief bibliography of further readings.   Bibliography.

D.   Program Control

See nos. 316, 335, 383, 505, 509.

E.   Fairness

See also nos. 186, 207, 518, 519, 663.

178 Friendly, Fred W.   The Good Guys, the Bad Guys, and the First Amendment: Free Speech vs.

Fairness in Broadcasting. New York: Random
House, 1976. 268 pp.
   Well-written narrative which wends its way down
paths legal and political, with many fascinating personalities along the path. Bibliography and index.

179 Geller, Henry. The Fairness Doctrine in Broadcasting:
     Problems and Suggested Courses of Action. Santa
     Monica, Calif.: Rand Corp., 1973.

F. Copyright

180 Ashley, Paul P. Say It Safely: Legal Limits in Pub-
     lishing, Radio, and Television. 5th edition. Seattle:
     University of Washington Press, 1976. 238 pp.
        The primary concern of this book throughout is
     not with how to secure a copyright, or deal with it
     as a proprietor, but rather with how to identify vio-
     lations of the rights of the copyright holder. The
     fifth edition is revised and enlarged, incorporating
     the results of recent court decisions and illustrating
     them with dozens of examples. Index.

181 Radio Corporation of America. Before the Federal
     Communications Commission. New York: RCA,
     1953. 697 pp.
        Petition of Radio Corporation of America and
     National Broadcasting Company, Inc. for approval
     of color standards for the RCA color television sys-
     tem. Charts, illustrations, index, and photographs.

G. General

See also nos. 38, 114, 156, 251, 272, 324, 398, 448, 506,
507, 508, 510, 511, 514, 522, 568, 576, 590, 657, 770,
809, 815, 816, 835, 858, 889.

182 Ashmore, Harry S. Fear in the Air: Broadcasting
     and the First Amendment--The Anatomy of a Consti-
     tutional Crisis. New York: W. W. Norton, 1973.
     180 pp.
        This book traces the alterations of First Amend-
     ment theory under the impact of licensed broadcast-
     ing; defines the new issues arising out of the presi-
     dential challenge to journalism's historic adversary

role, and the rising populist demand for right of access to communications channels; spells out the in-
adequacy of formal regulation by the FCC, and of
self-regulation bounded only by marketplace conside-
rations; and recounts the stormy effort to augment
commercial broadcasting with public service network.

183 Baer, Walter S.; Henry Geller; and Joseph A. Gund-
       fest. Newspaper-Television Station Cross-Ownership:
       Options for Federal Action. Santa Monica, Calif.:
       Rand Corp., 1974.

184 Borchardt, Kirk. Structure and Performance of the
       U.S. Communications Industry: Government Regula-
       tion and Company Planning. Cambridge, Mass.:
       Harvard University Graduate School of Business,
       1969. 180 pp.
       Discusses the economic basis for public policy in
       communications, the relationship between different
       kinds of communication entities, development of new
       media competition, etc. Index.

185 Cherington, Paul W.; Leon V. Hirsch; and Robert
       Brandwein, eds. Television Station Ownership: A
       Case Study of Federal Agency Regulation. New
       York: Hastings House Publishers, 1971. 304 pp.
       Essentially a reprinting of a private 1966 re-
       search study purporting to show that multiple own-
       ership of television stations is not such a bad thing,
       in that multiple owners offer more diversity of pro-
       gramming and offer no economic threat to inde-
       pendent operations.

186 Chester, Edward. Radio, Television, and American
       Politics. New York: Sheed & Ward, 1969. 342 pp.
       Represents the first comprehensive attempt to
       answer such questions as: how does Section 315 dif-
       fer from the Fairness Doctrine?, what types of
       ideas have censors most often barred from the air-
       waves?, how has Congress attempted to regulate
       the broadcasting industry?, and many more. Bib-
       liography and index.

187 Clark, David G. and Earl R. Hutchinson, eds. Mass
       Media and the Law: Freedom and Restraint. New
       York: Wiley/Interscience, 1970. 461 pp.
       A collection of 40 articles illustrating both the

protective and the restrictive influences of legal
process upon free expression.   Bibliography.

188   De Vol, Kenneth, ed.   Mass Media and the Supreme
      Court: The Legacy of the Warren Years.   2nd edi-
      tion.   New York: Hastings House Publishers, 1976.
      400 pp.
           In this newly revised and updated edition, major
      cases and selected reprints of important articles
      from leading law journals about obscenity, censor-
      ship, rights of privacy, and other First Amendment
      problems are included.   Glossary and index.

189   Francois, William E.   Mass Media Law and Regulation.
      Columbus, Ohio: Grid, 1975.   470 pp.
           Contains authoritative, documented and readable
      presentations on the major areas where law and the
      mass media confront one another.   Charts, glossary,
      and index.

190   Franklin, Marc A.   Communications Law: Cases and
      Materials.   Mineola, N.Y.: Foundation Press,
      1976.
           The first course book for law teachers and stu-
      dents focusing on the legal problems of mass media
      intended exclusively for use in law schools.

191   Gillmor, Donald M. and Jerome A. Barron.   Mass
      Communication Law: Cases and Comment.   2nd
      edition.   St. Paul, Minn.: West Publishing Co.,
      1974.
           A must for the serious student of communications
      law.   Its collection of cases, materials, and thought
      provoking notes from the editors is simply invalu-
      able.

192   Green, Mark J., ed.   The Monopoly Makers: Ralph
      Nader's Study Group Report on Regulation and Com-
      petition.   New York: Grossman, 1973.   400 pp.
           This book shows how, in industry after industry,
      agencies of the federal government ignore economic
      competition in order to become, both actively and
      passively, the makers of monopoly.   The first sec-
      tion deals with the FCC and AT&T.   Bibliography
      and index.

193   Herring, James M. and Gerald C. Gross.   Telecom-
      munications: Economics and Regulation.   New York:

Arno Press, 1936.

Written by an economist and a former staff member of the FCC, this work is extremely valuable today because of its detailed coverage of the organization and development of many key precepts still considered basic to the economic regulation of the electronic media. The authors write extensively about
the interrelationship of economic and regulatory aspects of public policy and provide an historical overview as well as a close look at regulatory machinery
and its functions in the 1930s. Their book is well-
documented and includes appendices with several key
legislative acts and treaties.

194   Kittross, John M. , ed.   Documents in American Tele-
      communications Policy, 2 volumes.   New York:
      Arno Press, 1976.

Included in this set of books are the first national government report on control of wireless, a detailed analysis of and plea for government control
of telegraph and telephone, the complete reports of
the Bureau of Navigation and Radio Division of the
Department of Commerce, recommendations of the
Hoover Radio Conferences of the 1920s, and the best
analysis of the FRC's operations and role ever published. Volume 2 includes the Truman administration's key policy report on telecommunications, one
of the first and most important discussions of use
of the radio spectrum, and a fine analysis of the
structure and policy of electrical communications in
the U.S. and abroad. These two volumes are to be
supplemented in 1977 with a third volume devoted to
administration of telecommunications policy also to
be edited by John M. Kittross. Bibliography,
charts, and index.

195   Kohlmeier, Louis M. , Jr.   The Regulators: Watchdog
      Agencies and the Public Interest.   New York:
      Harper & Row, 1969.   339 pp.

This book is about the major independent administrative, or regulatory, agencies Congress has
created to regulate or promote private industry for
stated public purposes and it is about the relationships of these agencies to other federal laws and
programs which also concern the "consumer interest. "   Index.

196   Krasnow, Erwin G. and Lawrence D. Longley. The
       Politics of Broadcast Regulation. New York: St.
       Martin's Press, 1973. 150 pp.
         By focusing on the very real case histories of
       regulation--of FM broadcasting, of UHF television,
       of proposed limits on broadcast commercial time,
       and of license renewal policies--the authors have
       shown how the regulatory process actually works,
       how it is influenced by political realities, and how
       decisions are really made. Bibliography, charts,
       illustrations, and index.

197   Krislov, Samuel and Lloyd Musolf. The Politics of
       Regulation: A Reader. Boston: Houghton-Mifflin,
       1964. 261 pp.
         Discusses regulation in a mold that is intellectu-
       ally, professionally, and didactically more useful
       than the rubrics of administrative law.

198   Lawhorne, Clifton O. Defamation and Public Officials:
       The Evolving Law of Libel. Carbondale: Southern
       Illinois University Press, 1971. 356 pp.
         This is the first comprehensive treatment of the
       changes in and evaluation of the law of libel over
       the years at last filling the gap in the existing legal
       texts and journalism books dealing with press law
       and public officials. This is a valuable reference
       for those people working in the field of journalism
       plus others working in communications. Bibliography
       and index.

199   Le Duc, Don R. , ed. Issues in Broadcast Regulation.
       Broadcast Education Association Monographs No. 1.
       Washington, D. C. : BEA/NAB, 1974. 151 pp.
         The first in what is intended to be a continuing
       series of monographs on major subject areas in
       broadcasting. This publication presents more than
       two dozen brief essays outlining arguments and
       issues on a variety of topics.

200   Leive, David M. International Telecommunications and
       International Law: The Regulation of the Radio
       Spectrum. Dobbs Ferry, N. Y. : Oceana Publica-
       tions, 1970. 386 pp.
         Concentrates on ITU decision-making, internal
       operation, and administration. A highly detailed
       advanced text in international administrative law.

201   Levin, Harvey J.   Broadcast Regulation and Joint Own-
        ership of Media.   New York: New York University
        Press, 1960.   219 pp.
           For the students of journalism and mass commu-
        nications who are curious to see first hand what an
        economist finds when he explores the interrelations
        of the mass media and, more particularly, the con-
        sequences of diversifying their ownership.   Charts
        and index.

202   Miller, Merle.   The Judges and the Judged.   Garden
        City, N. Y. :   Doubleday, 1952 (reprinted by Arno
        Press, 1971).   220 pp.
           This book tells with accuracy and objectivity a
        factual story of subversion and sabotage of freedom
        in the United States of America.   It is the report
        (sponsored by the American Civil Liberties Union)
        of the author's investigation of blacklisting in the
        radio and television industry.

203   Mosco, Vincent.   The Regulation of Innovations in the
        Broadcasting Market.   Cambridge, Mass. :   Harvard
        University Program on Information Technologies
        and Public Policy, 1975.   56 pp.
           Deals mainly with FM, UHF television, cable,
        and pay TV as examples of new technologies trying
        to break into the established broadcast industry--
        and what the government (FCC, etc.) and industry
        did about it.

204   Nelson, Harold L. and Dwight L. Teeter.   Law of
        Mass Communications: Freedom and Control of
        Print and Broadcast Media.   2nd edition.   (Accom-
        panying Instruction Manual.)   Mineola, N. Y. :
        Foundation Press, 1973.   713 pp.
           Offers only a glimpse at broadcast regulation
        under a chapter entitled "Public Access to the Mass
        Media. "   More than 100 pages are devoted to a
        thorough review of libel law.   Bibliography, glos-
        sary, and index.

205   Noll, Roger G. ; Merton J. Peck; and John McGowan.
        Economic Aspects of Television Regulation.   Wash-
        ington, D. C. :   Brookings Institute, 1973.   342 pp.
           Analyzes the complex relationships between eco-
        nomics, politics, and technology in the regulation of
        television and cable technology.

206   Pember, Don. <u>Privacy and the Press: The Law, the</u>
       <u>Mass Media, and the First Amendment</u>. Seattle:
       University of Washington Press, 1972. 298 pp.
          Traces the development of privacy as a legal
       issue, especially as that issue affects the press and
       broadcasting.

207   Pennybacker, John H. and Waldo W. Braden, eds.
       <u>Broadcasting and the Public Interest</u>. New York:
       Random House, 1969. 176 pp.
          The body of the book contains four parts: (1) the
       FCC, (2) programming, (3) Section 315 and the Fair-
       ness Doctrine, (4) implications of the communica-
       tion revolution. Bibliography.

208   Rivers, William L. and Michael J. Nyhan. <u>Aspen</u>
       <u>Notebook on Government and the Media</u>. New York:
       Praeger, 1973. 208 pp.
          "Meanings of the First Amendment," "Adversaries
       or Cronies?," "Citizens Access to the Media" are
       among the problems of government-media relation
       explored through essays and dialogue in this report
       of three seminars held by the Aspen Program on
       Communications and Society.

209   Shapiro, Andrew O. <u>Media Access: Your Right to Ex-</u>
       <u>press Your Views on Radio and Television</u>. Boston:
       Little, Brown, 1976. 297 pp.
          Combines a how-to-do-it approach with a good
       deal of useful background information on the peculiar
       position broadcast regulation finds itself in. Index.

210   Signitzer, Benno. <u>Regulation of Direct Broadcasting</u>
       <u>from Satellites: The UN Involvement</u>. New York:
       Praeger, 1976. 124 pp.
          Traces the development of the UN role and the
       political and administrative functions and limitations
       of that body in this regard. Bibliography and index.

211   Simons, Howard and Joseph A. Califano, Jr., eds.
       <u>The Media and the Law</u>. New York: Praeger, 1976.
       225 pp.
          This book is an edited version of the transcripts
       of a weekend discussion in March 1975 of journalists,
       lawyers, and government officials on the knotty sub-
       ject of the media and the law. Index.

212 Smead, Elmer E. Freedom of Speech by Radio and Television. Washington, D. C. : Public Affairs Press, 1959. 182 pp.

This book is a simple but comprehensive picture of the relation of the government to the licensees who receive monopoly grants to operate for the public interest in the mass distribution of education and entertainment over the air. Index.

213 Socolow, A. Walter. The Law of Radio Broadcasting, 2 volumes. New York: Baker, Voorhis, 1939.

214 Stonecipher, Harry W. and Robert Trager. The Mass Media and Law in Illinois. Carbondale: Southern Illinois University Press, 1976. 207 pp.

This book defines the present status of laws regarding the mass media, specifically as applied to the Illinois newsmen-publishers-broadcasters. This is a valuable model for other needed state studies. Charts and index.

215 Toohey, Daniel W. ; Richard D. Marks; and Arnold P. Lutzker. Legal Problems in Broadcasting: Identification and Analysis of Selected Issues. Lincoln, Neb. : Great Plains Instructional Television Library, 1974.

Contains major aspects of legal problems in television broadcasting.

216 Vaughn, Robert. Only Victims: A Study of Show Business Blacklisting. New York: Putnam, 1972. 355 pp.

The author, a noted film and TV star, has written a lively and incisive study of the effect of the House Committee on Un-American Activities on the entertainment industry from 1938 to 1958. Bibliography and index.

217 Warner, Harry P. Radio and Television Law. Albany, N. Y. : Matthew Bender, 1948.

A comprehensive reference book on the legal and regulatory structure of the radio and television law.

218 Wilson, H. H. Pressure Group: The Campaign for Commercial Television. New Brunswick, N. J. : Rutgers University Press, 1961. 232 pp.

This is an attempt to describe what was in

essence an intraparty conflict over the introduction
and passage of a single piece of legislation, the Independent Television Act.   Index.

4. ORGANIZATION

A. Radio Management

See also nos. 275, 702, 703.

219 Coddington, Robert H.   Modern Radio Broadcasting:
Management & Operation in Small-to-Medium Markets.   Blue Ridge Summit, Pa. : TAB Books, 1969.
288 pp.
A comprehensive guide to successful practices of
radio stations in small-to-medium-sized markets.
Charts, index, and photographs.

220 Hoffer, Jay.   Managing Today's Radio Station.   Blue
Ridge Summit, Pa. : TAB Books, 1968.   288 pp.
This book completely covers radio management,
programming, and sales.   Among the topics discussed are: how to get the most out of the station's staff; how to develop and maintain the proper
public image; how to deal with ad agencies and reps.
It thoroughly examines the cold, hard facts of station operation and offers in-depth coverage on audience ratings, advertising, automation, double bill-
ing, unionism, preventive maintenance, etc.   It
covers format control methods, station image, community involvement, news editorials, sports, copywriting, sources of air talent, and much, much
more.   Illustrations.

221 Johnson, Joseph S. and Kenneth K. Jones.   Modern
Radio Station Practices.   Belmont, Calif. : Wadsworth, 1972.   269 pp.
This book is written especially for the beginning
broadcaster and for the student who wants to know
about radio, either for merely understanding or for
pursuing a profession.   The authors have used a

management approach rather than a production approach, but the focus is on the product--the program. Bibliography, charts, glossary, and index.

222 Midgley, Ned. The Advertising and Business Side of Radio. New York: Prentice-Hall, 1948.
A practical textbook which contains information about the commercial scales of the major and regional networks, local station operation and management. Charts and illustrations.

223 National Association of Broadcasters. Broadcasting in the United States. Washington, D.C.: NAB, 1933. 191 pp.
Issued during the year when colleges were debating if this country should adopt the "essential features" of the British radio system, this is a defense of American radio and its role. Discussion of the American system is compared to that of the BBC, there is an outline of the key debate issues and arguments, a question-and-answer format review of the facts about U.S. broadcasting, and a discussion of the NAB code. Bibliography and charts.

224 Reinsch, J. Leonard and Elmo Israel Ellis. Radio Station Management. 2nd edition. New York: Harper & Row, 1960. 337 pp.
This new edition of Radio Station Management is an easy-to-read sourcebook into which the authors have distilled the know-how of their outstanding station operations. Bibliography, glossary, illustrations, index, and photographs.

225 Routt, Edd. The Business of Radio Broadcasting. Blue Ridge Summit, Pa.: TAB Books, 1972. 400 pp.
How to operate a station as a profitable business and serve the public interest as well. This is the first text to deal with broadcast station operation from beginning to end. Clearly explains proven techniques to follow and cautions to observe. Charts, glossary, and illustrations.

B. Radio Economics

See also nos. 90, 95, 220, 222, 266, 275, 459, 475, 476,

482, 866.

226 Dygert, Warren B. Radio as an Advertising Medium.
      New York: McGraw-Hill, 1939. 261 pp.
          One of the more solid advertising guides of the
      thirties, this volume remained in print well into the
      forties. The 25 chapters first review the audience,
      then program types, how to purchase radio time to
      best advantage, merchandising, ratings, the role of
      the agency, local station advertising, and a brief
      review of foreign advertising and upcoming technical
      developments (TV, FM, and facsimile). Charts and
      index.

227 Eoyang, Thomas T. An Economic Study of the Radio
      Industry in the United States of America. New
      York: Columbia University Press, 1936 (reprinted
      by Arno Press, 1974). 220 pp.
          A detailed, published Ph.D. dissertation with
      three major parts: technical aspects of radio, eco-
      nomics of the radio manufacturing industry, and
      economics of radio broadcasting. Detailed and at
      times advanced analysis, with valuable historical in-
      formation. Bibliography, charts, and index.

228 Federal Communications Commission. An Economic
      Study of Standard Broadcasting. New York: Arno
      Press, 1974.
          Contains a detailed analysis of changes in Ameri-
      can broadcasting in the post-war years of expansion
      when radio had to meet the challenge of FM and
      television.

229 Federal Radio Commission. Commercial Radio Adver-
      tising. New York: Arno Press, 1974.
          This is a letter from the FRC chairman to the
      Senate answering questions on commercial and edu-
      cational AM broadcasting.

230 Felix, Edgar H. Using Radio in Sales Promotion: A
      Book for Advertisers, Station Managers and Broad-
      casting Artists. New York: McGraw-Hill, 1927.
      386 pp.
          The first book-length treatment of radio advertis-
      ing, this volume is invaluable for its portrayal of
      radio in a key period--as advertising was being ac-
      cepted, and as the FRC was being established along

with radio networks. The 21 chapters cover all aspects of audience research, program features and
types, announcing, directing, technical factors in
station operation, structure of broadcasting, etc.
Illustrations, index, and photographs.

231 Goode, Kenneth M. What About Radio? New York:
     Harper & Bros., 1937. 255 pp.
        A 16-chapter review of radio advertising tech-
     niques as they were in the late 1930s, this volume
     reviews a good deal of information on the radio
     audience which is of value historically today, plus
     information on programs and approaches to adver-
     tising methods some of which is still applicable.
     Charts and index.

232 Hettinger, Herman S. A Decade of Radio Advertising.
     Chicago: University of Chicago Press, 1933 (re-
     printed by Arno Press, 1971). 354 pp.
        Essential for understanding of radio economics in
     its first decade, this published doctoral disserta-
     tion discusses the psychological role of radio, the
     network-station structure of broadcasting, the de-
     velopment of network advertising, role and impor-
     tance of early "spot" ads, local station advertising,
     detailed information on network programming, com-
     mercial announcement technique, role of the public
     interest, etc. Charts and index.

233 Hettinger, Herman S. and Walter J. Neff. Practical
     Radio Advertising. New York: Prentice-Hall,
     1938. 372 pp.
        A handbook written by an academic researcher
     and the owner of an advertising agency, this 25-
     chapter review offers a good deal of basic informa-
     tion on radio in 1936-1937, plus details on how
     radio advertising campaigns were then organized.
     Useful for its data on the radio audience and exist-
     ing advertising institutions in radio. Charts and
     index.

234 Jome, Hiram L. Economics of the Radio Industry.
     Chicago: A. W. Shaw, 1925 (reprinted by Arno
     Press, 1971). 332 pp.
        This is the first scholarly study of radio and
     broadcasting in the United States and is thus invalu-
     able as a balanced view of radio's development,

marketing of radio receivers, early means of station support, programming and copyright, patents
and public policy, need for regulation, and likely
future trends. Charts and index.

235 Morell, Peter. Poisons, Potions, and Profits: The
Antidote to Radio Advertising. New York: Knight,
1937. 292 pp.
A rare, early example of the consumer critic of
radio, this volume consists entirely of information
debunking then popular radio product advertisements.
Issued with a separate 35-page "Consumer's Radio
Log" of material received too late for inclusion, the
emphasis is on patent medicine and cosmetic products found to have negative properties. Written
from the files of the Consumer Union, the tone is
totally critical, with strong suggestions that radio
do a better job of policing advertising claims.
Charts and index.

236 Peck, William A. Radio Promotion Handbook. Blue
Ridge Summit, Pa.: TAB Books, 1968. 192 pp.
Here is a complete guide to help radio (and TV)
stations increase sales, develop better audience
ratings, and improve results. Illustrations.

237 Robinson, Sol. Radio Advertising--How to Sell It &
Write It. Blue Ridge Summit, Pa.: TAB Books,
1974. 228 pp.
This comprehensive volume presents an extremely practical approach to radio advertising sales--
new and useful methods which the time salesman
(and copywriter, too) can use to obtain better results for himself, the station, and the sponsor.
Index.

238 Willing, Si. How to Sell Radio Advertising. Blue
Ridge Summit, Pa.: TAB Books, 1970. 320 pp.
The author illustrates by theory and by practice
the right formula for sales which depends on the individual and the prospective advertiser.

239 Wolfe, Charles H., ed. Modern Radio Advertising.
2nd edition. New York: Funk & Wagnalls, 1953.
An authoritative account of radio advertising history with practical procedures for the agency representative and radio advertiser. Includes an

analysis of television advertising--how to plan it,
buy it, write it, and test it.

C.   Television Management

See also nos. 267, 275, 300, 428.

240   Roe, Yale, ed.   Television Station Management: The
        Business of Broadcasting.   New York: Hastings
        House Publishers, 1964.   251 pp.
            A number of television executives from various
        specialized fields within television have contributed
        timely and practical observations about the specific
        problems of television management.   The result is
        an anthology of forthright, from the shoulder de-
        scriptions of what works and what doesn't work in
        all phases of television's business operation.   Illus-
        trations and index.

D.   Television Economics

See also nos. 38, 236, 266, 275, 402, 432, 459, 475, 476,
482, 486, 660, 866, 894.

241   Agnew, Clark M. and Neil O'Brien.   Television Adver-
        tising.   New York: McGraw-Hill, 1958.   330 pp.

242   Bellaire, Arthur.   The Television Commercial Cost
        Control Handbook.   Chicago: Crain Communications,
        1972.

243   Bunce, Richard.   Television in the Corporate Interest.
        New York: Praeger, 1976.   150 pp.
            This study combines economics, regulation, and
        public policy in its discussion of business pluralism
        (the local ownership syndrome), legacies of cross-
        ownership (newspapers and broadcasting), what busi-
        ness control in television means, multinational em-
        pire building, the conglomerate complex (different
        kinds and their operations here in the U.S.), and
        television operating in the corporate (world's) inte-
        rest.   Charts and index.

244   Coleman, Howard W. , ed.   Color Television: The
        Business of Colorcasting.   New York: Hastings

House Publishers, 1968.   287 pp.
Seventeen experts in the field give a thorough appraisal of this important medium emphasizing the business angle.   Charts, glossary, illustrations, and index.

245 Costa, Sylvia Allen.   How to Prepare a Production Budget for Film and Video Tape.   2nd edition. Blue Ridge Summit, Pa. :   TAB Books, 1975. 196 pp.
A complete guide to determining the finances needed for any video tape or film production, from TV commercials to feature-length films.

246 Diamant, Lincoln.   Television's Classic Commercials: The Golden Years 1948-1958.   New York: Hastings House Publishers, 1971.   305 pp.
This study of 69 "classic" commercials aired on U.S. television between 1948 and 1958 assesses not only their sales impact, but also their overall marketing and sociological significance.   Each commercial is illustrated and transcribed in analytic script form, with notes and critical commentary on creative marketing and production aspects.   Glossary and photographs.

247 Galanoy, Terry.   Down the Tube: Or, Making Television Commercials Is Such a Dog-Eat-Dog Business It's No Wonder They're Called Spots.   Chicago: Regnery, 1970.

248 McMahan, Harry Wayne.   The Television Commercial: How to Create and Produce Effective TV Advertising. New York: Hastings House Publishers, 1957.
One of the few books devoted exclusively to television commercials.   Shows how to create and produce effective television advertising, along with do's and don'ts on production.

249 Ogden, Warde B.   The Television Business: Accounting Problems of a Growth Industry.   New York: Ronald Press Co. , 1961.   197 pp.
Study by a partner of Price Waterhouse of the business, accounting, and financial practices involved in the production, distribution, and broadcasting of television programs.   Glossary.

250   Ogilvy, David.   Confessions of an Advertising Man.
      New York: Dell, 1964. 172 pp.
      The complete, forthright guide to the world of
      advertising and advertising agencies, including the
      making of a television commercial.   Index.

251   Owen, Bruce M.; Jack H. Beebe; and Willard G. Man-
      ning, Jr. Television Economics. Lexington, Mass.:
      Lexington Books, 1974. 218 pp.
      For the general reader interested in television
      policy.   The content of this book will be of assist-
      ance to students of the television industry in their
      research and to policy makers and their advisors
      in seeking better answers to the great issues of
      mass communication regulation in the United States.
      Bibliography, charts, illustrations, and index.

252   Robinson, Sol. Broadcast Station Operating Guide.
      Blue Ridge Summit, Pa.: TAB Books, 1969.
      256 pp.
      This comprehensive reference encompasses every
      level of broadcasting.   The secret to success in
      broadcasting, as in any other business, is knowing
      what to do and how to do it.   This book tells it like
      it is.   Illustrations.

253   Rowsome, Frank.   Think Small: The Story of Those
      Volkswagen Ads.   Brattleboro, Vt.: Greene, 1970.
      128 pp.
      Here, from behind the scenes, are the origins
      and development of a unique advertising campaign.
      Pioneering in 1959 and going strong a decade later,
      a campaign assessed by international experts as
      among the most successful and most influential ever
      to have appeared in print and TV anywhere.   Photo-
      graphs.

254   Settel, Irving and Norman Glenn.   Television Advertis-
      ing and Production Handbook.   New York: Crowell,
      1953.   480 pp.
      This book covers the whole broad field of tele-
      vision advertising and production, and includes such
      aspects as operating and financing a TV station,
      staging and producing the TV live program and film
      commercial, advertising research, publicity, cover-
      age, package production and syndication, casting,
      writing, and personnel requirements.   Bibliography,

charts, glossary, illustrations, index, and photographs.

255 Wainwright, Charles Anthony. Television Commercials:
     How to Create Successful TV Advertising. Revised
     edition. New York: Hastings House Publishers,
     1970. 318 pp.
          This book is concerned with the creative aspects
     of television commercials. Some chapters are
     slightly technical, but the author's purpose has been
     to explore the area of ideas. Illustrations and in-
     dex.

256 Wrighter, Carl P. I Can Sell You Anything. New
     York: Ballantine Books, 1972. 245 pp.
          An incredible and informative guide to the world
     of TV advertising--how commercials are made, why
     they work, how to separate fakery from fact. In a
     devastating analysis of well-known commercials in-
     volving brand names of food, cars, drugs, and other
     products, the author--a veteran in the field--gives
     insight into secrets of the trade and tricks by which
     advertising slips glibly through the holes that sup-
     posedly protect customers. Illustrations.

E. Networks

See also nos. 18, 30, 36, 89, 113, 143, 163, 232, 292,
383, 385, 388.

257 Park, Rolla E. , ed. New Television Networks. Santa
     Monica, Calif. : Rand Corp. , 1974.

F. General

See also nos. 33, 64, 83, 185, 201, 205, 319, 511, 512,
568, 683, 732, 811, 1007, 1035, 1078.

258 Arnold, Frank A. Broadcast Advertising: The Fourth
     Dimension (Television Edition). 2nd edition. New
     York: John Wiley, 1933. 284 pp.
          A 21 chapter guide to radio advertising, this edi-
     tion is of particular interest because the last three
     chapters deal with the prospects of TV as an adver-
     tising medium, including discussion of TV in the
     lab and its likely commercial introduction. Charts.

259   Baer, Walter S. , et al.   Concentration of Mass Media
      Ownership: Assessing the State of Current Knowl-
      edge.   Santa Monica, Calif. :   Rand Corp. , 1974.
      202 pp.
            The best analysis of writing and research on
      media ownership, with lengthy discussion of findings
      and a detailed listing of writings (pp. 173-202).

260   Barton, Roger, ed.   Handbook of Advertising Manage-
      ment.   New York: McGraw-Hill, 1970.
            Book was written primarily for corporate adver-
      tising managers.   Covers every aspect of advertis-
      ing and would be a useful reference for individuals
      interested in the field.   Contains 32 chapters writ-
      ten by knowledgeable individuals in the field of ad-
      vertising.   Glossary, illustrations, index, and photo-
      graphs.

261   Bauer, Raymond and Stephen Greyser, eds.   Advertis-
      ing in America: The Consumer View.   Boston:
      Harvard Graduate School of Business Administration,
      1968.   473 pp.
            Reporting on a comprehensive study of the atti-
      tudes held by a cross-section of Americans, both
      toward advertising as an institution in our society
      and toward advertisements themselves, the authors
      have focused their research on attitudes and behavior
      in four basic areas: 1) the relative salience of ad-
      vertising, 2) the public's attitude toward advertising,
      3) how the public reacts to advertisements, 4) why
      the public reacts favorably and unfavorably to ad-
      vertisements.   Charts.

262   Berg, Thomas L.   Mismarketing: Case Histories of
      Marketing Misfires.   Garden City, N.Y. : Double-
      day, 1970.   253 pp.
            Book deals more with marketing misses than
      misfires.   It analyzes some marketing mistakes in
      terms of the original forces and strategies that
      caused those operations to go astray.   Index.

263   Bickel, Karl A.   New Empires: The Newspaper and
      the Radio.   Philadelphia: J. B. Lippincott Co. ,
      1930.   112 pp.
            Interesting early view of radio's relationship to
      print journalism written by then president of United
      Press agency.   Five short chapters explore briefly

the development of journalism and the likely effects
of radio on news reporting and as economic competi-
tor.   Many pages detail then-apparent beginnings of
press-radio "war." Appendix lists newspaper affili-
ated radio stations, and offers 25-page review of
broadcasting in other countries.   Index.

264   Coleman, Howard W.   Case Studies in Broadcast Man-
        agement.   New York: Hastings House Publishers,
        1970.   96 pp.
        This work is designed to shed light, delineate,
        and encourage thinking and discussion about the
        problems of operating commercial radio and tele-
        vision stations.   Charts.

265   Etkin, Harry A.   AM/FM Broadcast Station Planning
        Guide.   Blue Ridge Summit, Pa. : TAB Books,
        1970.   192 pp.
        Whether one plans to build a new station or re-
        model and update an existing one, this book covers
        every aspect of planning, building, and equipping
        the facility.   Illustrations.

266   Federal Communications Commission (Engineering De-
        partment).   Report on Social and Economic Data
        Pursuant to the Informal Hearing on Broadcasting,
        Docket 4063, Beginning October 5, 1936.   Washing-
        ton, D. C. : Government Printing Office, 1937.
        197 pp.
        Don't let the forbidding title scare you from a
        valuable source of statistical and general data view-
        ing the American system.   Discussion and tabular
        material on the organization of broadcasting, physi-
        cal service (types, location, and power of stations),
        financial support, program service, competition,
        suggested technical improvements, etc.   Charts.

267   Finnegan, Patrick S.   Planning the Local UHF-TV Sta-
        tion.   Rochelle Park, N. J. : Hayden Book Co. ,
        296 pp.
        Requirements for planning, building, and operat-
        ing a small UHF-TV station.

268   Gormley, William T. , Jr.   The Effects of Newspaper-
        Television Cross-Ownership on News Homogeneity.
        Chapel Hill: University of North Carolina Press,
        1976.   276 pp.

Examines in detail the actual effects of cross-
ownership of newspapers and broadcast stations in
the same market. Bibliography and charts.

269   Heighton, Elizabeth J. and Don R. Cunningham.   Ad-
       vertising in the Broadcast Media.   Belmont, Calif. :
       Wadsworth, 1976.   349 pp.
          A comprehensive text covering the theoretical,
       practical, and social aspects of broadcast advertis-
       ing.   The book includes a history of advertising in
       the broadcast media, an overview of the structure
       of the present industry, and a comprehensive sec-
       tion on the development of radio and television cam-
       paigns.   Bibliography, charts, illustrations, and
       photographs.

270   Hiebert, Ray Eldon; Donald F. Ungurait; and Thomas
       W. John.   Mass Media: An Introduction to Modern
       Communication.   New York: David McKay, 1974.
       295 pp.
          Twenty-seven chapters dealing with the process,
       development, economics, and effects of mass com-
       munications.   Bibliography, charts, illustrations,
       and index.

271   Hoffer, Jay.   Organization & Operation of Broadcast
       Stations.   Blue Ridge Summit, Pa. :   TAB Books,
       1971.   256 pp.
          A clear-cut delineation of station duties and re-
       sponsibilities that takes the guesswork out of who
       does what, and how it should be done.

272   Koenig, Allen E. , ed.   Broadcasting and Bargaining:
       Labor Relations in Radio and Television.   Madison:
       University of Wisconsin Press, 1970.   344 pp.

273   Quaal, Ward L. and James A. Brown.   Broadcast
       Management: Radio and Television.   2nd edition.
       New York: Hastings House Publishers, 1976.
       480 pp.
          Discusses the major aspects of managing a sta-
       tion.   Especially useful to the producer who would
       like to learn the management's point of view.
       Charts and index.

274   Rucker, Bryce W.   The First Freedom.   Carbondale:
       Southern Illinois University Press, 1968.   322 pp.

Looks specifically at issues of monopoly and economics in print and broadcast media.   Index.

275 Seehafer, Gene F. and Jack W. Laemmar. Successful
     Television and Radio Advertising.   New York:
     McGraw-Hill, 1959.   648 pp.
        A comprehensive look at both radio and television
     advertising.   The book is broken down into five
     parts: elements of the American Commercial Broad-
     casting System, creating television and radio com-
     mercials, research for radio and TV advertising,
     TV and radio campaigns, and TV and radio station
     management.   This is a good reference for those
     interested in broadcast advertising.   Charts, glos-
     sary, index, and photographs.

276 Wood, James Playsted.   The Story of Advertising.
     New York: Ronald Press Co., 1958.   512 pp.
        This book attempts to tell some of the long and
     richly varied history of advertising and to appraise
     critically some of advertising's characteristics, ac-
     complishments, and shortcomings.   Bibliography,
     illustrations, and index.

5.   PROGRAMMING

A.   News/Political

See also nos. 57, 64, 75, 135, 263, 420, 422, 424, 452, 463, 464, 470, 473, 480, 485, 487, 488, 489, 502, 517, 528, 531, 545, 549, 564, 567, 663, 773, 914, 936, 1063.

277   Bagdikian, Ben H.   The Information Machines: Their Impact on Men and the Media.   New York: Harper & Row, 1971.   359 pp.
　　　The focus of this book is on what the content of daily information will be, what form it will be delivered in, and how it will be distributed throughout the population. Bibliography, charts, and index.

278   Batscha, Robert M.   Foreign Affairs News and the Broadcast Journalist.   New York: Praeger, 1975. 254 pp.
　　　This book examines the behavior of the individuals who control the composition of television news. Bibliography and charts.

279   Berry, Thomas E.   Journalism in America: An Introduction to the News Media.   New York: Hastings House Publishers, 1976.   380 pp.
　　　This volume provides 14 chapters on all aspects of writing and reporting for print and broadcast news media.   Bibliography, glossary, and index.

280   Blumler, Jay G. and Denis McQuail.   Television and Politics: Its Uses and Influence.   Chicago: University of Chicago Press, 1969.   379 pp.
　　　The purpose of this study is to determine how voters use political television during an election and how political outlooks are influenced by televised propaganda.   Based on the 1964 British general election.

281   CBS News. Face the Nation 1975: The Collected
       Transcripts from the CBS Radio and Television
       Broadcasts. Metuchen, N.J.: Scarecrow Press,
       1976. 390 pp.
          Face the Nation transcripts are fascinating his-
       tory and provide a unique primary reference source
       for students, historians, researchers, political
       scientists, and the general reader. All transcripts
       have been fully indexed by name, subject, and is-
       sue. Index.

282   CBS News. Television News Reporting. New York:
       McGraw-Hill, 1958. 182 pp.
          This news manual is a compilation of information
       gathered by a large group of men and women en-
       gaged in electronic journalism and is intended as a
       newsroom and classroom handbook. Illustrations
       and index.

283   Calmer, Ned. The Anchorman. Garden City, N.Y.:
       Doubleday, 1970. 365 pp.
          A novel about one of TV's most important news-
       casters and the men and women who control him.
       Dominating the background of this novel are the
       enormous pressures and endless intrigues of tele-
       vision news itself.

284   Charnley, Mitchell. News by Radio. New York:
       Macmillan, 1948.
          A text in which are described the special prac-
       tices, principles, and characteristics of radio news
       and an evaluation of them in the light of their ef-
       fectiveness or their failure.

285   Cirino, Robert. Don't Blame the People. New York:
       Vintage Books, 1972. 339 pp.
          A documented account of how the news media use
       bias, distortion, and censorship to manipulate pub-
       lic opinion. Charts and index.

286   Clor, Harry M., ed. The Mass Media and Modern
       Democracy. Chicago: Rand McNally, 1974.
       232 pp.
          Based on a college conference, the seven papers
       included here focus on journalistic topics--especially
       political journalism.

287   Culbert, David Holbrook.   News for Everyman: Radio
      and Foreign Affairs in Thirties America.   Westport,
      Conn. : Greenwood Press, 1976.   238 pp.
         A discussion of several selected radio commen-
      tators, and their effect both on listeners, and on
      radio's developing news function in the late 1930s.

288   Dary, David.   How to Write News for Broadcast &
      Print Media.   Blue Ridge Summit, Pa. : TAB Books,
      1973.   190 pp.
         A complete handbook on journalism for the stu-
      dent or practicing newsman in both print and broad-
      cast fields.   The concept of "news"--the meaning of
      the term and its nature--is thoroughly discussed,
      including the fine-line definitions of what is news
      and what is not, and the classification of news.   A
      reporter's qualifications are clearly defined, as are
      the methods used to gather news.   Illustrations and
      photographs.

289   Dary, David.   Radio News Handbook.   2nd edition.
      Blue Ridge Summit, Pa. : TAB Books, 1970.
      192 pp.
         This updated and revised handbook, written for
      both aspiring and experienced broadcast journalists,
      serves not only as a day-to-day guide, but also as
      a source of vital information for those practicing
      newsmen who are endeavoring to improve their pro-
      fessional status.   Among the topics discussed are:
      a brief history of radio news; the radio newsroom;
      sources of news; radio news writing; putting the
      newscast together; radio news on the air; the mo-
      bile news unit; law, courts, and radio news; and
      editorializing.   Glossary, illustrations, and index.

290   Diamond, Edwin.   The Tin Kazoo--Television, Politics,
      and the News.   Cambridge, Mass. : MIT Press,
      1975.   269 pp.
         Edwin Diamond, a veteran journalist, teacher,
      and broadcast commentator himself, looks at tele-
      vision as a dynamic medium and records--in non-
      ephemeral print--the radical and/or subtle changes
      in its format and impact that have taken shape from
      the late 1940s to the present.   The book analyzes
      a number of misconceptions, demonstrating that
      television news in particular is neither as influen-
      tial as it is thought to be nor as "on top" of its

stories as it ought to be. The author does not
spare the print media but it is the local and network news that is the focus of his attention. Index.

291 Dickerson, Nancy. Among Those Present. New York:
Ballantine Books, 1976. 280 pp.
The inside story of the first female national network news correspondent, her journalistic scoops,
and her personal and professional relationships with
four American presidents from Kennedy to Ford.
Photographs.

292 Epstein, Edward Jay. News from Nowhere: Television
and the News. New York: Random House, 1973.
321 pp.
A detailed examination of the evening news programs of ABC, CBS, and NBC, which suggests that
internal corporate policy, rather than external circumstances or long-range goals, shapes the directions of TV news coverage. Bibliography, charts,
and index.

293 Fang, I. E. Television News. 2nd edition. New
York: Hastings House Publishers, 1972. 478 pp.
Analyzing the who, what, when, where, and especially the how of newscasting, this book examines
all the skills required by the TV journalist, and
delves into sources of news stories, interviewing
techniques, writing, and editing. Bibliography,
charts, glossary, illustrations, index, and photographs.

294 Field, Stanley. The Mini-Documentary--Serializing TV
News. Blue Ridge Summit, Pa.: TAB Books, 1975.
252 pp.
The author brings to the reader interviews with
producers, cameramen, editors, and sound men.
He has distilled the years of experience and talent
of mini-documentary producers from the four commercial television stations in the nation's capital.
Actual written or transcribed on-air scripts for
eight mini-documentary series--many of them award-
winners--are part of this valuable text. Bibliography, illustrations, and index.

295 Fixx, James F., ed. The Mass Media and Politics.
New York: Arno Press, 1972. 636 pp.

Facsimiles of New York Times articles and reviews of political communication (especially broadcasting) from 1936 through 1971.

296   Foote, Edward; Veda Gilp; and George L. Hall, eds.
CBS and Congress: "The Selling of the Pentagon"
Papers. Washington, D.C.: National Association
of Educational Broadcasters, 1971.   144 pp.
This is a special issue of the Educational Broad-
casting Review which assumes book-like proportions.
Good reference for those investigating the TV pro-
gram "Selling of the Pentagon."

297   Frank, Robert Shelby.   Message Dimensions of Television News.   Lexington, Mass.: Lexington/Heath,
1973.   120 pp.
This book is a study of the message content of
television newscasts.   It is hoped that the findings
here will present a more accurate picture of the
characteristics of television news.   Charts and index.

298   Gilbert, Robert E.   Television and Presidential Politics.   North Quincy, Mass.: Christopher, 1972.
335 pp.
Coverage of television's effects on campaigning
from 1952 through 1968 with details on varied uses
of the medium.

299   Gordon, George N. and Irving A. Falk.   TV Covers
the Action.   New York: Julian Messner, 1968.
189 pp.
A full-length look at the past, present, and future of the newest giant of the news media.

300   Green, Maury.   Television News: Anatomy and Process.   Belmont, Calif.: Wadsworth, 1969.   352 pp.
A clear study of the technical process of television as a news medium, this book covers writing,
reporting in the field and on the air, film and videotape editing, production, and news-department management.   A stimulating discussion of larger issues
that go beyond techniques is also presented: television news ethics, social values, and the impact of
television on politics.   This is the first book to
show how TV affects such things as politics, wars,
and urban violence.   Bibliography, glossary, illustrations, index, and photographs.

301 Herschensohn, Bruce. The Gods of Antenna. New
       Rochelle, N.Y.: Arlington House, 1975. 155 pp.
       Identifies dozens of ways in which TV news--all
       news--can be presented to accomplish a planned
       result.

302 Hofstetter, C. Richard. Bias in the News: Network
       Television Coverage of the 1972 Election Campaign.
       Columbus: Ohio State University Press, no date.
       215 pp.
       Between July 10 and November 6 of 1972, a
       specially trained staff monitored the content of all
       of the more than 4,000 weekday evening news
       stories broadcast by the three major television net-
       works. Employing advanced techniques of social-
       scientific analysis, the staff attempted not only to
       spot bias in those less subtle of its manifestations
       that result directly from conscious purpose or un-
       wittingly from ideological position or party affiliation,
       but also to detect it in those less apparent and more
       elusive forms in which in the absence of any expli-
       cit statement or clear visual image, a clear im-
       pression of preference for one candidate or party is
       nonetheless somehow distinctly conveyed. The re-
       sults of that survey and study are presented here
       for the first time in a volume that provides a valu-
       able corrective to the easy assumptions and gross
       oversimplifications that have been the basis for the
       passionate asseverations of advocates and critics on
       both sides of the debate. Charts and index.

303 Hulteng, John L. The Messenger's Motives: Ethical
       Problems of the News Media. Englewood Cliffs,
       N.J.: Prentice-Hall, 1976. 262 pp.
       Takes a hard look at how the news is presented
       and at the ethical problems that concern those who
       write, edit, produce, and report. Bibliography,
       index, and photographs.

304 Kraus, Sidney, ed. The Great Debates: Background-
       Perspective-Effects. Bloomington: Indiana Univer-
       sity Press, 1962. 439 pp.
       Includes articles by social scientists and broad-
       casters as well as a production diary and the text
       of the four debates. Charts, illustrations, index,
       and photographs.

305   Lang, Kurt and Gladys Engel Lang. Politics and Tele-
          vision. Chicago: Quadrangle, 1968. 315 pp.
              In this book the authors look at the ways in
          which television, through its presentation of events,
          shapes public images of political life and personali-
          ties. Charts and index.

306   Lang, Kurt and Gladys Engel Lang. Voting and Non-
          Voting. Waltham, Mass.: Blaisdell, 1968. 172 pp.
              Based on post-election interviews with 364 regis-
          tered voters in California who had not voted by
          4 p.m. P.S.T. on November 3, 1964, when elec-
          tion broadcast coverage had begun locally.

307   Lefever, Ernest W. TV and National Defense: An
          Analysis of CBS News, 1972-1973. Boston, Va.:
          Institute for American Strategy Press, 1974.
          209 pp.
              This study is a content analysis of CBS evening
          news programs (and some specials and 60 Minutes,
          too) for 1972 and 1973, as recorded by the Vander-
          bilt News Archive. While the emphasis is on how
          CBS covered military and national defense issues,
          other things are covered and reported as well.
          Bibliography, charts, glossary, and index.

308   LeRoy, David J. and Christopher H. Sterling, eds.
          Mass News: Practices, Controversies, and Alter-
          natives. Englewood Cliffs, N.J.: Prentice-Hall,
          1973. 334 pp.
              Several articles on television newscasts and docu-
          mentaries--and problems in creative production of
          both.

309   Lyle, Jack. The News in Megalopolis. San Francisco:
          Chandler Publishing Co., 1967. 208 pp.
              Offers a detailed analysis of the news media's
          role in Los Angeles. Bibliography, charts, illus-
          trations, and index.

310   Lyons, Louis M., ed. Reporting the News. Cam-
          bridge, Mass.: Belknap Press of Harvard Univer-
          sity, 1965. 443 pp.
              Contains an article dealing with TV news by
          John F. Day. Mr. Day is the former Director of
          CBS News. Index.

311   MacNeil, Robert. The People Machine: The Influence
      of Television on American Politics. New York:
      Harper & Row, 1968. 362 pp.
         A highly critical review of network television
      news methods and reporting, with emphasis on po-
      litical coverage both in and after campaigns. Index.

312   Mendelsohn, Harold and Irving Crespi. Polls, Tele-
      vision, and the New Politics. Scranton, Pa. :
      Chandler Publishing Co. , 1970. 329 pp.
         This book challenges some widely-held concep-
      tions about how American politics has been affected
      both by public opinion polls and television. Bibli-
      ography, charts, and index.

313   Mickelson, Sig. The Electric Mirror: Politics in an
      Age of Television. New York: Dodd, Mead, 1972.
      304 pp.
         Former head of CBS News examines television
      coverage of national political campaigns and conven-
      tions. Bibliography, index, and photographs.

314   Miles, Donald W. Broadcast News Handbook. Indian-
      apolis: Howard W. Sams & Co. , 1975. 392 pp.
         Focuses on radio because of its increasing news
      role. Bibliography, glossary, index, and photo-
      graphs.

315   Minor, Dale. The Information War. New York:
      Hawthorn Books, 1970. 212 pp.
         Describes the bitter conflict between reporters
      and government officials working in Vietnam. "The
      press" as used in this book refers to both print
      and non-print media. Index.

316   Minow, Newton N. ; John Bartlow Martin; and Lee M.
      Mitchell. Presidential Television: A Twentieth
      Century Fund Report. New York: Basic Books,
      1973. 232 pp.
         This report deals with the dangers to the nation's
      system of checks and balances posed by presidential
      access to television. The authors suggest a num-
      ber of reforms to preserve the constitutional balance
      in an era of technological change. Bibliography,
      charts, and index.

317   Morgan, Edward P. Clearing the Air. Washington,

D. C. :   Robert B. Luce, Inc. , 1963.   267 pp.
    The author, a Washington news reporter, has set
down his daily reactions to events and the people
who made them.   The book is a collection of his
wonderment about our soft lives and hard times, of
alternating complaints and cheers over the behavior
and behaviorisms of people.

318   Patterson, Thomas E. and Robert D. McClure.   The
      Unseeing Eye: The Myth of Television Power in
      National Elections.   New York: Putnam, 1976.
      218 pp.
          Based on extensive research into the 1972 cam-
      paign, the authors claim that TV has no effect in
      helping voters decide who or which party to vote
      for.   Charts.

319   Peterson, Sheldon, ed.   The Newsroom and the News-
      cast.   New York: Time-Life Broadcasting, 1966.
      112 pp.
          A brief conference symposium issued by the
      Radio Television News Directors' Association and
      Time-Life Broadcast, this book stresses newsroom
      operations and staffing.

320   Peterson, Sheldon, ed.   Television Newsfilm: Content.
      New York: Time-Life Broadcasting, 1965.   86 pp.
          A brief conference symposium issued by the
      Radio Television News Directors' Association and
      Time-Life Broadcast, this book discusses newsfilm
      content.

321   Porter, William E.   Assault on the Media: The Nixon
      Years.   Ann Arbor: University of Michigan Press,
      1976.   320 pp.
          This is the first lengthy treatment of the Nixon
      battle with the press from the point of view of gov-
      ernment vs. media interrelationships.   Index.

322   Pye, Lucian W. , ed.   Communications and Political
      Development.   Princeton, N. J. : Princeton Univer-
      sity Press, 1963.   381 pp.
          Contributors speak specifically on media in po-
      litical communication within a country.

323   Rivers, William L.   The Opinionmakers.   Boston:
      Beacon Press, 1965.   207 pp.

This book is about the interplay of politics and
the press--all the mass media--in Washington.
Charts and index.

324   Rivers, William L. and Michael J. Nyhan, eds.   Aspen
Notebook on Government and the Media.   New York:
Praeger, 1975.   192 pp.
Gives information and viewpoints on reporters vs.
politicians, the public's right to know, rules for re-
porters, citizen access to media, etc.

325   Robinson, Sol.   Guidelines for News Reporters.   Blue
Ridge Summit, Pa.:   TAB Books, 1971.   192 pp.
In this guidebook, the author relates quite specifically and to the point, the techniques he has
found to be successful during his many years as a
newsman and as a part of management.   The volume
discusses exactly what is required of a broadcast
journalist and the problems he faces, and the solutions, as well as how to deal with news sources
and how to prepare news stories understandably and
accurately.   Charts and photographs.

326   Rubin, Bernard.   Political Television.   Belmont,
Calif.:   Wadsworth, 1967.   200 pp.
This is an account of the dramatic reshaping of
elections and the Presidency by television, the mass
communications medium that brings current history
into the home.   This story of the five years preced-
ing the general election of 1964 is told in the context of two presidential campaigns, in an attempt to
show why and how television has become able to
exert such profound political influences.   Charts
and index.

327   Sevareid, Eric.   In One Ear.   New York: Knopf,
1952.
A collection of what the author refers to as individual snapshots taken from some of his daily
broadcasts.

328   Sevareid, Eric.   This Is Eric Sevareid.   New York:
McGraw-Hill, 1964.   306 pp.
This volume includes many of the author's broad-
casts and columns.

329   Siebert, Fred S.; Walter Wilcox; and George Hough, III.

(Edited by Chilton R. Bush.) Free Press and Fair
Trial: Some Dimensions of the Problem. Athens:
University of Georgia Press, 1970. 133 pp.
This volume presents findings from studies conducted by each of the authors: Dr. Siebert inter-
viewed a national sample of trial judges on the question of miscarriage of justice in their courts as the
result of publication of news about crime; George
Hough conducted an analysis of the magnitude of the
situation by analyzing the disposition in the Detroit
Recorder's Court and the reporting in one Detroit
newspaper of all felony cases for which warrants of
arrest had been issued over a six-month period;
Dr. Wilcox conducted a search of the literature on
the subject of jurors and the effect on verdicts of
published or broadcast pretrial news.   Charts.

330   Siller, Bob; Ted White; and Hal Terkel.   Television
      and Radio News.   New York: Macmillan, 1960.
      227 pp.
      A useful production book though now out of date.

331   Skornia, Harry J.   Television and the News: A Criti-
      cal Appraisal.   Palo Alto, Calif. :   Pacific Books,
      1968.   232 pp.
      There is increasing evidence that Americans are
      still not receiving from TV and radio the diversity
      and depth of news, clarification, and interpretation
      of the right type, from the right places, that they
      need for responsible decision making.   This book
      examines the causes of certain weaknesses and fail-
      ures of this nature and proposes some possible im-
      provements for public and industry consideration.

332   Small, William.   To Kill a Messenger: Television
      News and the Real World.   New York: Hastings
      House Publishers, 1970.   320 pp.
      From his vantage point as News Director and
      Bureau Manager of CBS News in Washington, the
      author thoughtfully and thoroughly examines the role
      of television news in our society.   Index.

333   Thomson, Charles A. H.   Television and Presidential
      Politics: The Experience in 1952 and the Problems
      Ahead.   Washington, D. C. :   Brookings Institute,
      1956.   173 pp.
      Examines the relationship of television to the

political process and the issues of public policy that
are presented by this use of the medium.   Charts
and index.

334   Whale, John.   The Half-Shut Eye: Television and Politics in Britain and America.   New York: St. Martin's Press, 1969.   219 pp.
Discusses the impact television has had on politics both in the U.S. and Britain.   Compares how
each nation uses the media for political advantage.
Index.

335   Whalen, Charles W. , Jr.   Your Right to Know: How
the Free Flow of News Depends on the Journalist's
Right to Protect His Sources.   New York: Vintage
Books, 1973.   206 pp.
A plea that journalists be legally protected from
having to reveal their sources in order to ensure
that the news gets to the people.   Illustrated by
case histories.

336   White, Paul.   News on the Air.   New York: Harcourt,
Brace, 1947.
An analysis of news gathering and preparation for
broadcasting.

337   Wilhelmsen, Frederick D. and Jane Bret.   Telepolitics:
The Politics of Neuronic Man.   Plattsburgh, N.Y.:
Tundra Books, 1972.   254 pp.
Deals with the effects of television, specially the
effect of media coverage of politics on news events.
The authors suggest the form rather than content of
media have created a new age of what they term
"neuronic man. "

338   Wolf, Frank.   Television Programming for News and
Public Affairs: A Quantitative Analysis of Networks
and Stations.   New York: Praeger, 1972.   203 pp.
Studies the identification and analysis of major
factors that account for the quality and proportion
of news and public affairs programming shown on
commercial television.   Bibliography and charts.

339   Wyckoff, Gene.   The Image Candidates: American
Politics in the Age of Television.   New York:
Macmillan, 1968.   274 pp.
A behind-the-scenes look at the making of a

political candidate's image for television. Interesting look at the image makers and their techniques.

B.   Public Affairs

See also nos. 338, 428, 512.

340 Swallow, Norman.   Factual Television.   New York:
     Hastings House Publishers, 1966.
        The role of television in public affairs, the arts,
     and education is discussed here by a top British
     director.

341 Wolff, Perry.   A Tour of the White House with Mrs.
     John F. Kennedy.   New York: Doubleday, 1962.
     258 pp.
        This well-illustrated book, based on the famous
     CBS-originated television program, includes not only
     the text of the broadcast but much of the background
     material gathered for its production.   Photographs.

C.   Documentaries

See also nos. 294, 422, 424, 507.

342 Bluem, A. William.   Documentary in American Tele-
     vision.   New York: Hastings House Publishers,
     1968.   311 pp.
        This knowledgeable, sometimes controversial,
     book presents a critical analysis of the documentary
     movement in American television.   Covered are:
     its history, its forms and functions, its achieve-
     ments, its problems and prospects, its shapers.
     Bibliography, index, and photographs.

343 Yellin, David G.   Special: Fred Freed and the Tele-
     vision Documentary.   New York: Macmillan, 1973.
     289 pp.
        Chronicles the development of television docu-
     mentary--from its beginnings after World War II to
     the present--through the life and work of Fred
     Freed, pioneer in the radio and television docu-
     mentary.   Index and photographs.

D. Drama

See also nos. 409, 416, 436, 487, 531.

344 Brauer, Ralph and Donna Brauer. The Horse, the
     Gun and the Piece of Property. Bowling Green,
     Ohio: University Popular Press, 1975. 246 pp.
         Includes discussions of just what a Western is,
     the old-fashioned Western and the TV Code, the law-
     man and associates defend the organization man, the
     male group and the emerging community, and the
     role of property in Westerns. Other topics dealt
     with include Indians, minority groups, women, etc.
     Illustrations.

345 Cantril, Hadley. The Invasion from Mars: A Study in
     the Psychology of Panic. New York: Harper &
     Row, 1966. 224 pp.
         The study reported in this book was launched im-
     mediately after Orson Welles' dramatization of H. G.
     Wells' fantasy, War of the Worlds. The book gives
     an account of people's reactions. Charts and index.

346 Edmondson, Madeleine and David Rounds. The Soaps:
     Daytime Serials of Radio and TV. New York:
     Stein & Day, 1973. 190 pp.
         A short and informal analysis with useful behind-
     the-scenes information on production.

347 Gerrold, David. The World of Star Trek. New York:
     Ballantine Books, 1973. 274 pp.
         Discusses Gene Roddenberry's brilliant concept
     of the first viable science-fiction world designed
     for a TV series; the writers, technicians, and stars
     who made the show happen; the fans who kept Star
     Trek alive in the face of network opposition. Photo-
     graphs.

348 Higby, Mary Jane. Tune in Tomorrow or How I Found
     the Right to Happiness with Our Gal Sunday, Stella
     Dallas, John's Other Wife, and Other Sunday Radio
     Serials. New York: Cowles Educational Corp.,
     1968. 226 pp.
         Offers insight into the soap operas by someone
     who was there. Photographs.

349 La Guardia, Robert. The Wonderful World of TV Soap

Operas. New York: Ballantine Books, 1974.
342 pp.
A complete guide to television's most unique
genre, the book discusses "soap addiction," the ratings war, the history of radio and TV soap operas,
up-to-date plot summaries, and a behind-the-scenes
taping of an actual soap opera. Photographs.

350 Mackey, David R. Drama on the Air. New York:
Prentice-Hall, 1951.
A text which integrates the three main facets of
radio dramatic presentations--script, production,
and acting--with emphasis on acting.

351 Olfson, Lewy. Radio Plays of Famous Stories. Bos-
ton: Plays, Inc., 1956. 250 pp.
Radio scripts written for half-hour broadcasts.
Glossary.

352 Stedman, Raymond William. The Serials: Suspense
and Drama by Installment. Norman: University of
Oklahoma Press, 1971. 514 pp.
Scholarly yet eminently readable history of the
serial form in film, radio, and television, the lat-
ter being one of the best available analyses of content and impact of this format.

353 Whitfield, Stephen E. and Gene Roddenberry. The
Making of Star Trek. New York: Ballantine Books,
1968. 414 pp.
Probably the best study of a commercial network
program ever published. Recommended even for
those who did not care for the program, as it provides detail on early conception of the idea, character and actor development, sets and props, writer
guidelines, pilot production, etc.

E. Variety

See also no. 487.

354 Andrews, Bart. Lucy, Ricky, Fred and Ethel: The
Story of "I Love Lucy." New York: Dutton, 1976.
278 pp.
Deals with interesting behind-the-scenes information for early filmed television productions. The

last 100 pages is an episode-by-episode log of all programs of the original series. Index and photographs.

355 Blumenthal, Norman. The TV Game Shows. New York: Pyramid Books, 1975. 272 pp.
      Popular discussion of program types, operations and economics, personalities, and details on network shows. Useful for "behind-the-scenes" approach even though aimed mainly at quiz show viewers.

F. Children

See also nos. 388, 554, 630, 709, 712, 713, 714, 718, 777, 834, 846, 851, 875, 892, 931, 932.

356 Callahan, Jennie Waugh. Radio Workshop for Children. New York: McGraw-Hill, 1948. 398 pp.
      This book was written to aid instructors of college courses and to serve as a text for the college students who are preparing to use radio broadcasting as a teaching tool. This is the first book in the field of radio broadcasting to set forth the step-by-step process of auditioning children for the school workshop, of planning and writing scripts on all school subjects, and of rehearsing and airing the programs. Bibliography, glossary, illustrations, index, and photographs.

357 Cater, Douglass and Stephen Strickland. TV Violence and the Child: The Evolution and Fate of the Surgeon General's Report. New York: Russell Sage Foundation, 1975. 167 pp.

358 Garry, Ralph; F. B. Rainsberry; and Charles Winick. For the Young Viewer. New York: McGraw-Hill, 1962. 181 pp.
      This book is for all those who hold a prime concern with improving children or television or both. It is for broadcasters, parents, creators of programs, and educators. Bibliography and photographs.

359 Gordon, Dorothy (Terner). All Children Listen. New York: G. M. Stewart, Inc., 1942. 128 pp.

Discusses how children can be influenced by radio
in terms of continuing our democratic way of government. Bibliography.

360   Hackett, Walter Anthony. Radio Plays for Young
      People. Boston: Plays, Inc. , 1950.   277 pp.
      Collection of radio scripts of plays for children.
      The scripts in this book have been produced over
      the air by both professionals and amateurs.

361   Kaye, Evelyn.   The Family Guide to Children's Tele-
      vision: What to Watch, What to Miss, What to
      Change. New York: Pantheon, 1974. 194 pp.

362   Kline, F. Gerald and Peter Clarke, eds. Mass Com-
      munications and Youth: Some Current Perspectives.
      Beverly Hills, Calif. : Sage, 1971. 128 pp.
      Eight original articles dealing with parents' role
      with children's media habits, the role of popular
      music and children, media effects on learning, etc.

363   Lesser, Gerald S. Children and Television: Lessons
      from Sesame Street. New York: Random House,
      1975. 290 pp.
      The author describes how "Sesame Street" was
      put together. He tells the story of the people who
      created it, the ideas that went into it, and the in-
      sights about children that emerged from it. Bibli-
      ography, illustrations, index, and photographs.

364   Liebert, Robert M. ; John M. Neale; and Emily S.
      Davidson. The Early Window: Effects of Televi-
      sion on Children and Youth. New York: Pergamon
      Press, 1973. 193 pp.
      The authors have written about what the child
      views in the "early window"--television--and how he
      is influenced by it. Bibliography, charts, illustra-
      tions, index, and photographs.

365   Melody, William. Children's Television: The Eco-
      nomics of Exploitation. New Haven, Conn. : Yale
      University Press, 1973. 164 pp.
      This study, commissioned by Action for Children's
      Television, focuses on the economic aspects of com-
      mercial children's television and their relation to
      FCC public-policy options. Bibliography and illus-
      trations.

366   Mielke, Keith W. , et al.   The Federal Role in Fund-
      ing Children's Television Programming.   Washing-
      ton, D. C. :   National Association of Educational
      Broadcasters, 1975.   283 pp.

367   Mukerji, Rose.   Television Guidelines for Early Child-
      hood Education.   Bloomington, Ind. :   National In-
      structional Television, 1969.   57 pp.
          A guide for those in decision-making positions in
      children's TV programming.

368   Noble, Grant.   Children in Front of the Small Screen.
      Beverly Hills, Calif. :   Sage, 1975.   256 pp.
          This book is the result of the author's original
      research with children in Britain, Ireland, and Can-
      ada.   It presents a rich array of findings and ideas
      that will interest not only the specialist, but teach-
      ers and parents as well, and hopefully encourage
      TV planners to look again at children's programs.

369   Polsky, Richard M.   Getting to Sesame Street: Ori-
      gins of the Children's Television Workshop.   New
      York: Praeger, 1974.   160 pp.
          Describes and analyzes the genesis and early de-
      velopment of the Children's Television Workshop,
      creators of "Sesame Street. "

370   Rutstein, Nat.   "Go Watch TV!"   What and How Much
      Should Children Really Watch?   New York: Sheed
      & Ward, 1974.

371   Schramm, Wilbur; Jack Lyle; and Edwin Parker.   Tele-
      vision in the Lives of Our Children.   Stanford,
      Calif. :   Stanford University Press, 1961.   324 pp.
          This book represents three years of research
      and analysis in ten communities in the United States
      and Canada.   It is the first full-length study of the
      impact of television on North American children.
      Both children and entire families were interviewed.
      Bibliography, charts, and index.

372   Shayon, Robert Lewis.   Television and Our Children.
      New York: Longmans, Green & Co. , 1951.   94 pp.
          This book is a revealing explanation of the basis
      upon which the radio-television industry operates,
      and the limitations within which the Federal Com-
      munications Commission must act.

373   Treadwell, Bill. Head, Heart and Heel. New York:
         Mayfair Books, 1958. 212 pp.
         Biography of famous children's radio program host
         "Uncle Don" Carney, written by a long-time associate
         and program director. Index and photographs.

374   Watson, Katherine (Williams). Radio Plays for Chil-
         dren. New York: H. W. Wilson Co., 1947.
         281 pp.
         Dramatizations for radio of children's books and
         stories.

375   Winick, Charles; Lorne G. Williamson; Stuart F. Chuz-
         mir; and Mariann P. Winick. Children's Television
         Commercials: A Content Analysis. New York:
         Praeger, 1973. 156 pp.
         Charles Winick and his colleagues have selected
         145 fundamental elements, most of which are the
         outgrowth of basic thinking about the potential ef-
         fects of advertising: how it fits into the fantasy
         world of the child, how the type of delivery might
         affect the child's compliance, etc. In a final sec-
         tion of this study, the authors lay out a broad plan
         for future research where it will be possible to in-
         terview or observe children directly. Bibliography
         and index.

376   Yin, Robert K. The Workshop and the World: Toward
         an Assessment of the Children's Television Work-
         shop. Santa Monica, Calif.: Rand Corp., 1973.

G.   Religious

See also nos. 1034, 1039, 1053, 1065.

377   Bluem, A. William. Religious Television Programs:
         A Study of Relevance. New York: Hastings House
         Publishers, 1969. 220 pp.
         This authoritative survey, commissioned by the
         Television Office, examines the current status of
         religious television programming in America, pri-
         marily at the local level. Bibliography, index, and
         photographs.

378   Ellens, J. Harold. Models of Religious Broadcasting.
         Grand Rapids, Mich.: Eerdmans, 1974. 168 pp.

Useful and sometimes humorous analysis of the
varied types of religious programs on the air and
the people behind them.

379 Lee, Alfred McClung and Elizabeth Briant Lee, eds.
     The Fine Art of Propaganda: A Study of Father
     Coughlin's Speeches. New York: Harcourt, Brace,
     1939. 140 pp.
         A classic analysis of the methods used by the
     famous "radio priest" in the 1930s, this volume of-
     fers detailed definitions and practical examples of
     such approaches as name calling, glittering general-
     ity, transfer, testimonial, plain folks, card stack-
     ing, band wagon building--and then all are shown in
     a typical Coughlin speech. This was one of the
     most important publications of the short-lived "Insti-
     tute for Propaganda Analysis" in the late 1930s,
     and was perhaps the best of the popular treatments
     of Coughlin's radio speeches. Bibliography.

380 Morris, James. The Preachers. New York: St.
     Martin's Press, 1973. 418 pp.
         In-depth look at the men who have been preach-
     ing on radio and television for years. Discusses
     the peculiarities of each, such as the one preacher
     who maintained he could raise the dead and ran into
     a problem when his listeners started sending him
     corpses for the miracle. Bibliography, illustra-
     tions, and index.

H. General

See also nos. 20, 29, 36, 52, 57, 93, 96, 110, 111, 113, 117,
124, 142, 153, 207, 221, 425, 509, 529, 530, 533, 541,
542, 551, 585, 614, 652, 656, 658, 704, 708, 893, 895,
935, 1015, 1036, 1068, 1077.

381 Arlen, Michael J. The View from Highway I. New
     York: Farrar, Straus & Giroux, 1976. 293 pp.
         Twenty-one essays from the period 1974-1976
     dealing with all kinds of television programming. A
     sequel to the author's Living Room War of 1969.

382 Cantor, Muriel G. The Hollywood Television Producer:
     His Work and His Audience. New York: Basic
     Books, 1971. 256 pp.

Author's Ph.D. dissertation and the only study of
its type. Explores the job constraints and activities
of prime-time program producers from a sociological perspective.

383 Clift, Charles and Archie Greer, eds. Broadcast Programming: The Current Perspective. Washington,
D.C.: University Press of America, 1976. 148 pp.
Sections of material are built around ratings,
network prime time programming 1973-1976, network television programming types, local television,
local radio programming, program regulation on the
local level, general program regulation, and a section entitled "Radio and Television Under Pressure."

384 Duff, Willis. The Talk Radio Handbook. San Francisco: The Author, 1969. 61 pp.
A Metromedia station manager's collection of
useful memos and advice on all kinds of talk radio
formats.

385 Federal Communications Commission (Office of Network
Study). Television Network Program Procurement.
Washington, D.C.: FCC, 1963. Part I, 494 pp.;
Part II, 838 pp.
An exhaustive analysis of a process that has
changed little in the past decade. Based on exten-
sive hearings and including many quotations from
testimony of network and package agency personnel
on program decisions and content.

386 Fisher, Hal. Radio Program Ideabook. Blue Ridge
Summit, Pa.: TAB Books, 1968. 256 pp.
Here's a new, exciting, comprehensive source of
all the programming ideas needed to build and hold
an audience--a thesaurus of ideas on radio show-
manship--written for everyone involved in radio programming by a seasoned broadcast veteran. Illustrations.

387 Gaines, J. Raleigh. Modern Radio Programming.
Blue Ridge Summit, Pa.: TAB Books, 1973. 192 pp.
Details duties and responsibilities of a program
director and covers music control and research,
public service and community involvement, maintaining the quality of the "air sound," use of jingles
and promotion, the various formats from contemporary

to "block" programming, the multitude of programming components, how to determine a need and to
fit it in the program schedule, plus the importance
and use of news, weather, sports, community service, and other special features. Glossary and illustrations.

388   Glut, Donald F. and Jim Harmon. The Great Televi-
      sion Heroes. New York: Doubleday, 1975. 245 pp.
          Short illustrated study written for the nostalgia
      market and covering network programs up to about
      1960. Discusses both children's and adult programs
      of various types. Illustrations.

389   Harmon, Jim. The Great Radio Heroes. Garden City,
      N.Y.: Doubleday, 1967. 263 pp.
          Description of early radio programs and the
      people who made it all happen.

390   Johnson, William O. Super Spectator and the Elec-
      tronic Lilliputians. Boston: Little, Brown, 1971.
      238 pp.
          The only lengthy study of television's effect on
      professional sports, and vice versa. Taken from
      articles in Sports Illustrated. Good data here on
      just how television manages to cover different types
      of sports events.

391   Klages, Karl W. Sportscasting. Lafayette, Ind.:
      Sportcasters, 1963. 154 pp.
          Deals with all aspects of sports broadcasting with
      detailed coverage of play-by-play sports newscasting
      and related areas.

392   McNamee, Graham (in collaboration with Robert Gordon
      Anderson). You're On the Air. New York: Harp-
      er & Bros., 1926. 207 pp.
          One of the earliest of radio memoirs by one of
      the first important radio personalities, this is both
      one man's early radio career and an engaging view
      of radio in the midst of its first decade of mad
      growth. Concentration here is on special programs
      (particulary political and sports events) as handled
      by New York station WEAF. Photographs.

393   Manning, Willard G. The Supply of Prime-Time En-
      tertainment Television Programs. Stanford, Calif.:

Center for Research in Economic Growth, 1973.

394 Michael, Paul and James Robert Parish. The Emmy
     Awards: A Pictorial History. New York: Crown,
     1970. 384 pp.
        A detailed review of the Academy of Television
     Arts and Sciences' annual "Emmy" awards for out-
     standing television programs, covered from the first
     awards in 1948 through the 22nd annual awards in
     1970. Pictures from each awarded program and
     listing of all awards--plus the losers in each cate-
     gory. Index and photographs.

395 Miller, Merle and Evan Rhodes. Only You Dick Dar-
     ing! New York: Sloane, 1964. 350 pp.
        Tongue-in-cheek, but an essentially true tale of
     an attempt to sell a program idea to then CBS Tele-
     vision President James Aubrey--and the reasons for
     this venture's failure. Useful analysis of program
     idea development problems.

396 Milton, Ralph. Radio Programming: A Basic Training
     Manual. London: Geoffrey Bles, 1968. 384 pp.
        This manual was designed to help international
     students learn the art of radio programming. Pro-
     duced for the Association of Christian Broadcasting.
     Glossary, illustrations, and photographs.

397 Newcomb, Horace. TV: The Most Popular Art. New
     York: Doubleday Anchor, 1974. 272 pp.
        Characters divided along network program genre
     lines, covering both entertainment and information
     formats. Discusses content types and conventions
     with many examples from specific series.

398 Shayon, Robert Lewis, ed. The Eighth Art: Twenty-
     Three Views of Television Today. New York:
     Holt, Rinehart & Winston, 1962. 269 pp.
        Originally commissioned for a CBS-backed quar-
     terly that never appeared, this is a collection of
     articles stressing programming types and opportuni-
     ties, but covering other areas (the audience, critics,
     worldwide systems, effects on reading and sports,
     needed research, coverage of court trials, etc.) as
     well. The authors read like a "who's who" of TV
     and society.

399 Shulman, Arthur and Roger Youman. How Sweet It
     Was: Television--A Pictorial Commentary. New
     York: Shorecrest, 1966 (reprinted by Bonanza,
     1968). 448 pp.
         An excellent review of developments in TV pro-
     gramming, this 12-chapter compendium (divided along
     program type lines) is a wealth of personalities and
     programs of TV networks' first two decades. Index
     and photographs.

400 Taylor, Sherril W. , ed. Radio Programming in Action:
     Realities and Opportunities. New York: Hastings
     House Publishers, 1967. 183 pp.
         Based on the 1966 programming seminars of the
     NAB, 27 broadcast executives representing radio
     stations throughout the country, present their origi-
     nal essays and viewpoints within six broad program-
     ming categories: News and Public Service, Modern
     Music, Country Music, "Beautiful" Music, FM Radio,
     Sports. Index.

401 Thomey, Tedd. The Glorious Decade. New York:
     Ace Books, 1971. 224 pp.
         A popular review of network television programs
     of the 1950s, this short book has chapters on Imo-
     gene Coca and Sid Caesar, anthology drama pro-
     grams, "adult" westerns, Lucille Ball, crime and
     detective programs, radio stars (mainly comedians)
     on TV, and the quiz scandals. Light nostalgia, but
     a good feel for typical programming of the era.
     Photographs.

402 Tuchman, Gaye, ed. The TV Establishment: Pro-
     gramming for Power and Profit. Englewood Cliffs,
     N.J.: Prentice-Hall, 1974. 186 pp.
         Highly anti-establishment view of the networks,
     concentrating on programming and economic issues.

403 West, Robert. The Rape of Radio. New York: Rodin
     Publishing Co. , 1941. 546 pp.
         A 16-chapter review of radio that in no way lives
     up to its title suggestion that someone was misusing
     the medium. This is a wandering discussion of an-
     nouncers, radio drama, music on the air, children's
     programs, educational applications, radio comedy,
     religion, propaganda and news, sports, political
     programming, censorship, role of advertisers, the

potential of television, and (lastly) what the public
wants.

404   Wilson, Angus. Tempo: The Impact of Television on
      the Arts.   London: Studio Vista, 1964.   99 pp.
        Illustrates the highlights of Tempo programs in-
      quiring into what television can do to foster pleasure
      in music, painting, poetry, drama, ballet, and
      architecture.   Photographs.

405   Wood, William A.   Electronic Journalism.   New York:
      Columbia University Press, 1967.   175 pp.
        This book is a favorable report on television
      journalism and on the men responsible for it.   In-
      dex.

406   Wylie, Max. Best Broadcasts of 1938-39. New York:
      Whittlesey House, 1940.
        An anthology of radio programs presented on all
      three major networks.

6. PRODUCTION

A. Audio

See also nos. 289, 356, 384, 490.

407 Alkin, Glyn. TV Sound Operations. New York: Hastings House Publishers, 1975. 176 pp.
Deals with a wide variety of audio production problems and techniques. Comprehensive and well illustrated. Bibliography, glossary, and illustrations.

408 Aspinal, Richard. Radio Programme Production: A Manual for Training. New York: Unipub, Inc. (UNESCO), 1971. 151 pp.
Offers a new basic guide to program production for radio operations in developing nations and gives major emphasis to type of programs.

409 Barnouw, Erik, ed. Radio Drama in Action. New York: Rinehart & Co., 1945. 397 pp.
Collection of radio dramas by well-known writers.

410 Carlile, John S. Production and Direction of Radio Programs. New York: Prentice-Hall, 1939. 397 pp.
Includes the details of radio production including hand signals and studio diagrams. The purpose of the book is to provide a useful volume on radio production for those who are already in, the radio industry and those who hope to enter it. The author has provided, above all, a practical book. Bibliography, glossary, illustrations, index, and photographs.

411 Chase, Gilbert. Music in Radio Broadcasting. New York: McGraw-Hill, 1946. 152 pp.

A text developed for a course covering all aspects of music used in broadcasting without attempting to teach the applied techniques of any one of them. Index.

412 Columbia Broadcasting System. Radio Alphabet. New York: Hastings House Publishers, 1946. 85 pp.
A glossary of radio terms and radio's sign language. Illustrations.

413 Crews, Albert. Radio Production Directing. New York: Houghton-Mifflin, 1944. 550 pp.
This volume gives the basic concepts on which all sound production work is founded. Illustrations, index, and photographs.

414 Dimond, Sidney A. and Donald M. Andersson. Radio and Television Workshop Manual: A Practical Guide to Creative Radio and Television. Englewood Cliffs, N.J.: Prentice-Hall, 1952. 301 pp.
A practical guide to creative radio and television production with emphasis on the more simplified types of programming for the small station. Illustrations.

415 Hoffer, Jay. Radio Production Techniques. Blue Ridge Summit, Pa.: TAB Books, 1974. 192 pp.
Covers every phase of radio production from announcements to the overall station "sound"--in fact, every creative aspect of today's radio. Illustrations.

416 Krulevitch, Walter. Radio Drama Production. New York: Rinehart & Co., 1946. 330 pp.
Written with the beginner in mind, this text includes chapters on script editing for producers, scoring from records, sources of radio plays, and sound effects. Bibliography, illustrations, and index.

417 Nisbett, Alec. The Technique of the Sound Studio. 2nd edition. New York: Hastings House Publishers, 1970. 559 pp.
This authoritative, standard work is essential reading for all who work with sound in television and film, as well as radio. It is intended for those with a creative interest in sound whether they are directors, writers, performers, or more directly

concerned with operational techniques.   Bibliography,
glossary, illustrations, and index.

418   Nisbett, Alec.   The Use of Microphones.   New York:
      Hastings House Publishers, 1974.   168 pp.
          A very useful guide to the various types of micro-
      phones and how they are best used in the recording
      and television studios.   Bibliography, glossary, and
      illustrations.

419   Oringel, Robert S.   Audio Control Handbook: For
      Radio and Television Broadcasting.   4th edition.
      New York: Hastings House Publishers, 1972.
      192 pp.
          Here, in clear and non-technical language, are
      complete step-by-step directions and full explana-
      tions of every phase of audio control in all types of
      broadcasting.   For the newcomer or seasoned pro-
      fessional it is an extremely practical aid.   Glossary,
      illustrations, index, and photographs.

420   Schwartz, Tony.   The Responsive Chord.   New York:
      Doubleday, 1973.   210 pp.
          Almost McLuhanesque discussion of the aesthe-
      tics of audio communication (including TV sound),
      especially in commercial and political advertising.

B.   Television

See also nos. 254, 300, 308, 320, 347, 349, 353, 363, 410,
414, 493, 494, 650, 820, 821, 826.

421   Alkin, E. G. M.   Sound with Vision: Sound Tech-
      niques for Television and Film.   New York: Crane,
      Russak, 1973.   283 pp.
          Deals specifically with production techniques in
      broadcasting.   Offers the basis of the writer's long
      BBC experience.   Illustrations.

422   Atkins, Jim, Jr. and Leo Willette.   Filming TV News
      and Documentaries.   New York: Chilton Books,
      1965.   158 pp.
          Book covers the entire field of news and infor-
      mation filmmaking, from philosophy to how-to-do-it.
      Glossary and photographs.

423   Banathy, Bela H.   Instructional Systems.   Belmont,
        Calif.: Fearon Publishers, 1968.   106 pp.
          Clear introduction to basic instructional systems.
        Useful as a guide for systems design in television
        production.   Bibliography and illustrations.

424   Barrett, Marvin, ed.   The Alfred I. DuPont-Columbia
        University Survey of Broadcast Journalism.   New York:
        Grosset & Dunlap, 1969-1971; Crowell, 1972-date.
          Originally an annual and now biennial.   Offers
        the best overview of developments in both network
        and local television news and documentary produc-
        tion.   Each year's volume has different main title.

425   Becker, Samuel L. and H. Clay Harshbarger.   Tele-
        vision: Techniques for Planning and Performance.
        New York: Henry Holt, 1958.   182 pp.
          A study of this text will be helpful in gaining an
        understanding of the speaking process in television.
        There are a variety of program assignments in this
        book which will acquaint the reader with the prob-
        lems of television programming, production, and
        broadcasting.   Bibliography, charts, illustrations,
        and index.

426   Bensinger, Charles.   Petersen's Guide to Video Tape
        Recording.   Los Angeles: Petersen Publishing Co.,
        1973.   80 pp.
          Publication tables about video, how it works, the
        equipment needed, portapaks, editing video and pro-
        duction tips.   Illustrations and photographs.

427   Bettinger, Hoyland (revised by Sol Cornberg).   Tele-
        vision Techniques.   New York: Harper & Bros.,
        1955.   236 pp.
          Basic television production book emphasizing both
        audio and video techniques as well as writing, di-
        recting, and producing for television.   Illustrations,
        index, and photographs.

428   Bluem, A. William; John F. Cox; and Gene McPherson.
        Television in the Public Interest: Planning, Pro-
        duction, Performance.   New York: Hastings House
        Publishers, 1961.   192 pp.
          This book supplies needed background to those
        given responsibility for an organization's efforts in
        the medium of television.   It suggests what television

can help to accomplish; it gives a behind-the-screen
acquaintance with a station and its facilities; it af-
fords guidance in initial planning, approaching a station, detailed planning and scripting, performance
and audience promotion.   Charts, glossary, illustrations, index, and photographs.

429   Bretz, Rudy.   Techniques of Television Production.
       2nd edition.   New York: McGraw-Hill, 1962.
       517 pp.
       The aim of this book is to bridge the gap between
the creative production man and the technically
minded engineer.   The book is directed toward the
production man, the director, producer, or worker
in any of the dozens of service departments, such
as graphic arts, costume, make-up, special effects,
or lighting.   It is written from their point of view
and in answer to their problems.   Charts, illustrations, index, and photographs.

430   Brodhead, James E.   Inside Laugh-In.   New York:
       Signet, 1969.   159 pp.
       The only fairly serious published study of how
this once popular program developed and how a typical show was produced.

431   Davis, Desmond.   The Grammar of Television Produc-
       tion.   2nd edition.   London: Barrie & Jenkins,
       1966.   80 pp.
       Offers a brief "grammar" which consists of an
annotated listing of conventions (must-do rules),
rules (to be broken only on occasion, with good
reason), and hints or tips (non-binding suggestions)
on TV production.   Glossary and illustrations.

432   Diamant, Lincoln, ed.   The Anatomy of a Television
       Commercial: The Story of Eastman Kodak's "Yes-
       terdays." New York: Hastings House Publishers,
       1970.   191 pp.
       How Kodak's now classic two-minute commercial
"Yesterdays" (winner of 13 international awards)
was created and produced by a cooperative advertising fraternity of writers, photographers, cameramen, editors, musicians, directors, and producers.
Includes the film commercial "Yesterdays." Glossary, illustrations, index, and photographs.

433   Dondis, Donis A.   A Primer of Visual Literacy.
        Cambridge, Mass.:   MIT Press, 1973.   194 pp.
           Applicable to television, films, or graphic arts
        work and pulls information and ideas from the fine
        arts as well as media.

434   Efrein, Joel.   Video Tape Production and Communica-
        tion Techniques.   Blue Ridge Summit, Pa.:   TAB
        Books, 1971.   256 pp.
           Here is an authoritative, practical guide on how
        to create effective video tape productions--the per-
        fect guidebook for businessmen, educators, tele-
        casters, CATV operators and others interested in
        using video tape for audio-visual communications.
        It is a complete how-to-do-it handbook on video
        production, direction, and program creation for edu-
        cational, industrial, broadcast, and CATV applica-
        tions.   Glossary, illustrations, and index.

435   Ewing, Sam (in collaboration with R. W. (Ozzie) Abo-
        lin).   Don't Look at the Camera!   Blue Ridge Sum-
        mit, Pa.:   TAB Books, 1973.   224 pp.
           Explains the basic techniques of TV photography,
        including dozens of tried-and-proven shortcuts for
        getting pictures on the air quickly and economically.
        Emphasis is placed on low-cost production.   Fully
        covered are such subjects as developing ease and
        tact in dealing with touchy and difficult advertisers;
        fresh, exciting new techniques for filming low-cost
        commercials; continuity writing and production plan-
        ning; the six important elements required in film
        production; the difficulties of filming on location;
        and a seven-point plan to help produce a better com-
        mercial film.   Also included is a step-by-step
        chronicle of a sound-on-film assignment.   Bibliog-
        raphy, glossary, illustrations, and index.

436   Heald, Tim.   The Making of Space 1999.   New York:
        Ballantine Books, 1976.   224 pp.
           The complete story behind the making of the
        popular science fiction television series.   Photo-
        graphs.

437   Jones, Peter.   The Techniques of the Television Cam-
        eraman.   Revised edition.   New York: Hastings
        House Publishers, 1969.   243 pp.
           This book is devoted wholly and specifically to

the work of the television cameraman. Primarily
intended to help the newcomer, directors and others
will find it helpful in program planning.

438   Lewis, Bruce. The Technique of Television Announc-
      ing. New York: Hastings House Publishers, 1966.
      264 pp.
      This is the only book that covers all facets of
      television announcing completely.

439   Lewis, Colby. The TV Director/Interpreter. New
      York: Hastings House Publishers, 1968. 255 pp.
      Describes all aspects of television direction.
      Many fine principles for the television director to
      consider. Good teaching text. Illustrations and
      index.

440   McCavitt, William. Television Studio Operations Manu-
      al. Revised edition. Indiana, Pa.: A. G. Halldin
      Publishers, 1975. 104 pp.
      Basic manual for beginners in television produc-
      tion. Includes responsibilities for each position in
      a production team, script writing, and set design.
      Bibliography, illustrations, and photographs.

441   Mattingly, Grayson and Welby Smith. Introducing the
      Single-Camera VTR System. New York: Charles
      Scribner's Sons, 1973.
      A rather simple, yet useful, introductory text to
      small-format television operation. Does not include
      small-format color.

442   Millerson, Gerald. Basic TV Staging. New York:
      Hastings House Publishers, 1974. 173 pp.
      A simplified text, including some of the principles
      of television staging, as elaborated upon in the au-
      thor's Technique of Television Production. Bibliog-
      raphy, glossary, and illustrations.

443   Millerson, Gerald. Effective TV Production. New
      York: Hastings House Publishers, 1976. 196 pp.
      This book presents the fundamentals of TV di-
      recting techniques outlining in an at-a-glance break-
      down the principles, practices, and opportunities of
      TV directing. Bibliography, glossary, and illustra-
      tions.

444   Millerson, Gerald.   TV Camera Operation.   New York:
      Hastings House Publishers, 1974.   160 pp.
      A small, simple, yet useful guide to the begin-
      ner of television production.   Bibliography, glossary,
      and illustrations.

445   Millerson, Gerald.   TV Lighting Methods.   New York:
      Hastings House Publishers, 1975.   150 pp.
      A simple version of the author's TV and film
      lighting book for the beginner.   Bibliography, glos-
      sary, and illustrations.

446   Millerson, Gerald.   The Technique of Lighting for
      Television and Motion Pictures.   New York: Hast-
      ings House Publishers, 1972.   366 pp.
      This book progresses from fundamental principles
      to lighting in its most advanced forms.   Invaluable
      for student and practitioner alike, it shows how
      light influences portraiture and atmospheric illu-
      sion; it explains how to display subjects persuasive-
      ly and how to set about lighting in all its artistic
      applications.   Bibliography, illustrations, and photo-
      graphs.

447   Millerson, Gerald.   The Technique of Television Pro-
      duction.   6th edition.   New York: Hastings House
      Publishers, 1968.   440 pp.
      Perhaps the best single volume on television pro-
      duction available.   Its coverage is complete, its
      diagrams are numerous and of value, and this edi-
      tion has more coverage of color.   A bit involved
      for new students, but unexcelled for those with at
      least minimal experience.   Charts, illustrations,
      and index.

448   Oswald, Ida and Suzanne Wilson.   This Bag Is Not a
      Toy: Handbook for the Use of Video-Recording in
      Education for the Professions.   New York: Council
      on Social Work Education, 1971.   133 pp.
      Concentrates on videotape itself with a well dia-
      grammed treatment of technical problems supple-
      mented with information on past projects, conceptu-
      alizing videotape recorder productions, and exam-
      ining legal and ethical issues involved.   Illustrations.

449   Quick, John and Herbert Wolff.   Small Studio Video
      Tape Production.   Reading, Mass. :   Addison-

Wesley, 1972. 229 pp.
A useful guide to studiotape use aimed at those
with studio facilities of a limited nature. A simplified one-volume guide for those in industry, business, government, and education who have had little
or no previous video experience.

450 Robinson, Richard. The Video Primer: Equipment,
Production, and Concepts. New York: Links Books,
1974. 380 pp.
An excellent, comprehensive discussion of small-
format television equipment and its operation. Also
includes basic production concepts. Glossary and
illustrations.

451 Stasheff, Edward; Rudy Bretz; John Gartley; and Lynn
Gartley. The Television Program: Its Direction
and Production. 5th edition. New York: Hill &
Wang, 1976. 243 pp.
Its comprehensiveness makes it an indispensable
handbook for students, anyone aspiring to a television career, and for professionals in the many fields
where television is finding new applications. Charts,
illustrations, and photographs.

452 Stone, Vernon and Bruce Hinson. Television Newsfilm Techniques. New York: Hastings House Publishers, 1974. 191 pp.
Offers a detailed analysis of all aspects of shoot-
ing newsfilm for television use.

453 Videofreex. The Spaghetti City Video Manual. New
York: Praeger, 1973.
Despite the "far-out" title, the book contains con-
ventional, useful information on small-format television equipment and operation techniques.

454 Wade, Robert J. Designing for Television. New York:
Pelligrini & Cudahy, 1952.
Entire book is extremely useful as a text for the
person seriously interested in scene design for television. Very thorough and well illustrated; most
useful for its completeness and full attention to the
problem of television set design. Illustrations.

455 Wade, Robert J. Staging TV Programs and Commercials. New York: Hastings House Publishers, 1954.

This book considers in some detail the relationship of the scene designer to the remainder of the
production crew. Well illustrated and comprehensive. Illustrations.

456   Weiner, Peter. Making the Media Revolution: A Hand-
      book for Video-Tape Production. New York: Mac-
      millan, 1973. 217 pp.
          A book on portable video production methods in-
      cluding use of videotape. Illustrations.

457   Westmoreland, Bob. Teleproduction Shortcuts: A
      Manual for Low Budget Television Production in a
      Small Studio. Norman: University of Oklahoma
      Press, 1974. 264 pp.
          Covers all of production but focuses on the low
      budget operation in a small studio. Details equip-
      ment and its effective use.

458   Zettl, Herbert. Television Production Handbook.
      Third edition. (Workbook also available.) Belmont,
      Calif.: Wadsworth, 1976. 450 pp.
          Provides a practical reference to all major ele-
      ments of television production, including cameras
      and camera operation, lights and lighting techniques,
      audio, videotape and film, and post-production edit-
      ing. This edition offers up-to-date information on
      production tools and techniques of television. Color
      is stressed throughout the book, but there is ample
      reference to traditional black-and-white production
      techniques. Bibliography, glossary, illustrations,
      index, and photographs.

C.   Writing

See also nos. 58, 279, 282, 288, 289, 293, 300, 351, 360,
374, 416, 427, 440.

459   Allen, Louise C.; Andre B. Lipscomb; and Joan C.
      Prigmore. Radio and Television Continuity Writing.
      New York: Pitman Publishing Co., 1962. 261 pp.
          Radio and TV are covered separately in well-
      illustrated format with lots of solid information on
      advertising, promotion, station image, and mer-
      chandising. Out-of-date. Illustrations.

460   Barnouw, Erik. Handbook of Radio Writing. Boston:
       Little, Brown, 1947.
       The techniques of writing for radio and markets
       for scripts. Concise, authoritative information for
       both professional and student radio writers.

461   Barnouw, Erik. The Television Writer. New York:
       Hill & Wang, 1962. 180 pp.
       Offers a long chapter on the world of the TV
       writer and over 50 facsimile pages of various TV
       scripts with important points demonstrated in each.

462   Bender, James F. (revised by Thomas Lee Crowell,
       Jr.). NBC Handbook of Pronunciation. 3rd edition.
       New York: Crowell, 1964. 418 pp.
       This book is designed solely to present a con-
       venient compilation of those pronunciations that will
       be immediately comprehensible to a great majority
       of Americans.

463   Bittner, John R. and Denise A. Bittner. Radio Jour-
       nalism. Englewood Cliffs, N.J.: Prentice-Hall,
       1976. 207 pp.
       The book offers thorough coverage of many areas,
       from how to obtain your job and how to gather and
       deliver the news, to how to build mini-documen-
       taries and news features. It shows you how to con-
       duct interviews and how to make the local radio
       news as professional as network radio news. Index.

464   Bliss, Edward, Jr. and John M. Patterson. Writing
       News for Broadcast. New York: Columbia Univer-
       sity Press, 1971. 298 pp.
       This timely volume is designed to serve as a
       text on how to write news for radio and television.
       Bibliography, index, and photographs.

465   Burack, A. S. Television Plays for Writers. Boston:
       The Writers, Inc., 1957. 396 pp.
       Eight television plays with comment and analysis
       by the authors.

466   Chayefsky, Paddy. Television Plays. New York:
       Simon & Schuster, 1955. 268 pp.
       Contains the complete scripts of six of the au-
       thor's plays.

467   Cowgill, Rome. Fundamentals of Writing for Radio.
       New York: Rinehart & Co. , 1949.
           An intensive text stressing the importance of a
       sound understanding of the broadcasting medium in
       learning to write for radio.

468   Field, Stanley. Professional Broadcast Writer's Hand-
       book. Blue Ridge Summit, Pa. : TAB Books, 1974.
       396 pp.
           Complete how-to coverage of all forms of writ-
       ing--drama, documentary, children's and religious
       programming, news, and commercial copy--for both
       radio and TV. Bibliography, glossary, and index.

469   French, Florence Felten; William B. Levenson; and
       Vera Cober Rockwell. Radio English. New York:
       McGraw-Hill, 1952. 368 pp.
           Radio English is a document from the hands of
       three experts. They have organized their textbook
       first so that the newcomer can make brief expedi-
       tions into the exciting new country of radio. Later
       they show him how to penetrate more deeply. Bib-
       liography, glossary, illustrations, index, and photo-
       graphs.

470   Hall, Mark W. Broadcast Journalism: An Introduc-
       tion to News Writing. New York: Hastings House
       Publishers, 1971. 159 pp.
           The book covers all basics of radio-television
       news writing style as well as providing information
       and guidelines in handling the major types of stories
       that a broadcast journalist might be expected to
       cover during his career. Index.

471   Herman, Lewis Helmar. A Practical Manual of Screen-
       Play-Writing for Theatre and Television Films.
       Cleveland, Ohio: World Publishing Co. , 1952.
       294 pp.
           This book is a practical manual of screen-play
       writing. Its purpose is to supply practical rules
       and suggestions and to describe practices applicable
       to the writing of motion-picture screen plays for both
       theater and television presentation. Index.

472   Hilliard, Robert L. Writing for Television and Radio.
       3rd edition. New York: Hastings House Publishers,
       1976. 461 pp.

This is an updated version of a highly praised
text. It is practical for home study as the book
includes end-of-chapter exercises and notes. Bibliography, charts, index, and photographs.

473 Keirstead, Phillip. Journalist's Notebook of Live
Radio-TV News. Blue Ridge Summit, Pa.: TAB
Books, 1976. 252 pp.
Written to provide broadcast journalists with a
solid understanding of journalism concepts and techniques plus a complete knowledge of the technology
with which they work. Covers the techniques of
gathering, processing, writing, and broadcasting
live news, using the latest electronic equipment,
including mini-cams. Pulls together all the elements a reporter must have at his command to give
a convincing on-air performance. Glossary, illustrations, and photographs.

474 Meyer, Philip. Precision Journalism: A Reporter's
Introduction to Social Science Methods. Bloomington: Indiana University Press, 1973.
Offers the basic rudiments of social science methods for reporters, dealing with research methods
only insofar as the in-depth reporter may need.

475 Peck, William A. Anatomy of Local Radio-TV Copy.
4th edition. Blue Ridge Summit, Pa.: TAB Books,
1976. 140 pp.
This new, revised fourth edition is a complete
over-the-shoulder course in creative copywriting by
one of the best admen in the business, who gives
practical instruction on every step of the copywriting process--from ideas to polished results.

476 Ris, Thomas F. Promotional & Advertising Copywriter's Handbook. Blue Ridge Summit, Pa.: TAB
Books, 1971. 128 pp.
While providing text material emphasizing the
important aspects of preparing advertising or promotional copy for various media (newspapers, magazines, billboards, direct mail, radio, and television), it is essentially a copywriting course workbook which requires the student to complete some
18 different assignments.

477 Rivers, William L. The Mass Media: Reporting,

Writing, Editing. 2nd edition. New York: Harper
& Row, 1975.   644 pp.
    Offers 20 chapters on reporting, writing, and
editing for both broadcasting and print media.   The
last 50 pages offers a handbook for journalists.

478 Roberts, Edward Barry.   Television Writing and Sell-
     ing.   Boston: The Writers, Inc., 1960.   504 pp.
         An excellent how-to-do-it book covering all as-
     pects of writing for television and how to sell your
     television scripts.

479 Seldes, Gilbert.   Writing for Television.   Garden City,
     N.Y.: Doubleday, 1952.   254 pp.
         This is a practical analysis of the principles and
     practices of successful writing for television.   It
     provides the beginning writer with a complete pro-
     fessional survey of the techniques of the trade.
     Glossary.

480 Siller, Robert C.   Guide to Professional Radio & TV
     Newscasting.   Blue Ridge Summit, Pa.: TAB
     Books, 1972.   224 pp.
         Here is a practical self-study guide especially
     written for those who want to get started in the fas-
     cinating and expanding field of broadcast journalism.
     The author discusses all the basic elements needed,
     then goes on to show how the pros on both local
     and network levels prepare for a newscast.   Illus-
     trations and index.

481 Taylor, Cecil P.   Making a TV Play.   Boston: Rout-
     ledge & Kegan Paul, 1970.   96 pp.
         Apart from the technical and creative problems
     involved in writing a television play, the author re-
     cords also the processes involved in selling a play
     for television from the first outline submitted to
     its final acceptance.

482 Terrell, Neil.   The Power of Technique of Radio-TV
     Copywriting.   Blue Ridge Summit, Pa.: TAB
     Books, 1971.   224 pp.
         Here is a practical handbook for active copy-
     writers, broadcast salesmen, and students who aim
     for a career in broadcasting.   It graphically shows
     how to write copy that moves and inspires listen-
     ers--copy that sells.   It covers basic advertising

principles as they apply to radio. It shows how to recognize each client's prospects, then how to create copy that motivates those prospects, copy designed to move listeners to buy. Index.

483 Trapnell, Coles. An Introduction to Television Writing. Revised edition. New York: Hawthorn Books, 1974. A useful book with many good hints on writing for television. Most of the examples are limited to the writing for television film.

484 Trapnell, Coles. Teleplay: An Introduction to Television Writing. San Francisco: Chandler Publishing Co., 1966. 245 pp.
Offers two major parts: theory (with discussion of the actor, script form, writer-director roles, character creation), and practice (covering selling of scripts, role of unions, etc.). The book stresses creative writing within the television series format.

485 Tyrrell, Robert. The Work of the Television Journalist. New York: Hastings House Publishers, 1972. 180 pp.
Television journalism depends on a team of talents and skills. Each member should know something about the others' problems and methods. This book describes every job, and analyzes the role of each, from the work of the writer and producer to that of the cameraman, recordist, film editor, and newscaster. Charts, glossary, illustrations, and index.

486 Wainwright, Charles Anthony. The Television Copy-writer: How to Create Successful TV Commercials. New York: Hastings House Publishers, 1966. 318 pp.
This book is concerned with the creative aspects of television commercials. Some chapters are slightly technical. Charts, illustrations, and index.

487 Willis, Edgar E. Writing Television and Radio Programs. New York: Holt, Rinehart & Winston, 1967. 372 pp.
Over half is devoted to the dramatic form of radio and TV writing, doing a good job of covering its key elements, with the rest covering documentaries and news, children's programs, comedy shows,

commercials and general kinds of talk formats.
Bibliography, illustrations, and index.

488   Wimer, Arthur and Dale Brix. Workbook for Radio
      and TV News Editing and Writing. 3rd edition.
      Dubuque, Iowa: William C. Brown, 1970. 350 pp.
          Both text (in part one) and workbook, the latter
      offering news reading exercises, writing practice,
      and listening reports.

489   Wulfemeyer, K. Tim. Beginning Broadcast Newswrit-
      ing: A Self-Instructional Learning Experience.
      Ames: Iowa State University Press, 1976. 89 pp.
          This workbook features a programmed approach
      so that students can move at their own pace and
      find out how they did.

490   Wylie, Max. Radio Writing. New York: Rinehart &
      Co. , 1939. (Later published under the title Radio
      and Television Writing, 1950.) 550 pp.
          This is a textbook on how to write for radio with
      much illustrative material. The author has en-
      deavored to show both the student and the interested
      layman what the standard practices of modern broad-
      casting really are. Illustrations, index, and photo-
      graphs.

491   Wylie, Max. Writing for Television. New York:
      Cowles Book Co. , 1970. 456 pp.
          Contains 12 full scripts from recent network
      series programs and a lot of useful tips.

D.   Performance

See also nos. 58, 152, 900, 972, 1075, 1095.

492   Duerr, Edwin. Radio and Television Acting: Criti-
      cism, Theory, and Practice. Westport, Conn. :
      Greenwood Press, 1972. 417 pp.

493   Kingson, Walter K. and Rome Cowgill. Television
      Acting and Directing: A Handbook. New York:
      Holt, Rinehart & Winston, 1965. 298 pp.
          Basically a collection of scripts for practice
      with perhaps 40 pages of suggestions and instruc-
      tions.

E. General

See also nos. 29, 33, 58, 249, 330, 346, 382, 389, 1097.

494 Bay, Howard. Stage Design. New York: Drama Book
     Specialists, 1974. 218 pp.
         Good reference for all types of stage design.
     Useful for large-scale television productions. Illus-
     trations.

495 Coombs, Charles I. Window on the World. New York:
     World Publishing Co. , 1965. 125 pp.
         Describes in a simple, clear manner how a pro-
     gram is put together and broadcast.

496 Henneke, Ben Graf and Edward S. Dumit. The An-
     nouncer's Handbook. San Francisco: Rinehart &
     Co. , 1959. 293 pp.
         This book discusses the skills required of the
     successful radio and/or television announcer. Bib-
     liography, charts, illustrations, and index.

497 Kehoe, Vincent, Jr. The Technique of Film and Tele-
     vision Make-Up. Revised edition. New York:
     Hastings House Publishers, 1976. 280 pp.
         Here is all the latest information about the ad-
     vances made in compatible systems--requiring make-
     up to be photographed in both color and black-and-
     white simultaneously--that makes it possible for to-
     day's make-up to appear less like "make-up" than
     did the look of former foundations and procedures.

498 Skiles, Marlin. Music Scoring for TV & Motion Pic-
     tures. Blue Ridge Summit, Pa. : TAB Books,
     1976. 266 pp.
         Would-be composers and arrangers will learn
     what they have to know to turn out effective music
     scores that preserve the commercialism of the fast-
     paced world of TV and motion pictures, without
     sacrificing or unduly restraining their own artistic
     creativity. And the director, whose responsibility
     it is to amass a coherent package of story and
     music within an impossibly short time allotment,
     will learn how to use that time to produce the best
     possible marriage of story and score with the least
     possible investment of manpower and money. Illus-
     trations and index.

499   Turnbull, Robert B.   Radio and Television Sound Ef-
        fects.   New York: Rinehart & Co., 1951.   334 pp.
            Detailed discussion of various types of sound ef-
        fect devices.   Glossary, illustrations, index, and
        photographs.

500   Tyler, Kingdon S.   Modern Radio.   New York: Har-
        court, Brace, 1944.   238 pp.
            A simplified and general description of both radio
        and television equipment and studio development dur-
        ing the war years, this volume provides a useful
        guide to the state of the art at the time.   About
        half is devoted to each medium (with chapters on
        FM radio and radar included); major coverage is
        given to studios, microphones, tubes, antennas, re-
        ceivers, the CBS system of color television, and
        radio's future.   Illustrations, index, and photo-
        graphs.

501   Zettl, Herbert.   Sight-Sound-Motion: Applied Media
        Aesthetics.   Belmont, Calif.:   Wadsworth, 1973.
        401 pp.
            In a down-to-earth approach, this book shows how
        to use light and shadows to present a story with
        clarity and impact; to use the small space of the
        television screen or the large movie screen to show
        images in motion with the greatest effectiveness;
        and to use sound to complement, dominate, or
        merge with the visual image.   It also extends these
        elements to other media, including photography,
        painting, writing, and radio.   Serves as a guide for
        both media producer and media consumer.   Bibli-
        ography, glossary, illustrations, index, and photo-
        graphs.

7. MINORITIES

See also nos. 74, 166, 291, 334, 344, 518, 546, 681, 897, 998, 1026, 1027, 1028, 1082.

502 Gelfman, Judith S. Women in Television News. New York: Columbia University Press, 1976. 186 pp.
    Women in Television News takes us behind the cameras, through the bureaucracy of network personnel policies, to meet the women who have "made it" in the traditionally male-dominated world of television news. Through firsthand interviews and on-the-job observations, the author divulges what she learned from 30 women newscasters about their role in television news, from general topics--such as how they got their first job or the future of women in broadcast news--to specific ones--such as salaries and the importance of physical appearance. Bibliography, charts, index, and photographs.

503 Klever, Anita. Women in Television. Philadelphia: Westminster Press, 1975. 142 pp.

504 Lewels, Francisco J., Jr. The Uses of the Media by the Chicano Movement: A Study in Minority Access. New York: Praeger, 1974. 185 pp.
    The story of how the media have served the author's fellow Mexican-Americans. Bibliography, charts, and index.

8.   RESPONSIBILITY

See also nos. 38, 198, 204, 216, 225, 315, 323, 326, 335, 339, 358, 448, 529, 546, 548, 598, 602, 804.

505   Barron, Jerome.   Freedom of the Press for Whom? The Right of Access to Mass Media.   Bloomington: Indiana University Press, 1973.   368 pp.
      This provocative book by a noted authority on Constitutional law argues that freedom of expression is meaningless if all the important means of expression--press, television, and radio--are closed. The book chronicles the new effort throughout the country to open up the media by applying citizen group pressure, by bringing court action, and by prodding federal agencies.   Bibliography and index.

506   Bosmajian, Haig A. , ed.   Obscenity and Freedom of Expression.   New York: Burt Franklin & Co. , 1976. 348 pp.
      Collection of the most important court decisions (Supreme Court and lower courts) on all aspects of the subjects.   Bibliography and index.

507   CBS and Congress: "The Selling of the Pentagon" Papers.   (Special issue of the Educational Broadcasting Review.)   Washington, D. C. :   National Association of Educational Broadcasters, 1971.   144 pp.
      Provides pertinent letters and hearings for students and scholars interested in Congressional hearings concerning the CBS network and the documentary "Selling of the Pentagon. "   Charts and illustrations.

508   Cogley, John.   Report on Blacklisting II: Radio-Television.   New York: Fund for the Republic, 1956. (Reprinted by Arno Press, 1971.)

509   Coons, John E. , ed.   Freedom and Responsibility in
      Broadcasting.   Evanston, Ill. :   Northwestern Uni-
      versity Press, 1961.   252 pp.
            This book covers three areas: 1) some of the
      relevant facts about broadcasting life are revealed,
      2) problems of programming are analyzed, and 3) the
      reactions of the communications world to the real or
      supposed threat of governmental restraints are re-
      vealed.

510   Emerson, Thomas I.   The System of Freedom of Ex-
      pression.   New York: Random House, 1970.   754 pp.
            This book attempts to formulate the legal founda-
      tions for an effective system of free expression in
      the United States.   Based on the principles underly-
      ing such a system, the dynamics of its operation,
      and the role of law and legal institutions in main-
      taining it, the author develops a comprehensive
      theory of the First Amendment designed to achieve
      a workable system attuned to present-day conditions.
      Index.

511   Ernst, Morris L.   The First Freedom.   New York:
      Macmillan, 1946.   316 pp.
            Book is divided into three sections: 1) an ex-
      ploration of the philosophy of freedom; 2) trends in
      the controls of press, radio, movies; and 3) means
      of reversing the monopoly trend in press, radio,
      and movies.   Bibliography, charts, illustrations,
      and index.

512   Federal Communications Commission.   Public Service
      Responsibility of Broadcast Licensees.   Washington,
      D. C. :   Arno Press, 1946.
            Popularly known as the "Blue Book" because of
      its original paper cover, this now classic publica-
      tion includes information of the legal basis for FCC
      regulation.   It provides examples of programming
      practices, and discusses a survey of several years
      of the financial earnings of broadcasting that indi-
      cate the ways in which stations might be able to
      schedule a greater number of public service pro-
      grams.   The "Blue Book" continues to provide the
      clearest presentation of the Federal Communications
      Commission's attitudes about the programming stan-
      dards of broadcasting stations.

513   Gross, Gerald, ed.   The Responsibility of the Press.
      New York: Simon & Schuster "Clarion" Books, 1969.
      416 pp.
      Offers 31 articles on all aspects of the problems
      of all media.

514   Guimary, Donald L.   Citizens' Groups and Broadcast-
      ing. New York: Praeger, 1976. 171 pp.
      Deals with several selected early citizens' groups,
      broadcaster and government reaction to such groups,
      and finally provides detailed information on three
      current groups.

515   Lacy, Dan.   Freedom and Communications.   Urbana:
      University of Illinois Press, 1965. 108 pp.
      Offers a very brief overview of American media
      as they were in the late 1950s, concentrating on is-
      sues of freedom and censorship.

516   Lynch, William.   The Image Industries: A Construc-
      tive Analysis of Films and Television. New York:
      Sheed & Ward, 1959. 159 pp.
      Discusses importance of mass media to life in
      America with emphasis on moral aspects.

517   Merrill, John C. and Ralph D. Barney, eds.   Ethics
      and the Press: Readings in Mass Media Morality.
      New York: Hastings House Publishers, 1975.
      338 pp.
      A collection of 35 articles about the ethical con-
      siderations and implications the media must face in
      reporting the news. Bibliography, charts, and in-
      dex.

518   Rivers, William L. and Wilbur Schramm.   Responsi-
      bility in Mass Communication. New York: Harper
      and Row, 1969. 314 pp.
      Analyzes issues such as freedom, restraint,
      truth, fairness, and offers a chapter on media
      coverage of blacks. Bibliography and index.

519   Routt, Edd.   Dimensions of Broadcast Editorializing.
      Blue Ridge Summit, Pa.: TAB Books, 1974.
      204 pp.
      This text tells broadcasters why they should edi-
      torialize, how to establish an editorial policy, how
      to develop and write forceful and effective editorials,

how to present them, and how to avoid legal compli-
cations resulting from violations of the FCC "fairness" rules.

520 Schramm, Wilbur. Responsibility in Mass Communica-
     tion. New York: Harper & Row, 1957. 391 pp.
     This is a study on the problem of responsibility
     in mass communication sponsored by the Federal
     Council of the Churches of Christ in America. The
     book deals with the common problems of all practi-
     tioners in the mass media by its careful analysis of
     the salient moral problems which they confront, and
     by its wealth of detailed case studies which give
     substance to the conclusions of the author. Bibli-
     ography, charts, and index.

521 Skornia, Harry J. and Jack William Kitson, eds.
     Problems and Controversies in Television and Radio.
     Palo Alto, Calif. : Pacific Books, 1968. 503 pp.
     Readings by selected authors, mostly taken from
     unpublished speeches, statements, etc. Selections
     by Gunner Back and Thomas Guback are especially
     applicable to censorship and responsibility in broad-
     casting.

522 Stavins, Ralph L. , ed. Television Today: The End
     of Communication and the Death of Community.
     Washington, D. C. : Communication Service Corp. ,
     1971. 292 pp.
     This empirical study, statistical in nature,
     limits itself to an examination of two criteria.
     First, the mandatory survey of local leaders to as-
     certain the needs and interest of the local commu-
     nity as required by the FCC; second, a statistical
     history of the performance of a licensee, measured
     against his earlier promise. Charts.

523 Stein, Robert. Media Power, Who Is Shaping Your
     Picture of the World. Boston: Houghton-Mifflin,
     1972. 265 pp.
     The purpose of this book is to explore media
     power--how it has come into existence over the
     past generation, how the people who exercise it
     have largely failed to recognize the nature of their
     new problems and possibilities, and how the present
     conflicts suggest the new values and standards that
     are needed for the future.

9. SOCIETY

A. Role of Radio

See also nos. 4, 103, 359, 583, 605, 609, 610, 702, 703.

524 Bureau of Applied Social Research, Columbia University.
     Radio Listening in America: The People Look at
     Radio--Again. New York: Prentice-Hall, 1948.
     178 pp.
          Based on a study done under the auspices of the
     National Opinion Research Center to check the habits
     of radio listeners. Charts and index.

525 Marx, Herbert L. , Jr. Television and Radio in Amer-
     ican Life. New York: Wilson, 1953.
          A compilation of articles dealing with the impact
     of the two major means of mass communications on
     our society, and its significance.

B. Role of Television

See also nos. 300, 304, 332, 334, 339, 370, 382, 525, 587,
612, 707, 708, 709.

526 Adler, Richard, ed. Television as a Social Force:
     New Approaches to TV Criticism. New York:
     Praeger, 1975. 171 pp.
          This volume includes eight original papers from
     a 1974 Aspen conference, taking a broad view of
     television's social role.

527 Adler, Richard and Douglass Cater, eds. Television
     as a Cultural Force. Palo Alto, Calif. : Aspen
     Institute for Humanistic Studies, 1976. 210 pp.
          This book challenges old and outmoded ways of

108

thinking about television with some unique new approaches for both the TV critic and the TV viewer to consider. Bibliography.

528 Arlen, Michael J. Living Room War. New York: Viking Press, 1969. 242 pp.
     Arlen's collected writings about television from his column in the New Yorker, examining television news and other subjects.

529 Baker, Robert K. and Sandra J. Ball, eds. Mass Media and Violence. Washington, D. C. : Government Printing Office, 1969. 614 pp.
     Divided into three parts, the topics covered include: 1) an historic perspective, 2) the news media, and 3) television entertainment and violence. Good study of violence in the media with documented samples. Bibliography and charts.

530 Berger, Arthur Asa. The TV-Guided American. New York: Walker, 1976. 194 pp.
     A popular culture approach to specific entertainment shows--and what each tells about its viewers.

531 Bluem, A. William and Roger Manvell, eds. Television: The Creative Experience. New York: Hastings House Publishers, 1967. 328 pp.
     Included are 37 essays and dialogues by 63 leading writers, producers, directors, educators, performers, and technicians. A wide range of TV theory and practice is explored here, including the challenge of television as an outlet for serious expression, where creative pitfalls and frustrations lie, the outlook for educational TV, the impact of television on politics, and the art and techniques of TV drama. Index.

532 Bogart, Leo. The Age of Television. 3rd edition. New York: Frederick Ungar Publishing Co. , 1972. 515 pp.
     This classic work on the social impact of television viewing habits in America extensively updates and annotates the original text. Although much has been written on the subject since the first publication in 1956, The Age of Television remains the only comprehensive survey which ties together and discusses all relevant issues. Bibliography, charts, and index.

533   Elliott, Philip.   The Making of Television Series: A
       Case Study in the Sociology of Culture.   New York:
       Hastings House Publishers, 1973.   180 pp.
          Analyzes the process of assembling a television
       series, focusing not on production techniques, but
       on program building as a sociological process of
       material selection, program assembly, and audience
       feedback.

534   Elliott, William Y.   Television's Impact on American
       Culture.   East Lansing: Michigan State University
       Press, 1956.   382 pp.
          In this book, it was the author's aim to set tele-
       vision, for the first time, into a frame that shows
       how television fits into the culture which has created
       it, and to explore what its possibilities are in that
       setting.   Charts and glossary.

535   Gabriel, Juri.   Thinking About Television.   London:
       Oxford University Press, 1973.   143 pp.
          Attempts to describe and detail the operations of
       the television broadcast system within which the au-
       thor worked and to discuss some of the ramifica-
       tions of the influence of television on society.

536   Halloran, J. D.; R. L. Brown; and D. C. Chaney.
       Television and Delinquency.   Leicester: Leicester
       University Press, 1970.   221 pp.
          Much popular criticism of television is reviewed,
       as well as varieties of conceptual approaches to
       survey and experimental research in the area.

537   Johnson, Nicholas.   How to Talk Back to Your Tele-
       vision Set.   Boston: Little, Brown, 1970.   228 pp.
          This book is intended to be instructive and inte-
       resting for the thoughtful general reader and student
       of the mass media and a manual for practicing
       pragmatists--in school or out.   The author's inten-
       tion was to encourage bringing more national re-
       sources of talent and creativity to bear upon the na-
       tional policy questions involving broadcasting.

538   Mehling, Harold.   The Great Time-Killer.   New York:
       World Publishing Co., 1962.   352 pp.
          Many of the people, creative and administrative,
       who work in television are demoralized and embit-
       tered and want the story of television's degeneration

told in the hope that the medium can be rescued.
Charts and index.

539   Milgram, Stanley and R. Lance Shotland. Television
      and Antisocial Behavior: Field Experiments. New
      York: Academic Press, 1973. 183 pp.
           This book reports a pioneering study in which the
      experimenters have had control of the central ex-
      perimental variable--the content of television pro-
      gramming itself. Through the cooperation of a
      major television network, the investigators were
      able to produce and air three versions--with differ-
      ing antisocial content--of an episode of the popular
      prime time program, Medical Center. They then
      carried out a series of highly original field experi-
      ments designed to assess the effects of the antiso-
      cial elements in the programs on the subject popu-
      lation. The book is a clear and reasoned report of
      the history, design, and results of this research.
      Bibliography, charts, illustrations, index, and photo-
      graphs.

540   Newcomb, Horace, ed. Television: The Critical View.
      New York: Oxford University Press, 1976. 336 pp.
           Some of the best examples of the growing body
      of criticism that seeks to establish and define the
      role of television in American culture are brought to-
      gether in this unique anthology. In its broadest
      sense a collection of humanistic criticism, it ex-
      tends beyond journalistic criticism which at its best
      is often as ephemeral as the medium itself, and
      supplements the social scientific research that deals
      primarily with audience responses rather than with
      the content of television.

541   Simonson, Soloman. Crisis in Television: A Study of
      the Private Judgement in the Public Interest. New
      York: Living Books, 1966. 230 pp.
           This book reflects the crisis in society at large.
      Provides some insight into the problems of com-
      mercial stations burying cultural programs in less
      than prime time.

542   Surgeon General's Scientific Advisory Committee on
      Television and Social Behavior. Television and So-
      cial Behavior, Volume I: Media Content and Con-
      trol. Washington, D.C.: Government Printing

Office, 1972.   546 pp.
    Some 300 pages on U.S. television programming
as perceived by parents, the industry, and critics.
Also, four long essays on program content and
trends in four selected foreign countries.

C.   General

See also nos. 64, 79, 157, 164, 168, 175, 202, 266, 317,
516, 517, 518, 523, 589, 591, 597, 598, 602, 724, 732,
840.

543   Agee, Warren K. , ed.   Mass Media in a Free Society.
          Lawrence: University Press of Kansas, 1969.   96 pp.
          Six respected spokesmen from mass media dis-
      cuss the challenges and problems to be met by
      newspapers, TV, motion pictures, and magazines.

544   Allen, Don.   The Electric Anthology: Probes into
          Mass Media and Popular Culture.   Dayton, Ohio:
          Pflaum, 1975.   198 pp.
          Taking a strong popular culture emphasis, the
      30 selections include radio-TV, films, popular liter-
      ature, and pop music.

545   Aronson, James.   Deadline for the Media: Today's
          Challenges to Press, TV and Radio.   Indianapolis:
          Bobbs-Merrill, 1973.   327 pp.
          Begins with a discussion of the (pre-Watergate)
      Nixon administration on the news media, then pre-
      sents a good deal of data (in a favorable light) con-
      cerning the rise of the "underground" or non-estab-
      lishment news sources.

546   Broadcasting and Social Action: A Handbook for Station
          Executives.   Washington, D.C. : National Associa-
          tion of Educational Broadcasters, 1969.   77 pp.
          This handbook is a series of illustrations on
      what radio and television stations can affirmatively
      do in order to help solve our most urgent current
      problem--the confrontation between blacks and
      whites.   Bibliography, charts, and illustrations.

547   Bulman, David, ed.   Molders of Opinion.   Milwaukee:
          Bruce, 1945.   166 pp.
          Chapters written by a well-known journalist

covering a wide range of topics dealing with mass
communications and its influence on the public.
Photographs.

548   Casty, Alan, ed.   Mass Media and Mass Man.   New
      York: Holt, Rinehart & Winston, 1968.   260 pp.
         Focuses on the media as processors and convey-
      ors of culture and information.   Provides a survey
      of the approaches being made and what is said about
      the media.   There are two parts to the book: Part
      I, "The Mass Media and Culture" and Part II, "The
      Mass Media and Information. "   Bibliography and in-
      dex.

549   Chaffee, Steven H. and Michael J. Petrick.   Using the
      Mass Media: Communication Problems in American
      Society.   New York: McGraw-Hill, 1975.   264 pp.
         Includes discussions of the American media sys-
      tems, news and public information problem areas,
      persuasion in advertising and politics, social con-
      trol of the media, and social change in and because
      of the media.   Index.

550   Chaney, David.   Processes of Mass Communication.
      New York: Herder & Herder, 1972.   187 pp.
         Offers a sociological approach that combines
      findings of several fields into a brief analysis of
      mass communications centering on participation,
      production, and distribution.

551   Christenson, Reo M. and Robert O. McWilliams, eds.
      Voice of the People: Readings in Public Opinion
      and Propaganda.   New York: McGraw-Hill, 1967.
      632 pp.
         Nearly 100 readings on topics such as nature of
      public opinion, background of public opinion, role
      of the press, radio-television-film, mass mind,
      censorship and freedom, political propaganda, ad-
      vertising, etc.   Index.

552   Clark, David G. and William B. Blankenberg.   You
      and Media: Mass Communication and Society.   San
      Francisco: Canfield Press (Harper & Row), 1973.
      275 pp.
         Offers a 14 chapter topical (rather than media)
      subject division, dealing in a very basic fashion
      with structure and issues.

553 Cohen, Stanley and Jock Young, eds. The Manufacture
     of News: A Reader. Beverly Hills, Calif. : Sage,
     1973. 383 pp.
        An investigation into an area of public concern
     which contains much valuable material for sociologists,
     psychologists, criminologists, social workers, stu-
     dents, teachers, and all those at the receiving end
     of mass communications. Bibliography and illustra-
     tions.

554 De Fleur, Melvin L. and Sandra Ball-Rokeach.
     Theories of Mass Communication. 3rd edition.
     New York: David McKay, 1975. 304 pp.
        In this completely revised and updated version,
     the authors discuss the impact that the introduction
     of each new medium has had on Western civiliza-
     tion. New sections include the effects of television
     violence on children and on media in the future; al-
     so included is a section in which the authors formu-
     late an integrated theory on the effects of mass
     media on society. Index.

555 Dennis, Everette E. and William L. Rivers. Other
     Voices: The New Journalism in America. San
     Francisco: Canfield Press (Harper & Row), 1973.
     218 pp.
        Offers material on modern muckraking, journal-
     ism reviews, advocacy, counter-culture press, al-
     ternative broadcasting, in-depth research, etc.

556 Donner, Stanley T. , ed. The Meaning of Commercial
     Television: The Texas-Stanford Seminar. Austin:
     University of Texas Press, 1967. 157 pp.
        This is basically a collection of nine speeches
     homogenized by the editor into a high-octane distil-
     late of contemporary criticism, defense, and apolo-
     gia of the medium.

557 Gerbner, George; Larry P. Gross; and William H.
     Melody, eds. Communications Technology and So-
     cial Policy: Understanding the New "Cultural Revo-
     lution. " New York: John Wiley, 1973. 573 pp.
        Covers such topics as communications and com-
     puters, broadcasting technologies, communications
     satellites, CATV, etc. Charts.

558 Glessing, Robert J. and William P. White. Mass

Media: The Invisible Environment. Chicago: Science Research Associates, 1973. 314 pp.

This collection of essays and articles represents a trip through that information-heavy environment in the hope that when the journey is completed the reader will be better able to control and utilize information from the media rather than be manipulated by it. Charts, illustrations, index, and photographs.

559 Greenberg, Bradley S. and Brenda Dervin. Use of Mass Media by the Urban Poor. New York: Praeger, 1970. 251 pp.

This book presents an overview of the communication behavior of the poor with particular emphasis on mass communication behaviors. Purpose is to give the poverty practitioner and the social scientist a realistic picture of the communication behaviors of the poor. Bibliography.

560 Greenberg, Bradley S. and Edwin B. Parker, eds. The Kennedy Assassination and the American Public: Social Communication in Crisis. Stanford, Calif. : Stanford University Press, 1965. 392 pp.

A compilation of responses concerning the assassination of John F. Kennedy, how the mass media reported the news, and how people generally learned and responded to the news. There is a summation of social research findings. Charts and index.

561 Hall, Stuart and Paddy Whannel. The Popular Arts: A Critical Guide to the Mass Media. Boston: Beacon Press, 1964. 480 pp.

An attempt at a teacher-oriented guide to critical media appreciation with chapters on the various media and major content themes and including some specific mentions of American practice.

562 Jacobs, Norman, ed. Culture for the Millions? Mass Media in Modern Society. Princeton, N.J. : D. Van Nostrand Co. , 1961. 200 pp.

Reports on a symposium on culture and the mass media. Participants consisted of historians, philosophers, and artists. Although papers were to deal with mass culture in general, mass media was emphasized with television receiving a major share.

563 Jennings, Ralph M. and Pamela Richard. How to Pro-
     tect Your Rights in Television and Radio. New
     York: Office of Communication, United Church of
     Christ, 1974. 167 pp.

564 Keogh, James. President Nixon and the Press. New
     York: Funk & Wagnalls, 1972. 212 pp.
        The author, a former special assistant to Nixon,
     reports on the intensive efforts of the Nixon Admin-
     istration to combat biased news coverage and get its
     side of the story to the American public. Index.

565 McLuhan, Marshall and Quentin Fiore. The Medium
     Is the Massage: An Inventory of Effects. New
     York: Bantam Books, 1967. 159 pp.
        Reveals how the medium, or process, of our
     time-electric technology is reshaping and restructur-
     ing patterns of social interdependence and every as-
     pect of your personal life. Illustrations and photo-
     graphs.

566 Mendelsohn, Harold. Mass Entertainment. New
     Haven, Conn.: College & University Press, 1966.
     203 pp.
        A sociologically oriented discussion into the
     pleasure and entertainment role of mass media
     which strongly defends that role in the face of exist-
     ing criticism.

567 Merrill, John C. and Ralph L. Lowenstein. Media,
     Messages and Men: New Perspectives in Communi-
     cation. New York: David McKay, 1971. 293 pp.
        Explores topics like the role of news and opin-
     ion media, the media audience, and ethics and con-
     trols in news media. The book seeks to explore
     criticism of the press (meaning all media) while
     providing a conceptual background and viewpoints
     of its own. Bibliography and index.

568 Pember, Don R. Mass Media in America. Chicago:
     Science Research Associates, 1974. 380 pp.
        Twelve chapters discussing the role of media in
     society including media history, newspapers, radio,
     television and film, and material on regulation,
     economics and organization, and media effects.
     Bibliography, index, and photographs.

569 Rivers, William L.; Peterson, Theodore; and Jensen, Jay W. The Mass Media and Modern Society. 2nd edition. San Francisco: Rinehart & Co., 1971. 342 pp.

Although the authors write primarily about the mass media, they find it necessary to take account of the broad context in which the media operate. Their conviction is that the condition of the world affects the media and is affected by the media. Bibliography and index.

570 Rosenberg, Bernard and David M. White, eds. Mass Culture: The Popular Arts in America. Glencoe, Ill.: Free Press, 1957. 561 pp.

This volume draws together the insights of 51 observers commonly concerned with the social effects of the media on American life. Bibliography.

571 Sandman, Peter M.; David M. Rubin; and David B. Sachsman. Media: An Introductory Analysis of American Mass Communications. 2nd edition. Englewood Cliffs, N.J.: Prentice-Hall, 1976. 483 pp.

The basic question which the authors are attempting to answer is: What are the effects of the forms, practices, habits, and biases of the media today? It is written for the general consumer of the mass media. Bibliography, charts, and index.

572 Schiller, Herbert I. The Mind Managers. Boston: Beacon Press, 1973. 214 pp.

The author asks: Why and how does the massive knowledge industry--recreation and entertainment, polling, advertising, publishing, TV, and radio-- use our beliefs in freedom, individual choice, and objectivity in influencing if not creating our attitudes and behavior? Bibliography, charts, and index.

573 Schmidt, Benno C. Freedom of the Press vs. Public Access. New York: Aspen/Praeger, 1976. 296 pp.

This book is divided into four parts: 1) treating access to the media generally, 2) access in defamation and "public forum" cases, 3) access to broadcasting and cable, and 4) the future of access theory in light of the Tornillo decision.

574   Schwartz, Barry N. , ed. Human Connection and the
        New Media. Englewood Cliffs, N.J. : Prentice-
        Hall, 1973. 179 pp.
           Covers many facets of communication, relating
        the process to the new technological developments of
        cable, videotape, and cybernetics.

575   Seldes, Gilbert. The New Mass Media: Challenge to
        a Free Society. Washington, D.C. : Public Affairs
        Press, 1968. 100 pp.
           In this volume the author guides adult groups in
        exploring the new mass media--their implications
        for the individual and the free society. Ranging
        over the content, effects, and social control of tele-
        vision, radio, and motion pictures, he raises criti-
        cal issues for study and discussion. Bibliography.

576   Stanley, Robert H. and Charles S. Steinberg. The
        Media Environment: Mass Communications in Ameri-
        can Society. New York: Hastings House Publishers,
        1976. 281 pp.
           From I Love Lucy's pregnancy to Maude's abor-
        tion, from the National Association of Broadcasters
        television code to the allegedly indecent broadcast
        of a George Carlin album cut, Messrs. Stanley and
        Steinberg have pieced together the people, corpora-
        tions, events, and law that shaped the mass media.
        Bibliography and index.

577   Steinberg, Charles S. , ed. Mass Media and Communi-
        cation. 2nd edition. New York: Hastings House
        Publishers, 1972. 686 pp.
           Excellent book on the development of how the
        media and mass communications both serve and re-
        flect society. Thought provoking readings in this
        new and enlarged edition. Bibliography and index.

578   Voelker, Francis H. and Ludmilla A. Voelker, eds.
        Mass Media: Forces in Our Society. 2nd edition.
        New York: Harcourt, Brace, Jovanovich, 1975.
        431 pp.
           Contains five mini-studies of media coverage.
        Bibliography and illustrations.

579   Wells, Alan, ed. Mass Media and Society. 2nd edi-
        tion. Palo Alto, Calif. : Mayfield Publishing, 1975.
        412 pp.

This new edition contains some 20 new selections.
Good anthology on social impact of the mass media.

580   White, David Manning and Richard Averson, eds.
      Sight, Sound, and Society--Motion Pictures and Tele-
      vision in America.   Boston: Beacon Press, 1968.
      466 pp.
      An investigation of the ways by which American
      society communicates with itself.   The book con-
      sists of essays written by producers, writers, pro-
      fessional critics, educators, and government offi-
      cials.   The contributors are concerned with both
      motion pictures and television and their impact upon
      the lives of all of us.   Index.

581   Whitney, Frederick C.   Mass Media and Mass Commu-
      nications in Society.   Dubuque, Iowa: William C.
      Brown, 1975.   474 pp.
      Each of the mass media is examined in the light
      of its historical development, relationship to other
      media, and its effect on the audience.   Bibliography,
      illustrations, and index.

582   Wright, Charles R.   Mass Communications: A Socio-
      logical Perspective.   2nd edition.   New York:
      Random House, 1975.   179 pp.
      This book should serve as an important remind-
      er that there is far more to the mass communica-
      tions process than a simple linear relationship be-
      tween a source, a message, a medium, and a re-
      cipient.   Wright offers a pastiche of sociological
      variables that are to be taken into account in the
      exploration of the mass communication process.
      Bibliography.

10. CRITICISM

A. Radio

See also nos. 235, 403.

583 Williams, Albert N. Listening: A Collection of Critical Articles on Radio. Denver, Colo. : University
of Denver Press, 1948. 152 pp.
    Series of essays on the radio medium concerning
the materials, programming, commercials, etc.

B. Television

See also nos. 283, 296, 300, 302, 311, 312, 342, 398, 526,
527, 536, 537, 538, 540, 621, 939.

584 Ellison, Harlan. The Glass Teat: Essays of Opinion
on the Subject of Television. New York: Ace
Books, 1970; 317 pp. and The Other Glass Teat.
New York: Pyramid Books, 1975; 397 pp.
    Collected anti-establishment television criticism
by the Los Angeles Free Press critic.

585 Hazard, Patrick D. , ed. TV as an Art: Some Essays on Criticism. Champaign, Ill. : National
Council of Teachers of English, 1966. 160 pp.
    Discussion of dramatic, musical, and other pro-
gram formats in the arts.

586 Miles, Betty. Channeling Children: Sex Stereotyping
in Prime-Time TV. Princeton, N. J. : Women on
Words and Images, 1975.

587 Skornia, Harry J. Television and Society: An Inquest
and Agenda for Improvement. New York: McGraw-
Hill, 1965. 268 pp.

Although the most essential portion of this study
is the recommendations to which it leads, early
sections provide an examination of what appear to
be persistent, recurring, and critical weaknesses in
our broadcasting. Index.

588 Sopkin, Charles. Seven Glorious Days, Seven Fun-
     Filled Nights. New York: Simon & Schuster, 1968.
     241 pp.
     One man's somewhat cynical report of a solid
     week of viewing the New York television channels
     (all seven of them)--what he saw and what he
     thought about what he saw.

C. General

See also nos. 285, 331, 383, 492, 545, 556, 558, 561, 562,
565, 567, 569, 575, 1033, 1059.

589 Finkelstein, Sidney. Sense and Nonsense of McLuhan.
     New York: International Publishers, 1968. 122 pp.
     An interesting and revealing book about Marshall
     McLuhan, referred to in the text as the brilliant
     prophet of our time. Describes, discusses, and
     questions McLuhan's "media revolution."

590 Geller, Henry. A Modest Proposal to Reform the
     Federal Communications Commission. Santa Monica,
     Calif.: Rand Corp., 1974.

591 Guimary, Donald L. Citizens' Groups and Broadcast-
     ing. New York: Praeger, 1975.

592 Howitt, Dennis and Guy Cumberbatch. Mass Media
     Violence and Society. New York: Halstead Press/
     John Wiley, 1975. 167 pp.
     The central theme of this book is that the mass
     media do not have any significant effect on the level
     of violence in society. Index.

593 Hulteng, John L. and Roy P. Nelson. Fourth Estate:
     An Informal Appraisal of the News and Opinion
     Media. New York: Harper & Row, 1971. 356 pp.
     Seeks to explore criticism of the press (meaning
     all media) while providing a conceptual background
     and viewpoints of its own. Illustrations and index.

594 Hunt, Todd. Reviewing for the Mass Media. Phila-
       delphia: Chilton Books, 1972. 190 pp.
       Deals with the whys and wherefores of reviewing.
       Deals with book, movie, film, TV, and other kinds
       of reviews, discussing writing and content. Bibli-
       ography.

595 Larsen, Otto N. , ed. Violence and the Mass Media.
       New York: Harper & Row, 1968. 310 pp.
       Contains some 30 articles on all aspects of media
       violence. Index.

596 Lippmann, Walter. Public Opinion. New York: Mac-
       millan, 1961. 425 pp.
       Discusses the formulation of public opinion and
       argues for public opinion to be developed for mass
       communication instead of being formed by the media.
       Index.

597 Merrill, John C. The Imperative of Freedom: A
       Philosophy of Journalistic Autonomy. New York:
       Hastings House Publishers, 1974. 228 pp.
       Professor Merrill presents in this study a cheer-
       less assessment of media in the United States.

598 National Citizens Committee for Broadcasting. Demys-
       tifying Broadcasting. Washington, D. C. : NCCB,
       1974.

599 Rubin, Ronald I. The Objectives of the U. S. Informa-
       tion Agency: Controversies and Analysis. New
       York: Praeger, 1968. 251 pp.
       Provides an in-depth discussion of USIA objec-
       tives as seen by Congress, the Executive Branch,
       and in USIA itself.

600 Shayon, Robert Lewis. Open to Criticism. Boston:
       Beacon Press, 1971. 324 pp.
       Unique self-analysis of the then-critic for Satur-
       day Review. Includes many of his columns, the
       background of their writing, and his latest reaction
       to it all.

601 Smith, Robert R. Beyond the Vast Wasteland: The
       Criticism of Broadcasting. Falls Church, Va. :
       Speech Communication Association, 1976. 105 pp.
       Explores the aims and varieties of criticism in

general and then turns to criticism of broadcasting, reviewing the role of criticism in public policy and the criteria for evaluating broadcasting.

602 Steinberg, Charles H. , ed. Broadcasting: The Critical Challenges. New York: Hastings House Publishers, 1974. 320 pp.

11. PUBLIC BROADCASTING

A. Public Radio

See also nos. 97, 650, 906.

603 Harrison, Margaret. Radio in the Classroom. New
York: Prentice-Hall, 1937. 260 pp.
This book offers suggestions to those concerned
with the classroom use of radio. It is designed to
help supervisors, principals, and teachers make
use of programs broadcast throughout the country.
Bibliography and index.

604 Herzberg, Max J., ed. Radio and English Teaching:
Experience, Problems, and Procedures. New York:
D. Appleton-Century Co., 1941. 246 pp.
Gives examples of radio in education, English
literature, and a bibliography of publications. Bib-
liography and index.

605 Hill, Frank Ernst. Tune In for Education. New York:
National Committee on Education by Radio, 1942.
109 pp.
General summation of events in which the National Committee on Education by Radio had partici-
pated during the 11 years of its existence.

606 Koon, Cline M. The Art of Teaching by Radio. U.S.
Office of Education Bulletin No. 4. Washington,
D.C.: Government Printing Office, 1933. 32 pp.
Describes techniques used to teach by radio.
Bibliography.

607 Land, Herman W., Associates. The Hidden Medium:
A Status Report on Educational Radio in the United
States. Washington, D.C.: National Association

124

of Educational Broadcasters, 1967.   143 pp.
Covers all aspects of the field including station organization, the relationship of stations to their communities, data regarding the areas served by educational stations, the means by which stations determine listeners' needs and promote station activities, present and future budgetary requirements and sources of financing, technical details concerning station equipment and operating facilities, personnel, etc. Charts.

608 Lazarsfeld, Paul F. Radio and the Printed Page. New York: Duell, Sloan & Pearce, 1940 (reprinted by Arno Press, 1971).   354 pp.
Deals with the educational aspects of radio, listener research, and effects of radio on the reading of newspapers. Charts and index.

609 Milam, Lorenzo W.   Sex and Broadcasting: A Handbook on Starting Community Radio Stations.   2nd edition.   Saratoga, Calif.: Dildo Press, 1972. 352 pp.
Within its pages this book offers a cheap and dirty guide to obtaining a non-commercial radio license and putting a station on the air, with excursions into programming, the general state of the world, and advanced messing with the FCC.

610 Post, Steve.   Playing in the FM Band.   New York: Viking Press, 1974.   230 pp.
An insider's account of his experience with Pacifica's New York station, WBAI-FM.

611 Willey, Roy DeVerl and Helen Ann Young.   Radio in Elementary Education. Boston: D. C. Heath & Co., 1948.   450 pp.
Emphasizes the social impact of radio on children and suggests ways in which this "new medium" can be utilized in the classroom. Bibliography, illustrations, index, and photographs.

B.   Public Television

See also nos. 38, 531, 640, 695, 905, 907.

612 Blakely, Robert J.   The People's Instrument: A

Philosophy of Programming for Public Television.
Washington, D. C. :   Public Affairs Press, 1971.
179 pp.
    The author has captured the essence of public
broadcasting's purpose and goals.   He has set forth
its historical background and endeavored to give direction to its future.   He has truly specified "the
people's instrument" for the future use of all Ameri-
cans.   He has demonstrated that the message must
be the message if the great potential of these media
for the improvement of the quality of American life
is to be realized.

613   Carnegie Commission on Educational Television.   Pub-
       lic Television: A Program for Action.   New York:
       Harper & Row, 1967.   254 pp.
           This is a broadly conceived study of non-com-
       mercial television conducted by the Commission.
       Attention is focused principally on community-owned
       channels and their services to the general public.
       Lines along which non-commercial television sta-
       tions might most usefully develop in the years ahead
       are recommended.   Charts and illustrations.

614   Katzman, Natan.   One Week of Public Television No.
       7: April, 1972.   Washington, D. C. :   Corporation
       for Public Broadcasting, 1972.

615   Koenig, Allen B. and Ruane B. Hill, eds.   The Far-
       ther Vision: Educational Television Today.   Madi-
       son: University of Wisconsin Press, 1967.   371 pp.
           Explores those significant elements that consti-
       tute ETV and puts them into perspective.   Index.

616   Lee, S. Young and Ronald J. Pedone.   Summary Sta-
       tistics of Public TV Licensees, 1972.   Washington,
       D. C. :   Corporation for Public Broadcasting, 1973.
           Provides information on programming, ownership,
       costs of operation, employment, etc.   Charts.

617   Lyle, Jack.   The People Look at Public Television:
       1974.   Washington, D. C. :   Corporation for Public
       Broadcasting, 1975.   66 pp.

618   Macy, John, Jr.   To Irrigate a Wasteland: The Strug-
       gle to Shape a Public Television System in the
       United States.   Berkeley: University of California

Press, 1974.   186 pp.
Good description of the establishment of a public
television system in the U.S.   Appendix offers examples of the law establishing public broadcasting,
growth patterns of public stations, costs, etc.
Charts, glossary, and index.

619   National Association of Educational Broadcasters.   The
Needs of Education for Television Channel Alloca-
tions.   Washington, D.C. :   U.S. Government Printing Office, 1962.   181 pp.
This report is based on a study designed specifically to bring into focus the national picture of television facilities for educators that will be needed
during the next decade.   Charts, illustrations, and
index.

620   Powell, John Walker.   Channels of Learning: The
Story of Educational Television.   Washington, D.C. :
Public Affairs Press, 1962.   178 pp.
As President of the Fund for Adult Education,
created by the Ford Foundation, the author was giv-
en the mission of finding out how educational television could be brought into being, how its policies
could be developed, how new people could be found
and trained, how adequate programs could be produced, and how its support could be assured.   This
is the story of that mission.   Bibliography, charts,
glossary, and index.

621   Powledge, Fred.   Public Television: A Question of
Survival.   Washington, D.C. :   Public Affairs Press,
1972.   46 pp.
This brief report looks at the controversy over
how, or whether, federal money shall support a free
medium of communication.

622   Schramm, Wilbur, ed.   The Impact of Educational Television.   Urbana: University of Illinois Press, 1960.
247 pp.
Based on 50 research grants dealing with scientific inquiries into attitudes, motivations, audience
composition, audience size, viewing habits, pre-
sentational patterns, attitude change, and learning--
all relating to educational television.   Bibliography
and charts.

623   U. S. Department of Health, Education, and Welfare.
      Educational Television: The Next Ten Years.
      Washington, D. C. : Government Printing Office,
      1965. 375 pp.
        First published by the Institute for Communica-
      tion Research at Stanford. Interesting look into the
      future of educational television as seen by the ex-
      perts in 1965. Bibliography, charts, illustrations,
      and photographs.

C.   Instructional Television

See also nos. 369, 434, 650, 684, 689, 692, 710, 716, 717,
718, 873.

624   Adkins, Edwin P. , ed. Television in Teacher Educa-
      tion. Washington, D. C. : American Association of
      Colleges of Teacher Education, 1960. 72 pp.
        This report reflects the efforts of the A. A. C. T. E.
      to bring to the attention of institutions affiliated with
      the A. A. C. T. E. some of the possibilities of televi-
      sion for the education of teachers, for college in-
      struction in general, and for public schools. Glos-
      sary and illustrations.

625   Burke, Richard C. , ed. Instructional Television: Bold
      New Venture. Bloomington: Indiana University
      Press, 1971. 145 pp.
        Offers eight chapters by as many writers, most
      of which view the role of instructional television ad-
      ministrators and programmers on the elementary
      and secondary level.

626   Callahan, Jennie. Television in School, College, and
      Community. New York: McGraw-Hill, 1953.
      339 pp.
        This book deals in detail with the problems of
      educational television programming. Provides a
      factual and extensive record of educational televi-
      sion and shows how elementary, secondary schools,
      and higher education are using television in educa-
      tion. Bibliography, index, and photographs.

627   Carlisle, D. B. College Credit Through TV: Old
      Idea, New Dimensions. Lincoln, Neb. : Great
      Plains National Instructional Television Library,

1974.   200 pp.
Provides an overview of instructional television
with a chapter of history and a lengthy analysis of
current programs and administrative trends in this
area.

628   Cassirer, Henry R.   Television Teaching Today.
      Paris: UNESCO, 1960.   267 pp.
      Part I deals with ETV in the United States.   It
reports on and discusses how ETV is being used
around the country and the costs involved for equipment (although these costs are somewhat dated).
Part II looks at ETV in other countries.   Bibliography, charts, illustrations, and photographs.

629   Clarke, Beverly.   Graphic Design in Educational Tele-
      vision.   New York: Watson-Guptill, 1974.   96 pp.
      A guide to graphic design for educational televi-
sion with many examples written from a British
point of view.   Illustrations.

630   Cook, Thomas D. , et al.   "Sesame Street" Revisited.
      New York: Russell Sage Foundation (Basic Books),
      1975.   410 pp.
      An extensive re-examination of the data gathered
by the Educational Testing Service and others during the earlier evaluations.

631   Costello, Lawrence F. and George N. Gordon.   Teach
      with Television: A Guide to Instructional TV.   2nd
      edition.   New York: Hastings House Publishers,
      1965.   192 pp.
      This book deals with a non-technical viewpoint,
the entire spectrum of instructional television from
planning the studio to evaluating the results.   The
equipment used in ETV is described.   Bibliography,
glossary, illustrations, index, and photographs.

632   Diamond, Robert M. , ed.   A Guide to Instructional
      Television.   New York: McGraw-Hill, 1964.   304
      pp.
      This book is a collection of articles describing
the methods used by schools in applying ETV.
Both single room TV and the TV studio are considered.   The equipment used and problems en-
countered in each system are discussed.   Bibliography, glossary, illustrations, index, and photographs.

633   Gattegno, Caleb. Towards a Visual Culture: Educat-
        ing Through Television. New York: Outerbridge &
        Dienstfrey, 1969. 117 pp.
             The author outlines a series of specific programs
        for preschool children, including a way to teach
        them reading so that they could "probably master
        ... the English language in a few weeks of viewings
        at the rate of half an hour per day." Illustrations.

634   Gibson, Tony. The Use of ETV: A Handbook for Stu-
        dents and Teachers. London: Hutchinson Education-
        al, 1970. 127 pp.
             Offers brief administrative and programming
        guidelines.

635   Gordon, George N.   Classroom Television: New
        Frontiers in ITV. New York: Hastings House Pub-
        lishers, 1970. 248 pp.
             Classroom Television explores the strange past
        of television teaching at the hands of broadcasters,
        educators, foundation and government officials, and
        publicists. Dr. Gordon concludes that, while broad-
        cast ITV faces a dubious future, increasing use of
        videotape, pre-recorded and inexpensively produced
        local TV lessons should become indispensable teach-
        ing tools during the next 25 years. Bibliography,
        charts, glossary, illustrations, and index.

636   Gordon, George N. and Irving A. Falk. Videocassette
        Technology in American Education. Englewood
        Cliffs, N.J.: Educational Technology Publications,
        1972.
             This book is concerned with the possible interac-
        tions between emerging videocassette technology and
        emerging patterns of education.

637   Griffith, Barton L. and Donald W. MacLennan, eds.
        Improvement of Teaching by Television. Columbia:
        University of Missouri Press, 1964. 238 pp.
             The University of Missouri and the Instructional
        Division of the NAEB sponsored a conference at the
        University of Missouri in 1964. The resulting
        papers are contained in this book and are frank
        assessments of the status of instructional television,
        made by administrators, television specialists, and
        teachers at every level of education. Index.

638 Hancock, Alan. Planning for ETV: A Handbook of Ed-
     ucational Television. New York: Humanities Press,
     1972. 263 pp.
          Offers a British view with some detail on the
     general role of instructional television, its applica-
     bility in all kinds of systems (from single class-
     rooms to schools, colleges, districts, cities, states,
     and countries), organization and operation, and re-
     cent technical developments. Illustrations.

639 Hilliard, Robert L. and Hyman H. Field. Television
     and the Teacher. New York: Hastings House Pub-
     lishers, 1976.
          This handbook is designed to help use television
     effectively in the classroom. It provides an over-
     view for the administrator and the communications
     student who wants to find out in basic, broad terms
     what it is all about.

640 Lewis, Philip. Educational Television Guidebook.
     New York: McGraw-Hill, 1961. 238 pp.
          This book is unique in approach and scope and is
     a non-technical guidebook offering a wealth of data
     and information covering the field of educational and
     instructional television. Bibliography, charts, glos-
     sary, illustrations, and index.

641 Meaney, John W. Televised College Courses: A Re-
     port About the College Faculty Releases Time-
     Program for Television Instruction. New York:
     Fund for the Advancement of Education, 1962.
     88 pp.
          This report is based primarily on field inter-
     views which the author had with administrators and
     faculty members of colleges and universities on
     various studies of student results and reactions to
     telecourses and two days of intensive discussions at
     a conference held in Austin, Texas. Charts, illus-
     trations, and photographs.

642 Moir, Guthrie, ed. Teaching and Television: ETV
     Explained. Oxford, England: Pergamon Press,
     1967. 170 pp.
          Purpose of this work was to build up a compre-
     hensive picture of the achievements of ETV and to
     survey the growth points along with some of the
     problems which have arisen and are likely to arise.
     Bibliography.

643   Murphy, Judith and Ronald Gross. Learning by Tele-
        vision. New York: Fund for the Advancement of
        Education, 1966. 95 pp.
            In this book the authors have examined televi-
        sion's role in instruction. They convey the diver-
        sity of effort in this field, how the medium works,
        what the leading practitioners and critics think and
        feel about its achievements and failures, and what
        the future may hold. They have focused not on tele-
        vision but on education.

644   Schramm, Wilbur, ed. Quality in Instructional Televi-
        sion. Honolulu: University of Hawaii Press, 1973.
        226 pp.
            A collection which focuses on perceptions of in-
        structional television quality. Emphasis is on how
        broadcasters and effects researchers can aid one
        another in determining the value of ITV programs.

D.   General

See also nos. 28, 80, 776, 782, 788, 791, 800, 806, 807, 813,
817, 820, 857, 886, 888, 908, 909, 930, 946, 947, 948,
949, 950, 951, 952, 1076.

645   Advisory Council of National Organizations. Public
        Broadcasting and Education. Washington, D. C. :
        ACNO, 1975. 114 pp.
            Report of four Task Forces who identified 11
        major goals for public broadcasting with specific
        action proposals. Charts and photographs.

646   Cater, Douglass and Michael J. Nyhan, eds. The Fu-
        ture of Public Broadcasting. New York: Praeger,
        1976. 392 pp.
            Comprehensive series of 18 essays analyzing a
        wide variety of problems in public broadcasting.

647   Cater, Douglass and Michael Nyhan, eds. Public Tele-
        vision: Towards Higher Ground. Palo Alto, Calif.:
        Aspen Institute Program on Communications and So-
        ciety, 1975. 70 pp.
            Discusses an overview of public broadcasting,
        programming, the station program cooperative, and
        program rights in public broadcasting.

648 Kurtz, Edwin B. Pioneering in Educational Television:
1932-39. Ames: State University of Iowa Press,
1959. 166 pp.
A limited edition volume, this explains the development of Iowa educational TV operation W9XK
which from 1932-1939 used the mechanical (spinning
disk) system of TV to broadcast programs into
schools. Very useful today for details on operations of an early TV station, and for early educational applications. Illustrations and photographs.

649 Levenson, William B. and Stasheff, Edward. Teaching
Through Radio and Television. Revised edition.
New York: Rinehart & Co., 1952. 560 pp.
The purpose of this book is twofold: the improvement of school broadcasting and the encouragement of more effective use of educational programs.
This book has been written to stimulate the imagi-
nation and to create a thorough knowledge of the
working implements--radio and TV. Bibliography,
illustrations, index, and photographs.

650 Nyhan, Michael J., ed. The Future of Public Broadcasting. New York: Praeger, 1976. 372 pp.
Offers 15 original papers on such things as the
stations, the next decade in public radio, instructional television, the funding of public television,
the myth of public involvement, PTV audiences,
audience and program research, program funding
and the SPC, and the production process.

651 Tressel, George W., et al. The Future of Educational Telecommunication: A Planning Study. Lexington, Mass.: D. C. Heath Co., 1975. 126 pp.

12. AUDIENCE

A. Radio

See nos. 231, 233, 287, 345, 524, 608, 702, 703, 704, 705.

B. Television

See also nos. 347, 398, 530, 532, 533, 549, 617, 622, 749, 765, 899.

652 Bower, Robert T. Television and the Public. New
     York: Holt, Rinehart & Winston, 1973. 205 pp.
        This book gives an overview of the broad changes
     in attitude toward television as compared to a pre-
     vious survey conducted ten years earlier. The tele-
     vision audience, viewing habits, and programming
     are evaluated. Charts.

653 Fischer, Edward. The Screen Arts: A Guide to Film
     and Television Appreciation. New York: Sheed &
     Ward, 1960. 184 pp.
        The author explains many standards for motion
     pictures and for television and hopes that the book
     may lead the reader to a deeper appreciation of the
     good and the best in movies and television. Bibli-
     ography.

654 Kuhns, William. Why We Watch Them: Interpreting
     TV Shows. New York: Benzinger, 1970. 209 pp.
        Analysis of program genres and specific shows
     current at the time of publication, relating charac-
     ters and plot to their appeal for viewers.

655 Steiner, Gary A. The People Look at Television: A
     Study of Audience Attitudes. New York: Knopf,

1963.   422 pp.
The emphasis in this study is on the attitudes
and feelings associated with the television set and
what is on it.   The authors believe that an empiri-
cal reading on such feelings and attitudes is of in-
trinsic interest to the student of mass communications, and certainly relevant to informed and pro-
ductive discussion of the issues.   Charts and illustrations.

656   Surgeon General's Scientific Advisory Committee on
Television and Social Behavior.   Television and
Growing Up: The Impact of Televised Violence.
Washington, D. C. : Government Printing Office,
1972.   279 pp.
Summarizes one of the biggest research programs
on the effects of television violence.

C.   General

See also nos. 83, 324, 331, 364, 428, 558, 565, 567, 580,
581, 591, 650, 772, 925, 1062.

657   Bennett, Robert W.   A Lawyer's Sourcebook: Repre-
senting the Audience in Broadcast Proceedings.
New York: United Church of Christ, 1974.

658   Lichty, Lawrence W.   Broadcast Program and Audience
Analysis and Workbook.   Madison, Wisc. : American Printing & Publishing Co. , 1975.   150 pp.
Comes in two parts: a reader and a related
workbook.   The emphasis here is on program content and appeals, and on audience research and ratings and other means of measuring program effec-
tiveness.   The workbook assignments provide forms
and other means of putting the reader ideas to work.

659   Prowitt, Marsha O.   Guide to Citizen Action in Radio
and Television.   New York: United Church of
Christ, 1971.

660   Seiden, Martin H.   Who Controls the Mass Media?
Popular Myths and Economic Realities.   New York:
Basic Books, 1975.   246 pp.
Seiden suggests that the audience, not the so-
called media barons, really control what they see,

hear, and read. This long-time media consultant
deals with ownership, advertising, money, and control in American media.

661 Seldes, Gilbert. The Great Audience. New York:
     Viking Press, 1951. 299 pp.
        An investigation into the audiences of various
     media, including movies, radio, television, etc.

662 Singer, Benjamin D. Feedback and Society: A Study
     of the Uses of Mass Channels for Coping. Lexing-
     ton, Mass.: Lexington Books, 1973. 124 pp.
        Offers the first book-length study of that segment
     of the media audience which responds or "feeds
     back" reaction to media institutions. Based on
     early 1970s research in Canada, this book provides
     details on both audience make-up and media content
     tailoring to feed back (talk shows, letters to the
     editor, etc.). Bibliography, charts, and index.

663 Smith, Anthony. The Shadow in the Cave: The Broad-
     caster, His Audience, and the State. Urbana: Uni-
     versity of Illinois Press, 1974. 351 pp.
        Tensions between broadcasters, politicians, and
     the vast audience which they share have greatly in-
     creased in recent years. In the first book to ex-
     amine the real basis of the present world-wide con-
     troversy over fairness, access, and control in
     broadcasting, Anthony Smith discusses the causes of
     these tensions, showing how the controversy finds
     its roots in the very origins of mass society and
     the role of culture within such societies. Bibliog-
     raphy and index.

664 Trenaman, J. M. Communication and Comprehension.
     New York: Humanities Press, 1968. 212 pp.
        An ambitious and awesome investigation into the
     effects of television, radio, and print media upon
     listener comprehension.

13.   CABLE TELEVISION

A.   History

665   Cable Television: A Message About the Medium.   University Park: Continuing Education Services, The Pennsylvania State University, no date.   47 pp.
Discusses the history, technical aspects, and future of cable television.   Charts, illustrations, and photographs.

666   Phillips, Mary.   CATV: A History of Community Antenna Television.   Evanston, Ill. : Northwestern University Press, 1972.   209 pp.
Part I focuses on early CATV time and is essentially a detailed account of one representative system in Astoria, Oregon; Part II focuses on federal, state, and municipal regulations; and Part III on the future of CATV and federal, state, and municipal regulations.   Bibliography and index.

667   Smith, Ralph Lee.   The Wired Nation--Cable TV: The Electronic Communications Highway.   New York: Harper & Row, 1972.   128 pp.
Based on the author's well-received lengthy magazine treatment of cable in 1970, now updated to include the new FCC rules.   Offers essentially an historical view of developments to date.

668   Townsend, George R. and J. Orrin Marlowe.   Cable: A New Spectrum of Communications.   Spectrum Communications, Inc. , 1974.   102 pp.
Short comprehensive coverage of the development of cable television including the struggle for franchising.   Government regulations and pay TV.

B.   Regulation

See also nos. 167, 170, 205, 666, 667, 668, 681, 696, 842, 990, 1021.

669   Cable Communications and the States.   Albany: New
         York State Senate, 1975.   487 pp.
         Presents analysis of legal, statistical, and policy
      matters bearing on state involvement in cable.

670   Johnson, Leland L. and Michael Botein.   Cable Tele-
         vision: Process of Franchising. Santa Monica,
         Calif.: Rand Corp., 1973.   85 pp.

671   LeDuc, Don R.   Cable Television and the FCC: A
         Crisis in Media Control.   Philadelphia: Temple
         University Press, 1973.
         Early chapters of the book are devoted to an ex-
      amination of the Federal Radio Act, the 1934 Com-
      munications Act, and the FCC's early broadcast
      policies.   The author then turns to the development
      of cable and the FCC's regulatory response to that
      development.

672   Park, Rolla Edward, ed.   The Role of Analysis in
         Regulatory Decision-making: The Case of Cable
         Television.   Lexington, Mass.: Lexington/Heath,
         1973.   144 pp.
         Gives a series of brief original papers showing
      how cable groups--broadcasters, the public, the
      FCC, academics, and economists--visualize the
      likely impact and role of cable in the near future.

673   Seiden, Martin H.   Cable Television U.S.A.: An Analy-
         sis of Government Policy.   New York: Praeger,
         1972.   252 pp.
         This study is an analysis and detailed description
      of how the Federal Communications Commission has
      altered the concept of governmental regulations by
      involving itself unnecessarily in the innermost work-
      ings of a minor part of the communications industry
      --cable television (CATV).   Charts.

C.   Public Access

See also nos. 573, 691, 696.

674   Bretz, Rudy. Handbook for Producing Educational and
      Public-Access Programs for Cable Television.
      Englewood Cliffs, N. J. :   Educational Technology
      Publications, 1976.   160 pp.
          Provides the basic knowledge needed to begin "do-
      it-yourself" television on the educational and public-
      access channels provided by local cable system
      operators. Bibliography, glossary, and index.

675   Cable Television Information Center. Local Govern-
      ment Uses of Cable Television. Washington, D. C. :
      Cable Television Information Center, 1974.   66 pp.
          Discusses uses that local governments can make
      of cable television, with primary emphasis on utili-
      zation of the government access channel mandated
      by the FCC's 1972 cable TV rules.

676   Dordick, Herbert S. and Jack Lyle. Access by Local
      Political Candidates to Cable Television: A Report
      of an Experiment. Santa Monica, Calif. :   Rand
      Corp. , 1971.   26 pp.

677   Gillespie, Gilbert. Public Access Cable Television in
      the United States and Canada. New York: Praeger,
      1975.   172 pp.
          Surveys the individual and collective responses of
      major North American metropolitan governments to
      the decree or mandate delivered by the Canadian
      and American Federal Governments to the cable
      operators, instructing them to provide public access
      to at least one of their channels.

678   Kletter, Richard C. Cable Television: Making Public
      Access Effective. Santa Monica, Calif. :   Rand
      Corp. , 1973.

679   Othmer, David. The Wired Island: The First Two
      Years of Public Access to Cable Television in Man-
      hattan. New York: Fund for the City of New York,
      1973.

680   Pool, Ithiel de Sola, ed. Talking Back: Citizen Feed-
      back and Cable Technology. Cambridge, Mass. :
      MIT Press, 1973.   325 pp.
          Fifteen papers which focus on technology and the
      many potential benefits to be derived from properly
      designed cable systems. Illustrations.

681   Tate, Charles, ed. <u>Cable Television in the Cities:</u>
      <u>Community Control, Public Access, and Minority</u>
      <u>Ownership.</u> Washington, D. C. : Urban Institute,
      <u>1971. 1</u>84 pp.
            A detailed guide to developing and operating city
      cable systems, stressing problems of community ac-
      cess and local origination and ending with over 80
      pages of reference and bibliographical material.
      Bibliography.

D.   <u>Production</u>

<u>See also</u> nos. 434, 674, 683, 689.

682   Efrein, Joel. <u>Cablecasting Production Handbook.</u>   Blue
      Ridge Summit, Pa. : TAB Books, 1975. 210 pp.
            This guidebook is intended to serve both as an
      introduction to cablecasting production for the novice,
      as well as a working handbook for those already in
      the field.   It will help CATV planners, directors,
      and producers to make the right decisions in organ-
      izing a station and obtaining revenue through sub-
      scriptions, ad revenue, and programming.   It's a
      well seasoned exposition of the subject that will
      clear up the haze surrounding CATV and its appli-
      cations.   Anyone involved in a cable facility, or
      planning to get involved in one, will find this book
      an absolute must! Illustrations and index.

E.   <u>Technical</u>

<u>See also</u> nos. 665, 991, 993, 995, 997, 1000, 1001.

683   Knecht, Kenneth B.   <u>Designing & Maintaining the CATV</u>
      <u>& Small TV Studio.</u>   2nd edition.   Blue Ridge Sum-
      mit, Pa. : TAB Books, 1976.   288 pp.
            New, completely updated second edition is a sim-
      plified, yet detailed guide on the installation and
      maintenance of production facilities for cable TV,
      medical and industrial closed-circuit TV, instruc-
      tional TV, and small broadcast TV studios.   This
      all-in-one handbook is written specifically to help
      those who need expert, in-depth guidance on setting
      up a small to medium size TV studio.   Illustrations
      and index.

F. General

See also nos. 66, 80, 557, 820, 841, 865, 885, 943, 988,
989, 992, 994, 996, 998, 999, 1002, 1003, 1004, 1005,
1006, 1035, 1056, 1060.

684   Adler, Richard and Walter S. Baer. Aspen Notebook:
      Cable and Continuing Education. New York: Prae-
      ger, 1973. 210 pp.
         Centers attention on the potential adult or con-
      tinuing education role of the nation's expanding cable
      systems. Offers six general chapters on cable and
      education, and supplements these with three models
      of television-supported education which might be ap-
      plicable to cable work.

685   Adler, Richard and Walter S. Baer. The Electronic
      Box Office: Humanities and Arts on Cable. New
      York: Praeger, 1974. 160 pp.
         Details the potential of pay cable as an alterna-
      tive mechanism for supporting quality programming
      and as a source of revenue for the performing arts.
      Includes a survey of pay cable enterprises and
      their impact on the performing arts.

686   Baer, Walter S. Cable Television: A Handbook for
      Decisionmaking. Santa Monica, Calif.: Rand Corp.,
      1974. 244 pp.
         This volume presents basic information about
      cable television and outlines the political, social,
      economic, legal, and technical issues communities
      must face in cable decisionmaking. Bibliography,
      charts, glossary, illustrations, and index.

687   Baer, Walter S., et al. Cable Television: Franchis-
      ing Considerations. New York: Crane, Russak,
      1974.
         Contains five of the Rand cable studies originally
      issued in 1973.

688   Barnett, H. J. and E. A. Greenberg. A Proposal for
      Wired City Television. Santa Monica, Calif.: Rand
      Corp., 1967.

689   Cable Television Information Center. Educational Uses
      of Cable Television. Washington, D. C.: Cable
      Television Information Center, 1974. 105 pp.

Discusses uses educators can make of cable television, including an overview of current educational
programming, costs of programming and possible
sources of funds, and technical aspects of production.

690   Cable Television Information Center.   The Uses of
      Cable Communications. Washington, D. C. :   Cable
      Television Information Center, 1973.   47 pp.
          Introduces ranges of cable uses now possible and
      applications for the future.

691   Carpenter-Huffman, Polly, et al.   Cable Television:
      Developing Community Services.   New York: Crane,
      Russak, 1974.   276 pp.
          Contains four of the Rand cable studies originally
      issued in 1973.

692   Hanley, Anne.   Cable Television and Education: A Re-
      port from the Field.   Washington, D. C. :   National
      Cable Television Association, 1973.

693   Kamen, Ira.   Questions and Answers About Pay TV.
      Indianapolis: Howard W. Sams & Co. , 1973.

694   Land, Herman W. , Associates.   Television and the
      Wired City: A Study of the Implications of a Change
      in the Mode of Transmission.   Washington, D. C. :
      National Association of Broadcasters, 1968.
          The report is based on the premise that the
      choice presented is an abandonment of the present
      broadcast system in favor of a nationwide wire-grid
      system.   Not surprisingly, the report generally finds
      that the status quo is good.

695   National Education Association.   Schools and Cable
      Television.   Washington, D. C. :   NEA, 1971.
      66 pp.

696   Price, Monroe and John Wicklein.   Cable Television:
      A Guide for Citizen Action.   Philadelphia: Pilgrim
      Press, 1972.   160 pp.
          This is a guidebook for citizens as they seek to
      understand the implications of cable television, the
      decisions that are being made about it, and actions
      which only they can initiate.   Bibliography.

697 Ross, Leonard. Economic and Legal Foundations of
     Cable Television. Beverly Hills, Calif. : Sage,
     1974. 76 pp.

698 Sachman, Harold and Barry W. Boehm, eds. Planning
     Community Information Utilities. Montvale, N.J. :
     AFIPS Press, 1972. 501 pp.
        Specifically focuses on cable technology as a
     means of better two-way communication. The 17
     original papers deal with the many community infor-
     mation services needed, system design to meet
     those information needs, and system management
     problems.

699 Scott, James D. Cable Television: Strategy for Pene-
     trating Key Urban Markets. Ann Arbor: University
     of Michigan Graduate School of Business Administra-
     tion, 1976. 132 pp.
        An interesting business approach to the likely
     future of cable, this book deals with building cable
     penetration in the top 100 markets, two-way inter-
     active cable services (and market demand for same),
     analysis of alternative pay-cable services, local
     program origination, the development of CATV pro-
     gram networks, and the potential threat of the video-
     cassette. Charts.

700 Sloan Commission on Cable Communications. On the
     Cable: The Television of Abundance. New York:
     McGraw-Hill, 1971. 272 pp.
        Offers an introduction to cable television. Un-
     fortunately issued before the major FCC rule-making
     of February 1972.

701 Yin, Robert K. Cable Television: Applications for
     Municipal Services. Santa Monica, Calif. : Rand
     Corp. , 1973.

14.   RESEARCH

A.   Radio

See also nos. 345, 524, 607, 608.

702   Lazarsfeld, Paul F. and Harry N. Field.   The People
Look at Radio.   Chapel Hill: University of North
Carolina Press, 1946.
A survey by the National Opinion Center of the
University of Denver, as analyzed by Columbia Uni-
versity's Bureau of Applied Social Research.

703   Lazarsfeld, Paul F. and Patricia L. Kendall.   Radio
Listening in America: The People Look at Radio--
Again.   New York: Prentice-Hall, 1948.   178 pp.
The present report is based on a questionnaire
sponsored by the National Association of Broadcasters and conducted by the National Opinion Research
Center.   The questions were aimed at finding out
what people know and feel about the general policies
of the radio industry, and the way it is organized
and operated.   It is the second survey, the first
one appearing under the title The People Look at
Radio.   Charts and index.

704   Lazarsfeld, Paul F. and Frank N. Stanton, eds.
Radio Research, 1941.   New York: Duell, Sloan &
Pearce, 1942.
The first in a planned series as a supplement to
Dr. Lazarsfeld's own study, "Radio and the Printed
Page."   Contains six reports--three on different
types of programs and three on listener reactions.

705   Lazarsfeld, Paul F. and Frank N. Stanton, eds.
Radio Research, 1942-1943.   New York: Duell,
Sloan & Pearce, 1944.   599 pp.

Deals with radio research during World War II.
Good look at early attempts of audience analysis in
radio.   Charts, illustrations, and index.

706   National Broadcasting Company.   C. R. A. M. --Cumula-
      tive Radio-Audience Method.   New York: NBC,
      1966.

B.   Television

See also nos. 302, 307, 318, 338, 368, 371, 375, 398, 522,
536, 539, 540, 616, 622, 630, 641, 652, 655, 656, 749,
777, 834, 898, 899, 1071, 1072, 1073.

707   Arons, Leon and Mark A. May, eds.   Television and
      Human Behavior.   New York: Appleton-Century-
      Crofts, 1963.   307 pp.
          This book approaches television and mass com-
      munication generally in a somewhat unusual way.
      It is a book of research strategies in which re-
      search plans are developed for specific problems.
      The 18 research plans included are the award win-
      ners of a competition which was conducted by a
      group of eminent social scientists and scholars.
      Photographs.

708   Belson, W. A.   The Impact of Television: Methods
      and Findings in Program Research.   Hamden, Conn. :
      Archon, 1967.   400 pp.
          The book is divided into five sections.   Section
      I deals with the use of research to provide informa-
      tion about the population's interest.   Section II is
      concerned with the degree to which informative pro-
      grams can be understood by the people.   Section III
      deals with the effects of specific programs.   Section
      IV is about television's social impact.   Section V
      presents the case for making greater use of televi-
      sion research.   Bibliography and index.

709   Brown, Ray, ed.   Children and Television.   Beverly
      Hills, Calif. : Sage, 1976.   368 pp.
          An edited overview of research findings, remain-
      ing problems, and issues.   The 16 papers included
      fall into three main parts: children as an audience,
      individual and social factors which shape the view-
      ing experience, and processes of influence and some
      effects of exposure to television.   Index.

710   Chu, Goodwin and Wilbur Schramm.   Learning from
        Television: What the Research Says. Washington,
        D.C.: National Association of Educational Broad-
        casters, 1968. 116 pp.
           Review discussion of topics in instructional tele-
        vision keyed to bibliography, making whole book a
        literature review, and best to date. (1974 reprint
        includes 11-page update introduction.)

711   Comstock, George A., et al.   Television and Human
        Behavior: The Research Horizon, Future and Pres-
        ent. Santa Monica, Calif.: Rand Corp., 1975.
           Includes three volumes: Volume I--A Guide to
        Pertinent Scientific Literature (344 pp.); Volume II--
        The Key Studies (251 pp.); Volume III--The Research
        Horizon (120 pp.). A bibliography is in each of the
        three volumes. Bibliography.

712   Feshbach, Seymour and Robert D. Singer.   Television
        and Aggression: An Experimental Field Study.   San
        Francisco: Jossey-Bass, 1971. 186 pp.
           Presents the findings of a study designed to de-
        termine the effect of aggressive TV programs on the
        behavior of children. Evidence from the study sug-
        gests that, for some children at least, aggressive
        TV provides a fantasy outlet which reduces actual
        aggressiveness. Bibliography.

713   Ford Foundation.   Television and Children: Priorities
        for Research.   New York: Ford Foundation, 1975.
        38 pp.
           Highly condensed outline approach to a wide range
        of current research findings and problems. Offers
        many questions suitable for research projects.

714   Himmelweit, Hilde T.; A. N. Oppenheim; and Pamela
        Vince.   Television and the Child: An Empirical
        Study of the Effect of Television on the Young.
        London: Oxford Press, 1958. 522 pp.
           This book is the culmination of four years of
        research on the effects of television on children in
        Great Britain. This is one of the most compre-
        hensive studies to date on the effects of any mass
        medium on children.

715   Nelson, William A.   The Impact of Television: Me-
        thods and Findings in Program Research.

Hamden, Conn. :   Archon, 1967.

716   Rehak, Robert, ed.   Me and My TV.   Shabbona, Ill. :
      Journalism Education Association, 1976.   72 pp.
         A research report on the role of popular televi-
      sion in developing verbal skills and bringing together
      adolescents and adults.   Implications for the home
      and classroom.

717   Reid, J. Christopher.   Research in Instructional Tele-
      vision and Film.   Washington, D. C. :   Government
      Printing Office, 1967.   216 pp.
         Report of almost 350 research studies concerned
      with instructional TV and film.   Historical or de-
      scriptive studies, reports on surveys, surveys of
      research, and other non-experimental reports are
      not included.   Index.

718   Schramm, Wilbur, ed.   The Second Harvest of Two Re-
      search-Producing Events: The Surgeon General's
      Inquiry and "Sesame Street. "   Stanford, Calif. :
      National Academy of Education, 1976.   69 pp.
         A review of Recent Books on Children and Tele-
      vision.   Proceedings of the National Academy of
      Education.

C.   General

See also nos. 49, 71, 261, 262, 275, 329, 474, 555, 560,
592, 650, 658, 664, 770, 772, 785, 786, 802, 804, 810,
845, 850, 924, 927, 961, 1031, 1041, 1062.

719   Backstrom, Charles H. and Gerald D. Hursh.   Survey
      Research.   Evanston, Ill. :   Northwestern Univer-
      sity Press, 1963.   192 pp.
         This book is an introduction to survey research.
      Although intended as the initial volume in a series
      of similar teaching and research manuals, this
      book can be used by surveyors in general.   Illus-
      trations and index.

720   Berelson, Bernard.   Content Analysis in Communica-
      tion Research.   2nd edition.   New York: Hafner,
      1952 (reprinted by Free Press, 1971).   220 pp.
         This is a revision and expansion of The Analysis
      of Communication Content.   Book deals with content

analysis. The uses, the procedures, and the problems of this research method are the subject matter
of the book. Bibliography.

721 Blumler, Jay G. and Elihu Katz, eds. The Uses of
     Mass Communications: Current Perspectives on
     Gratifications Research. Beverly Hills, Calif.:
     Sage, 1974. 318 pp.
         A collection of essays on the uses and gratifica-
     tions approach to mass communication. Bibliography
     and charts.

722 Clarke, Peter, ed. New Models for Mass Communica-
     tion Research. Beverly Hills, Calif.: Sage, 1973.
     240 pp.
         Nine original papers suggesting models to guide
     mass communication research, including pioneering
     efforts to apply those models. Bibliography.

723 Davison, W. Phillips and Frederick T. C. Yu, eds.
     Mass Communication Research: Major Issues and
     Future Directions. New York: Praeger, 1974.
     248 pp.
         Review of current knowledge in selected topic
     areas; keyed to bibliography pp. 202-236. Bibli-
     ography.

724 Johnstone, John W. C.; Slawski, Edward J.; and Bow-
     man, William W. The News People: A Sociologi-
     cal Portrait of American Journalists and Their Work.
     Urbana: University of Illinois Press, 1976. 240 pp.
         This study, based on extensive interviews with
     more than 1,300 practicing journalists, is one of
     the first large-scale national inquiries dealing with
     any occupational group. The interview statistics
     are used to paint a portrait of the nearly 70,000
     men and women who make their living as full-time
     disseminators of news. These include persons who
     work in radio and television, wire services and syn-
     dicates, news magazines, daily and weekly news-
     papers, as well as some of the journalists in the
     alternative media. Charts.

725 Kelman, Herbert C. and Raphael S. Ezekiel. Cross-
     National Encounters. San Francisco: Jossey-Bass,
     1970. 368 pp.
         An in-depth study of the effects of a 1962 seminar

of foreign broadcasters brought to observe radio-TV
operations in America. The study evaluated the
personal impact of the seminar on the 28 participants and their impact at home.

726 Klapper, Joseph T. The Effects of Mass Communica-
     tion. New York: Free Press, 1960. 302 pp.
     Although out of date, offers a clear exposition of
     basic findings for beginning students. The author
     takes five hypotheses and then constructs his book
     around support of each in turn. The end result is
     clear understanding of research--to that time. Bib-
     liography.

727 Kline, F. Gerald and Phillip J. Tichenor, eds. Cur-
     rent Perspectives in Mass Communication Research.
     Beverly Hills, Calif.: Sage, 1972. 320 pp.
     Nine major and original articles reviewing litera-
     ture of mass communications, with bibliographies
     attached to each. Bibliography.

728 Lazarsfeld, Paul F. and Frank N. Stanton, eds. Com-
     munications Research, 1948-1949. New York:
     Harper, 1949. 332 pp.
     This volume contains mainly studies which were
     organized by Columbia University's Bureau of Ap-
     plied Social Research in the last two years of the
     war and in the time since. Charts and index.

729 McQuail, Denis. Towards a Sociology of Mass Com-
     munications. New York: Macmillan, 1969. 122 pp.
     Review of research knowledge supplemented by
     annotated bibliography. Bibliography.

730 Nafziger, Ralph O. and David Manning White, eds.
     Introduction to Mass Communications Research.
     Baton Rouge: Louisiana State University Press,
     1963. 281 pp.
     Concentrates on research methods in mass com-
     munication from a behavioral point of view. Charts
     and index.

731 Nielsen, A. C., Company. The Use of Random Num-
     ber Phone Samples for NSI Diary Placements. New
     York: Nielsen, 1972.

732 Pearce, Michael; Scott M. Cunningham; and Avon

Miller.   Appraising the Economic and Social Effects
of Advertising: A Review of Issues and Evidence.
Cambridge, Mass.:   Marketing Science Institute,
1971.   Approximately 200 pp.
   Gives an overview of a vast amount of previous
writing and research to provide a cogently organized
overview of the role and function of advertising, with
material on advertising effects on consumer behavior,
on industry advertising and competition, and on society in general.

733 Roper Organization.   Trends in Public Attitudes Toward
      Television and Other Mass Media, 1959-1974.   New
      York: Television Information Office, 1975.

734 Yu, Frederick T. C., ed.   Behavioral Sciences and
      the Mass Media.   New York: Russell Sage Founda-
      tion (Basic Books), 1968.   270 pp.
         Assembled from conference proceedings, its 20
      articles explore the relationship of media and media
      studies to the various behavioral sciences and me-
      thods.   The emphasis is on cooperative research
      project feasibility.   Index.

15. BROADCASTING CAREERS

A. Radio

See also no. 463.

735 Fisher, Hal. How to Become a Radio Disc Jockey.
Blue Ridge Summit, Pa.: TAB Books, 1971.
224 pp.
This book is expressly formulated to serve a dual
purpose--a comprehensive 25-lesson home-study
course of instruction for the talented young person
who wishes to go it alone with his tape recorder in
the privacy of his home, and as a classroom teacher's handbook for group instruction purposes. It
contains drills, exercises, illustrations, professional scripts and commercials--all the material needed
to polish one's skills. Illustrations and index.

736 Lowell, Maurice. Listen In: An American Manual of
Radio. New York: Dodge Publishing Co., 1937.
114 pp.
A brief examination of radio in four parts: a
glossary of radio terms, key jobs in radio (writer,
director, artists, and announcer), the role of radio
training in colleges, and a final 40 pages on the
radio industry in general, all written by a production director of NBC. Though written for a general
audience, most of the volume aims at prospective
career types.

B. Television

See also nos. 443, 887.

737 Shanks, Bob. The Cool Fire: How to Make It In

Television. New York: W. W. Norton, 1976. 318
pp.
    Bob Shanks writes.from the experience of one
who joined the television family as a soap opera
performer and now is an ABC programming vice
president. Through first-hand observations and
anecdotes and historical and technological explanations, Mr. Shanks provides the newcomer with a
travelogue to the industry.

C. General

See also no. 480.

738 Coleman, Ken. So You Want to Be a Sportscaster.
     New York: Hawthorn Books, 1973. 170 pp.

739 Ewing, Sam. You're On the Air! Blue Ridge Summit,
     Pa. : TAB Books, 1972. 224 pp.
        This book tells the beginning broadcaster how to
     find the shortcuts to a career in radio and televi-
     sion broadcasting. The author describes many job
     categories--both on and off the air--in the sound
     medium, and covers in detail the many skills needed
     in front of the camera, as well as the countless
     behind-the-scenes opportunities available--not only
     in broadcasting, but in cable TV as well. Index
     and photographs.

740 Falk, Irving A. and George N. Gordon. Your Career
     in TV and Radio. New York: Julian Messner,
     1966. 224 pp.
        Written by two broadcast educators who are also
     professional broadcasters, this book surveys the
     whole range of television-radio careers. Bibliog-
     raphy and photographs.

741 Gordon, George N. and Irving A. Falk. Your Career
     in TV and Radio. New York: Julian Messner, no
     date.
        Describes the work of producers, directors,
     writers, artists, public relations experts, actors
     and other personalities, advertisers, and educational
     broadcasters. Included are histories of radio and
     television, personal career anecdotes of people im-
     portant in their areas of broadcasting, and basic

information concerning necessary personal and educational qualifications.

742 Hauenstein, A. Dean and Steven A. Bachmeyer. Intro-
    duction to Communications Careers. Bloomington,
    Ill. : McKnight Publishing Co. , 1975.
        In this book, the basic elements of communica-
    tions (including listening) are covered in detail with
    students planning, writing, rehearsing, presenting,
    and taping a five-minute radio program complete
    with sound effects, music, and a commercial an-
    nouncement. Television and motion pictures are
    discussed.

743 Hyde, Stuart W. Television and Radio Announcing.
    2nd edition. Boston: Houghton-Mifflin, 1971.
    549 pp.
        Provides a realistic picture of the broadcasting
    industry today, describes the kind of jobs available
    for announcers, and discusses the skills and per-
    sonal characteristics necessary for success in the
    field. Index and photographs.

744 Jackson, Gregory. Getting into Broadcast Journalism.
    New York: Hawthorn Books, 1974. 156 pp.
        Written for young people who think they want to
    get into radio and television news but don't really
    know what they're getting into, how to prepare for
    it, or where to start looking for a job. Index.

745 Rider, John. Your Future in Broadcasting. New
    York: Richard Rosen Press, 1971. 125 pp.

16. INTERNATIONAL

A. Europe

See also nos. 223, 280, 334, 368, 714, 839, 852, 915, 919.

746 Briggs, Asa. The History of Broadcasting in the
United Kingdom. Volume I: The Birth of Broadcasting, 1961, 425 pp.; Volume II: The Golden Age
of Wireless, 1965, 688 pp.; Volume III: The War
of Words, 1970, 766 pp. London: Oxford University Press.
   The first volume is concerned largely with the
first four years in the history of the BBC. The
main theme of the second volume is the extension
and the enrichment of the activity of broadcasting.
The third volume deals directly with the role of the
BBC outside as well as inside Britain within the
context of the general history of the Second World
War. Bibliography, charts, illustrations, index,
and photographs.

747 Carter, Martin D. An Introduction to Mass Communications: Problems in Press and Broadcasting.
New York: Humanities Press, 1971. 142 pp.
   Provides an introductory analysis of press and
broadcasting issues as seen in Britain which gives
good insight into that country's major media.

748 Dowling, Jack; Lelia Doolan; and Bob Quinn. Sit Down
and Be Counted: The Cultural Evolution of a Television Station. Dublin: Wellington, 1969. 383 pp.
   This book is an analysis of the first decade of
Radio Telefis Eireann (RTE), the Irish television
station/system.

749 Goodhardt, G. J.; A. S. C. Ehrenberg; and M. A.

Collin. The Television Audience: Patterns of Viewing. Lexington, Mass.: Lexington Books, 1975.
159 pp.
This new British analysis is based mainly on
regular broadcast ratings information gathered over
the early 1970s. Bibliography and index.

750 Gorham, Maurice. Broadcasting and Television Since
1900. London: Andrew Dakers Ltd., 1952. 274 pp.
This book is mainly concerned with British broadcasting and British television. Index.

751 Harasymiw, Bohdan, ed. Education and the Mass
Media in the Soviet Union and Eastern Europe.
New York: Praeger, 1976.
Contains three essays on East European education
plus four on the mass media. Taken together, the
essays in this book contain some useful material
not readily available elsewhere. Even though intended as "papers" for a learned society, they are
not difficult reading. Mass media workers will find
them interesting.

752 Harris, Paul. When Pirates Ruled the Waves. Blue
Ridge Summit, Pa.: TAB Books, 1972. 232 pp.
Here's the complete story--with no holds barred
--of the pop radio pirates who operated unauthorized
radio ships off Britain's shores. Illustrations.

753 Hollander, Gayle Durham. Soviet Political Indoctrina-
tion: Developments in Mass Media and Propaganda
Since Stalin. New York: Praeger, 1972. 264 pp.
A broadly-based review of all means of communication and propaganda since the death of Stalin,
this book is a well thought out and heavily detailed
report on the Soviet Union.

754 Holt, Robert T. Radio Free Europe. Minneapolis:
University of Minnesota Press, 1958. 249 pp.
Dated (coverage ends with the Polish and Hun-
garian uprisings of 1956) but still offers solid data
on Radio Free Europe's inception and early years.

755 Hood, Stuart. The Mass Media. New York: Humanities Press, 1972. 96 pp.
A very brief overview of press and broadcast
development in Europe since the war, with a

discussion of problems of both media in Europe and
Britain.

756 Hood, Stuart. Radio and Television. North Pomfret,
        Vt. : David & Charles, 1976. 144 pp.
        Mr. Hood came up through the ranks of BBC and
     now, as a professor of film and television in Eng-
     land, provides a simple overview of both the BBC
     and commercial broadcasting there. From the
     anchorman to the obituary department to the camera
     crew, Mr. Hood details job responsibilities, piec-
     ing together the total broadcasting picture. His
     study even includes an appendix with salary grades.

757 Hopkins, Mark W. Mass Media in the Soviet Union.
        New York: Pegasus, 1970. 384 pp.
        An in-depth look at the mass media in Russia,
     with chapters on both print and non-print journalism.
     Good historical study on a subject that should be of
     interest to both students and practitioners of the
     mass media. Bibliography, charts, illustrations,
     index, and photographs.

758 Lisann, Maury. Broadcasting to the Soviet Union: In-
        ternational Politics and Radio. New York: Praeger,
        1975. 224 pp.
        Surveys the Soviet reaction to foreign radio broad-
     casting with special reference to the period 1963-
     1968 when there was virtually no jamming.

759 McGarry, K. J. Mass Communications: Selected
        Readings for Librarians. Hamden, Conn. : Linnet
        Books (Shoe String Press), 1972. 255 pp.
        Offers a selection of heavily British-based arti-
     cles on media problems, the audience, cultural is-
     sues related to media, and media content.

760 Markham, James W. Voices of the Red Giants: Com-
        munications in Russia and China. Ames: Iowa
        State University Press, 1967. 513 pp.
        Covers broadcasting (and other media) in the
     Soviet Union and Mainland China sequentially, with
     a heavy emphasis on print media.

761 Paulu, Burton. British Broadcasting: Radio and Tele-
        vision in the United Kingdom. Minneapolis: Uni-
        versity of Minnesota Press, 1956. 457 pp.

A survey of British broadcasting which presents
the BBC as ITA was just getting started.

762   Paulu, Burton.   British Broadcasting in Transition.
      Minneapolis: University of Minnesota Press, 1961.
      250 pp.
      Offers in-depth treatment of both BBC and ITA
      operations after the initial adjustment to a bifur-
      cated system.   Bibliography, charts, and index.

763   Paulu, Burton.   Radio and Television Broadcasting in
      Eastern Europe.   Minneapolis: University of Minne-
      sota Press, 1974.   592 pp.
      This comprehensive study of broadcasting in the
      socialist countries of Eastern Europe is of signifi-
      cance not only to specialists in communications but
      also to political scientists, government officials,
      historians, sociologists, and others who need accu-
      rate information about this aspect of the socialist
      regimes.   This is the first reasonably complete
      book about broadcasting in the Eastern European
      countries.   Bibliography and index.

764   Paulu, Burton.   Radio and Television Broadcasting on
      the European Continent.   Minneapolis: University
      of Minnesota Press, 1967.   290 pp.
      This book is a description and appraisal of radio
      and television broadcasting on the European conti-
      nent.   All aspects of broadcasting are discussed.
      Bibliography, charts, and index.

765   Piepe, Anthony; Miles Emerson; and Judy Lannon.
      Television and the Working Class.   Lexington,
      Mass.: Lexington Books, 1975.   170 pp.
      This book draws upon two recent studies to ex-
      amine the effects of television viewing on the work-
      ing class in the United Kingdom.

766   Polman, Edward W.   Broadcasting in Sweden.   Boston:
      Routledge & Kegan Paul, 1976.   80 pp.
      Shows how Sweden's broadcasting network is
      unique in the speed of its growth relative to popula-
      tion.

767   Priestley, J. B.   All England Listened.   New York:
      Chilmark Press, 1967.   146 pp.
      A selection of J. B. Priestley's wartime

broadcasts over the BBC with an introduction by
Eric Sevareid.

768 Quicke, Andrew. Tomorrow's Television: An Exami-
     nation of British Broadcasting Past, Present, and
     Future. Berkhamsted, England: Lion Publishing,
     1976. 240 pp.
        A highly literate and informal survey based more
     on observation and the writings of others than on
     original research. Index.

769 Robinson, John, ed. Educational Television and Radio
     in Britain. London: British Broadcasting Corp.,
     1966. 292 pp.
        Stresses the BBC role and covers radio as well
     as TV.

770 Tunstall, Jeremy, ed. Media Sociology: A Reader.
     Urbana: University of Illinois Press, 1970. 574 pp.
        Dealing largely with the British system of com-
     munication (though many of the articles are non-
     British in subject matter or authorship), this volume
     concentrates upon communications organizations and
     communicators, such as journalists and TV produc-
     ers. The 25 essayists examine how the organiza-
     tions function, what effect one form of communica-
     tion has upon another, to what extent the media af-
     fect politics or politics the media, and the reliabili-
     ty of methods used to measure these effects. Bib-
     liography and index.

771 Wedell, E. G. Broadcasting and Public Policy. Lon-
     don: Michael Joseph, 1968. 370 pp.
        In this single-volume treatment of British radio
     and television, Wedell examines the polity and plan-
     ning factor.

772 Who's Listening? The Story of BBC Audience Re-
     search. London: Allen & Unwin, 1974. 219 pp.
        A personal account of the origins and develop-
     ment of the Audience Research Department by its
     founder and director for 32 years. Highlights some
     of the problems related to conducting and using re-
     search in non-commercial broadcasting.

B. Africa

See also no. 848.

773 Hachten, William A. Muffled Drums: The News Media in Africa. Ames: Iowa State University Press, 1971. 314 pp.
This book both surveys generally and examines minutely the news media in contemporary Africa. Bibliography, charts, index, and photographs.

774 Head, Sydney W. , ed. Broadcasting in Africa: A Continental Survey of Radio and Television. Philadelphia: Temple University Press, 1974. 453 pp.
The present study divides the subject into three major parts: description of individual broadcasting systems; description, as well as appraisal, of cross-system functions on a continental scale; and a critique leading to an inventory of subjects suggested for further study. Bibliography, charts, illustrations, and index.

775 Wilcox, Dennis L. Mass Media in Black Africa: Philosophy and Control. New York: Praeger, 1975. 170 pp.
A descriptive, comparative survey of press-government relationships in independent black Africa. Bibliography, charts, illustrations, and index.

C. Asia

See also nos. 760, 802, 855, 927.

776 de Vera, Jose M. Educational Television in Japan. Rutland, Vt. : Charles E. Tuttle, 1967. 140 pp.
On the role of educational television (concepts, audience, and effects).

777 Furo, Takeo. The Function of Television for Children and Adolescents. Tokyo: Sophia University Press, 1971. 323 pp.
In-depth published research in Japanese broadcasting on the effects of television on young people.

778 Henderson, John W. The United States Information Agency. New York: Praeger, 1969. 324 pp.

Presents chapters on VOA and USIA in the Vietnam War. Bibliography, charts, index, and photographs.

779   Kyokai, Nippon Hoso. The History of Broadcasting in Japan. Tokyo: Radio and Television Culture Research Institute, 1967. 423 pp.
        Essentially this book is a resume of documents critical in the evolution of Japanese broadcasting.

780   Lerner, Daniel and Wilbur Schramm, eds. Communication and Change in the Developing Countries. Honolulu: East-West Center Press, 1967. 333 pp.
        Devotes most of its attention to case studies of Mainland China, the Philippines, and India, stressing economic and social factors.

781   Liu, Alan P. L. Communications and National Integration in Communist China. Berkeley: University of California Press, 1971. 225 pp.
        This is a study of the roles that the mass media in Communist China play in achieving national integration. Bibliography, charts, and index.

782   Nishimoto, Mitoji. The Development of Educational Broadcasting in Japan. Rutland, Vt.: Charles E. Tuttle, 1969. 287 pp.
        A complete history of educational radio and TV from the mid-1920s to the mid-1960s. Devotes extensive attention to administration, programs, audience surveys and observed effects, and the role of the teacher.

783   Rao, Y. V. Lakshmana. Communication and Development: A Study of Two Indian Villages. Minneapolis: University of Minnesota Press, 1966. 145 pp.
        Carefully examines media impact on two types of rural villages, one developing, and the other still locked in tradition. The author's field method and results are useful for Asia as a whole and other regions as well.

D.   Latin America

784   Deutschmann, Paul J.; H. Ellingsworth; and John T. McNelly. Communication and Social Change in

Latin America.   New York: Praeger, 1968.   142 pp.
Discusses media technology as one of several important change agents in the modernization process.

785   Rogers, Everett M.   (in collaboration with Lynne Sven-
ning).   Modernization Among Peasants: Impact of
Communications.   New York: Holt, Rinehart &
Winston, 1969.   429 pp.
A highly detailed and somewhat complicated analysis of media impact on five Colombian villages in
the Andes.

786   Rogers, Everett M. and F. Floyd Shoemaker.   Communication of Innovations: A Cross-Cultural Approach.   2nd edition.   New York: Free Press,
1971.   476 pp.
A massive summation of the literature of communications diffusion focusing on media applicability
in developing areas and reporting a number of Latin
American researchers.   Bibliography.

787   Wells, Alan.   Picture-Tube Imperialism?   The Impact
of U.S. Television on Latin America.   Maryknoll,
N.Y.:   Orbis Books, 1972.   197 pp.
An illustrated volume which puts a lot of stress
on industry organization and control along with a selection of readings on media effects and its socie-
tal role.

E.   Canada

See also nos. 677, 918, 920, 946, 964, 1003.

788   Faris, Ron.   The Passionate Educators: Voluntary Associations and the Struggle for Control of Adult
Education Broadcasting in Canada 1919-52.   Toronto:
Peter Martin Associates Ltd., 1975.   201 pp.
Traces the intricate relationships between voluntary associations and Canadian radio broadcasting
during the 1919-1952 period.

789   Firestone, O. J.   Broadcast Advertising in Canada:
Past and Future Growth.   Ottawa: University of
Ottawa Press, 1966.   358 pp.
A specialized study on Canadian broadcast adver-
tising.

790 Jamieson, Don. The Troubled Air. Fredericton,
        N. B. : Brunswick Press, 1966. 237 pp.
        Concentrates on the private broadcaster written
     from the author's vantage point as a member of
     Canada's Parliament.

791 Lambert, Richard S. School Broadcasting in Canada.
        Toronto: University of Toronto Press, 1963.
        223 pp.
        This is a detailed study of the growth and opera-
     tion of Canadian school broadcasting. Bibliography,
     charts, index, and photographs.

792 Peers, Frank W. The Politics of Canadian Broadcast-
        ing: 1920-1951. Toronto: University of Toronto
        Press, 1969. 466 pp.
        Covers in great detail the political-legal develop-
     ments up to the 1951 inception of television.

793 Weir, E. Austin. The Struggle for National Broadcast-
        ing in Canada. Toronto: McClelland & Stewart,
        1964. 477 pp.
        Concentrates on the history of the CBC from its
     inception to the early 1960s.

F. Propaganda

See also nos. 551, 753, 758, 778, 804, 854, 879, 1096.

794 Graves, Harold, Jr. War on the Short Wave. New
        York: Foreign Policy Association, 1941. 64 pp.
        Deals with propaganda and the Foreign Policy
     Association during World War II (1939-1945). Illus-
     trations.

795 Hale, Julian. Radio Power: Propaganda and Interna-
        tional Broadcasting. Philadelphia: Temple Univer-
        sity Press, 1975. 196 pp.
        The author, a former scriptwriter, producer, and
     organizer of the BBC's Romanian and Italian ser-
     vices, introduces his work by calling radio "the
     only unstoppable medium of mass communication"
     and thus "the most powerful weapon of international
     propaganda. " Bibliography and index.

796 Riegel, O. W. Mobilizing for Chaos: The Story of

the New Propaganda. New Haven, Conn. : Yale
University Press, 1934. 231 pp.
Discusses early efforts of propaganda utilizing
all methods of communication available during this
time in history, including radio. Index.

797 Sorensen, Thomas C. The Word War: The Story of
American Propaganda. New York: Harper & Row,
1968. 337 pp.
A history of USIA and its broadcasting arm,
Voice of America, with some information on govern-
ment activities which preceded it.

G. Satellites

See also nos. 66, 147, 151, 210, 557, 809, 815, 1014.

798 Brown, Donald. Telecommunications: The Booming
Technology. Garden City, N. Y. : Doubleday, 1970.
191 pp.
The author explores the past and present of
communications systems but deals mainly with the
developing systems of the near and far future. He
particularly describes the wide range of uses of
the communications satellite that will allow not only
direct intercontinental television reception but also
home computers connected to a central agency thou-
sands of miles away and intercontinental direct-dial
telephone systems. Bibliography, illustrations,
index, and photographs.

799 Twentieth Century Fund Task Force on International
Satellite Communications. The Future of Satellite
Communications: Resource Management and the
Needs of Nations. New York: Twentieth Century
Fund Task Force on International Satellite Communications, 1970. 80 pp.
A report on how communications satellites can
be fully utilized on a global scale to gather data
for scientific research, to spread education and
knowledge, and to achieve new dimensions of international understanding.

H. General

See also nos. 1, 5, 68, 69, 76, 80, 146, 200, 210, 398,
408, 542, 599, 628, 725, 856, 861, 871, 878, 880, 890,
896, 911, 921, 923, 929, 1009, 1010, 1011, 1012, 1013,
1015, 1016, 1031, 1041, 1093.

800 Arnove, Robert F. , ed. Educational Television: A
     Policy Critique and Guide for Developing Countries.
     New York: Praeger, 1976. 224 pp.
          This book is specially designed as a critical
     guide for educational planners and combines the
     points of view of non-TV specialists analyzing ETV
     after a decade of its application in developing na-
     tions. Charts.

801 Codding, George A. , Jr. Broadcasting Without Bar-
     riers. Paris: UNESCO, 1959. 167 pp.
          The task undertaken in this study is threefold:
     to determine the extent to which broadcasting has
     been made available to the world's peoples; to de-
     fine the obstacles--political, economic, and techni-
     cal--which impede its full and proper use as a
     medium of communication; and to examine possible
     ways and means of extending its benefits more wide-
     ly. Bibliography, charts, glossary, illustrations,
     index, and photographs.

802 Eguchi, H. and H. Ichinohe, eds. International Studies
     of Broadcasting with Special Reference to the Japa-
     nese Studies. Tokyo: NHK Radio and TV Culture
     Research Institute, 1971. 301 pp.
          Collection of ten articles, five of them covering
     most aspects of Japanese broadcasting, the other
     five being reprints of research articles on other
     countries' systems.

803 Emery, Walter B. National and International Systems
     of Broadcasting: Their History, Operation, and
     Control. East Lansing: Michigan State University
     Press, 1969. 752 pp.
          This book represents the first attempt by an au-
     thor to analyze in some depth the important broad-
     casting systems in all parts of the world and ex-
     plain their origin, development, and present opera-
     tions. Bibliography and index.

804 Fischer, Heinz-Dietrich and John C. Merrill, eds. International and Intercultural Communication. New York: Hastings House Publishers, 1976. 524 pp.
     A wide range of subjects are discussed including: communication systems and concepts in the world's media, problems of freedom and responsibility, national development and mass media, international news flow and propaganda, supranational communication efforts, international communication, theory and research in international communication. Bibliography, charts, and index.

805 Green, Timothy. The Universal Eye, the World of Television. New York: Stein & Day, 1972. 276 pp.
     This book is a first hand study of what is happening to television and what television is doing to and for every part of the world--from Japan to Nigeria, Caracas to Sidney, Moscow to Los Angeles. Bibliography and index.

806 Groombridge, Brian, ed. Adult Education and Television: A Comparative Study in Three Countries. Paris: UNESCO, 1966. 143 pp.
     Groombridge has succeeded in identifying the many concerns that any country must consider in promoting the use of television for adult education purposes.

807 International Institute for Educational Planning. New Educational Media in Action: Case Studies for Planners. 3 volumes. Paris: UNESCO, 1967. Volume I, 203 pp.; Volume II, 226 pp.; Volume III, 198 pp.
     Detail ETV growth and applications (plus a few radio studies) in both developed and developing countries.

808 Lee, John, ed. Diplomatic Persuaders: New Role of the Mass Media in International Relations. New York: John Wiley, 1968. 205 pp.
     Examines the broad role of media in diplomacy.

809 McWhinney, Edward, ed. The International Law of Communications. Leyden, Netherlands: A. W. Sijthoff, 1971. 170 pp.
     Collection of 11 papers, seven of which deal with satellites; offers views on direct broadcasting from many countries, including developing nations.

810   Markham, James W. , ed.   International Communica-
      tion as a Field of Study.   Iowa City: University of
      Iowa Publications Department, 1970.   158 pp.
         Offers an interesting collection of papers on the
      prospects and problems of teaching and doing re-
      search in international communications.

811   Namurois, Albert.   Structure and Organization of
      Broadcasting in the Framework of Radiocommunica-
      tions.   Geneva: European Broadcasting Union, 1972.
      211 pp.
         Contains a great deal of concise data on specific
      nations, financing of broadcast systems, and struc-
      tural diagrams illustrating the text.   Illustrations.

812   Schramm, Wilbur.   Mass Media and National Develop-
      ment: The Role of Information in the Developing
      Countries.   Stanford, Calif. :   Stanford University
      Press, 1964.   333 pp.
         This book looks closely at the relationship of
      mass communication to economic and social develop-
      ment in developing countries.   Four cases from
      four regions of the world are examined.   Bibliog-
      raphy, charts, illustrations, and index.

813   Schramm, Wilbur; P. H. Coombs; F. Kahnert; and
      Jack Lyle.   The New Media: Memo to Educational
      Planners.   Paris: UNESCO, 1967.   175 pp.
         Survey dealing specifically with educational media
      in developing countries.

814   Sherman, Charles and Donald Browne, eds.   Broad-
      cast Monographs No. 2:   Issues in International
      Broadcasting.   Washington, D. C. :   Broadcast Edu-
      cation Association, 1976.   171 pp.
         Includes 19 papers from a 1974 conference; thus
      all are original publications here.   They deal with
      the problem of culture imperialism from several
      points of view, the international flow of programs,
      national and international broadcast systems, teach-
      ing and research on this topic.

815   Smith, Delbert D.   International Telecommunication
      Control.   Leyden, Netherlands: A. W. Sijthoff,
      1969.   231 pp.
         Devotes about 50 pages to the legalities of satel-
      lite broadcasting, but on the way presents a current

analysis of the legal context of international broadcasting, the functions of ITU and regional broadcast
organizations, and the problem of illegal transmis-
sions.

816 Smythe, Dallas. The Structure and Policy of Electronic
     Communications. Urbana: University of Illinois
     Press, 1957. 103 pp.
         An excellent though dated description of the allo-
     cations basis of international broadcasting control,
     this book is an amazingly concise discussion with a
     wealth of detailed historical information.

817 Waniewicz, Ignacy. Broadcasting for Adult Education:
     A Guidebook to World Wide Experience. Paris:
     UNESCO, 1972. 132 pp.
         This book is directed mainly to those concerned
     with broadcasting for adult education in the so-called
     "developing" countries. Bibliography.

17. TECHNICAL

A. Audio

See also nos. 3, 99, 100, 101, 102, 104, 106, 110, 417, 418, 940, 1069.

818   Kiver, Milton S.   F-M Simplified.   3rd edition.
        Princeton, N.J.:   D. Van Nostrand Co., 1960.
        376 pp.
            The fundamentals of FM are presented in addi-
        tion to propagation, reception, and transmission of
        FM signals; FM receivers; circuit alignment; com-
        mercial FM receivers, their servicing and mainten-
        ance; and modern FM transmitters.   Bibliography,
        charts, illustrations, index, and photographs.

819   Lowman, Charles E.   Magnetic Recording.   New York:
        McGraw-Hill, 1972.   285 pp.
            This is an authoritative and practical guide to the
        technology of magnetic recorders used in such fields
        as audio recording, broadcast and closed-circuit TV,
        instrumentation recordings, and computer data sys-
        tems.   Glossary, illustrations, index, and photo-
        graphs.

B. Video

See also nos. 115, 118, 121, 122, 123, 127, 181, 426, 448, 450, 648, 665.

820   Berliner, Oliver.   Color TV Studio Design & Opera-
        tion: For CATV, School & Industry.   Blue Ridge
        Summit, Pa.:   TAB Books, 1975.   168 pp.
            Applicable to any small TV studio, this new
        easy-to-read book gives all the in-depth answers to

168

all the questions any studio owner or operator
might ask about how to equip and operate a low-cost
color TV studio--from design of the building itself,
to equipment maintenance and calibration. Of prime
interest to cable systems, schools and industrial
studios, this volume fully explains how to put out
professional-grade, network-quality productions on
a minimum budget. It provides a wealth of hard-
learned information in extremely condensed form.
Illustrations and index.

821 Bermingham, Alan, et al. The Small TV Studio:
     Equipment and Facilities. New York: Hastings
     House Publishers, 1975. 163 pp.
     This book deals with basic small television studio
equipment and production facilities. Useful reference. Bibliography, glossary, illustrations, and
photographs.

822 Chinn, Howard A. Television Broadcasting. New
     York: McGraw-Hill, 1957.
     Here is a highly technical discussion of televi-
sion. TV equipment, studios, lighting, and techniques are studied in much detail along with planning and installation. This book serves as an excellent reference of equipment, types of connectors
and their wiring, and techniques.

823 Costigan, Daniel M. FAX: The Principles and Prac-
     tice of Facsimile Communication. Philadelphia:
     Chilton Books, 1971. 270 pp.
     Discusses the current status of facsimile as well
as assessing its likely future. Bibliography, charts,
illustrations, index, and photographs.

824 Kiver, Milton S. and Kaufman, Milton. Television
     Simplified. 7th edition. New York: Van Nostrand /
     Reinhold, 1973. 616 pp.
     In simple and clear terms this book analyzes all
types of TV receivers now in service, from the
standpoint of theory, operation, troubleshooting,
and alignment. The emphasis is on solid-state and
integrated circuits and also on color, as well as
monochrome, TV circuits and receivers. It includes sufficient information on TV transmission and
transmitters to provide a full understanding of the
overall television system. Illustrations, index, and
photographs.

825 Robinson, Joseph F. and P. H. Beards. Using Video-
        tape. New York: Hastings House Publishers, 1976.
        208 pp.
           This book details the many possible applications
        of VTR, describes the machines and thier engineer-
        ing principles, and sets out the most reliable me-
        thods of operation. Bibliography, glossary, and il-
        lustrations.

826 Ross, Rodger L. Color Film for Color Television.
        New York: Hastings House Publishers, 1970.
           Currently available color films and processes
        which enable television producers to meet different
        program requirements.

827 Sheldon, H. Horton and Edgar Norman Grisewood.
        Television: Present Methods of Picture Transmis-
        sion. New York: D. Van Nostrand Co. , 1929.
        194 pp.
           In this book the authors have attempted to bring
        together, in a manner that can be understood by all,
        a summary of the achievements in the field of tele-
        vision together with a description of accessory equip-
        ment. Illustrations, index, and photographs.

828 Wilkie, Bernard. The Technique of Special Effects in
        Television. New York: Hastings House Publishers,
        1971. 392 pp.
           This unique work is both pioneering and astonish-
        ingly comprehensive. The treatment is detailed,
        giving full descriptions of equipment, working prin-
        ciples, safety precautions, and type of effect ob-
        tained.

C. General

See also nos. 130, 147, 500, 877, 981, 982, 983, 984, 985,
986, 987, 1035, 1064, 1080.

829 Ennes, Harold E. Broadcast Operator's Handbook.
        2nd edition. New York: John F. Rider Publisher,
        1951. 440 pp.
           This edition of Broadcast Operator's Handbook
        covers the technical aspects of production and pro-
        gramming. The first four parts cover the operat-
        ing practice in control rooms, the master control,

remote controls, and the transmitter. Parts 5 and
6 are concerned with technical data for operators
and engineers. Bibliography, charts, illustrations,
index, and photographs.

830   Finnegan, Patrick S.   Broadcast Engineering & Maintenance Handbook.   Blue Ridge Summit, Pa. :   TAB
Books, 1976.   532 pp.
This new data-packed volume is the reference
work for all broadcast engineers, technicians, and
managers--for anyone involved in the planning, con-
struction, installation, start-up, calibration, operation, updating, maintenance, modification, and re-
pair of commercial or educational broadcasting facilities.   It totally engulfs the subject of aural broadcasting, and is the sum total of the author's over
30 years of unmatched know-how and experience in
broadcasting.   Illustrations and index.

831   Gould, Jack.   All About Radio and Television.   New
York: Random House, 1953.   144 pp.
Explains in simple language the nature of television and radio waves and how to transmit and receive them.   Illustrations.

832   Safford, E. L. , Jr.   A Guide to Radio & TV Broadcast Engineering Practice.   Blue Ridge Summit,
Pa. :   TAB Books, 1971.   256 pp.
Essentially a "how-to" handbook on operation,
maintenance, and troubleshooting, the volume is divided into two parts--Radio and Television.   Operator qualifications, preventive maintenance, FCC violations, AM antenna systems, equipment used in
radio and TV stations, maintenance philosophy, and
technical problems and solutions are among the topics
discussed.   Illustrations.

18. BIBLIOGRAPHIES

833 Adkins, Gale R. <u>Books on Radio-Television-Film: A Collection of Recommendations.</u> Lawrence: University of Kansas Radio-Television Research, 1962. 50 pp.
   Collection of short responses to a college survey requesting teacher evaluation of books useful as texts. Covers 29 subject areas and 348 different titles, offering an interesting collection of critical reactions to pre-1960 volumes.

834 Atkin, Charles; John P. Murray; and Oguz B. Nayman, compilers. <u>Television and Social Behavior: An Annotated Bibliography of Research Focusing on Television's Impact on Children.</u> Rockville, Md. : National Institute of Mental Health, Public Health Service, 1971. 150 pp.
   A detailed discussion of research findings issued as a part of the early 1970s government investigation of TV's effects, especially violent programming's effects on children. Some 300 studies are annotated in detail and another 250 are listed. A valuable review bibliography of scholarly research in a controversial area. Index.

835 "A Bibliography of Articles About Broadcasting in Law Periodicals, 1920-1968. " <u>Journal of Broadcasting</u> 14: 83-156; Winter 1969-70, No. 1, Part II.
   A separately-issued three-part annotated bibliography which consists of a bibliography on broadcast rights from 1920-1955, general articles on broadcast law and regulation from 1920-1955, and an inclusive listing of legal citations from 1956-1968. A valuable author, title, and subject guide to nearly 50 years of writing on legal aspects of broadcasting. Index.

836   Blum, Eleanor. Basic Books in the Mass Media: An
       Annotated, Selected Booklist Covering General Com-
       munications, Book Publishing, Broadcasting, Film,
       Magazines, Newspapers, Advertising, Indexes, and
       Scholarly and Professional Periodicals.   Urbana:
       University of Illinois Press, 1972.   252 pp.
            This volume is set in typescript and details 665
       items, 123 of which relate specifically to radio and
       television here and abroad.   Index.

837   Blum, Eleanor, ed. New Books in the Journalism and
       Communications Library. Urbana: University of
       Illinois College of Communications.
            Annotated, arranged by subject. Issued quarterly.

838   Blum, Eleanor. Reference Books in the Mass Media.
       Urbana: University of Illinois Press, 1962.   103 pp.
            A major starting place for student research proj-
       ects by one of the most knowledgeable people in the
       country on media bibliography.

839   British Broadcasting Corporation. British Broadcasting:
       A Bibliography. London: BBC, 1958 (with a four-
       page supplement, 1960).   53 pp.
            Annotated discussion of books, government docu-
       ments, BBC publications, and periodicals from
       1920s to 1960 on history, monopoly and commercial
       broadcasting, general, external services, technique of
       broadcasting, biography, education, music, religion,
       television, public corporations, finance, BBC annual
       reports, constitutional documents on BBC and ITA,
       parliamentary debates, BBC serials, and periodicals.
       The definitive source for the period covered. Index.

840   Broderick, Gertrude (Golden). Radio and Television
       Bibliography. Washington, D.C.: U.S. Department
       of Health, Education, and Welfare, Office of Educa-
       tion, Bulletin No. 2, 1956.   46 pp.
            Emphasis is on historical, philosophical, and
       sociological aspects of media.

841   Cable Television Information Center. Bibliocable.
       Washington, D.C.: Cable Television Information
       Center, 1972, 1974.   59 pp.
            Lists and annotates the best sources of informa-
       tion on cable communications written to date, and
       tells where to find them. Update supplement in-
       cluded.

842   Cable Television Information Center.   Legal Bibliogra-
        phy: Synopses of Cases on Cable Television.   Wash-
        ington, D. C. :   Cable Television Information Center,
        1974.   21 pp.
        Useful for attorneys involved in cable franchising.

843   Comstock, George, et al.   Television and Human Be-
        havior: A Bibliography.   3 volumes.   Santa Monica,
        Calif. :   Rand Corp. , 1975.

844   Cooper, Isabella M.   Bibliography on Educational Broad-
        casting.   Chicago: University of Chicago Press,
        1942 (reprinted by Arno Press, 1971).   576 pp.
        Coverage of this annotated 1800-item bibliography
        is far broader than title suggests with sections on
        law, technical developments, commercial programs,
        freedom and censorship, allocations, political uses,
        etc. being among the 61 classifications.   Covering
        books and periodicals from 1920 through 1940, stress
        is on the thirties.   Annotations are lengthy, detailed,
        and both descriptive and evaluative.   An essential
        guide to writing on radio before World War II, it
        concludes with an author and title index.   Index.

845   Danielson, Wayne A. and G. C. Wilhoit.   A Computer-
        ized Bibliography of Mass Communication Research:
        1944-1964.   New York: Magazine Publisher's As-
        sociation, 1967.   399 pp.
        Nearly 2,300 entries listed first by key word and
        then in full citation form, this volume has a maga-
        zine emphasis but contains a heavy dosage of broad-
        casting and broadcast-related periodical citations as
        well.   Coverage is from 48 scholarly social science
        journals with emphasis on content of mass communi-
        cations and a heavy dosage of methodology articles.

846   Fairman, Edith M.   The Effects of Television Violence
        on Children: A Selected Annotated Bibliography.   Wash-
        ington, D. C. :   Library of Congress, Congressional Re-
        search Service, 1973.   14 pp.

847   Gordon, Thomas F. and Mary Ellen Verna.   Mass Media
        and Socialization: A Selected Bibliography.   Philadel-
        phia: Temple University School of Communications
        and Theater, 1973.   47 pp.

848   Hachten, William A.   Mass Communication in Africa: An
        Annotated Bibliography.   Madison: University of

Wisconsin Center for International Communication
Studies, 1971. 121 pp.

849 Hamill, Patricia Beall. Radio and Television: A Selected Bibliography. Washington, D. C. : U. S. Government Printing Office, 1960. 46 pp.
A revision of an annotated bibliography first issued
(by Gertrude Broderick) from the Office of Education
in 1948, this pamphlet contains book discussions under
headings of general-historical, program techniques,
educational uses, scripts and plays, technical aspects,
plus a listing of periodicals and general information
sources. Index.

850 Hansen, Donald A. and J. Herschel Parsons, compilers.
Mass Communication: A Research Bibliography. Santa
Barbara, Calif. : Glendessary Press, 1968. 115 pp.
Subject-divided review of periodical articles.

851 Harris, Dale B. Children and Television: An Annotated Bibliography. Urbana, Ill. : National Association of Educational Broadcasters, 1959.

852 Harwood, Kenneth. Radio and Television Works Added
to the Library of the British Museum, 1881-1950:
A Bibliography. Los Angeles: University of
Southern California Department of Telecommunications, 1965. 184 pp.
Approximately 1,800 books and pamphlets are listed
under five-year sections with all but the first two subject divided. Gives data on author, title, publisher,
date of publication, number of pages, and British Museum call number. Most are in English, but perhaps
100 are in other languages.

853 Kaid, Lynda Lee; Keith R. Sanders; and Robert O.
Hirsch. Political Campaign Communication: A Bib-
liography and Guide to the Literature. Metuchen,
N. J. : Scarecrow Press, 1974.

854 Lasswell, Harold D. ; Ralph D. Casey; and Bruce Lannes Smith. Propaganda and Promotional Activities:
An Annotated Bibliography. Minneapolis: University of Minnesota Press, 1935 (reprinted by University of Chicago Press, 1969). 450 pp.
The first of a classic trio, this annotated volume
covers communications in a broad sense and includes
many references to radio (especially on pages 319-27).

Index.

855   Lent, John A. Asian Mass Communications: A Compre-
      hensive Bibliography. Philadelphia: Temple Univer-
      sity School of Communications and Theater, 1975.
      708 pp.
          Provides an annotated listing of publications, or-
      ganizations, and other sources of media data.

856   Lichty, Lawrence W. , compiler. World and Interna-
      tional Broadcasting: A Bibliography. Washington,
      D. C. : Association for Professional Broadcasting
      Education, 1970.   881 pp.
          An unannotated listing divided basically along
      region and country lines (and within those categories
      chronologically), this is a valuable listing of books
      and periodical articles over five decades.

857   Lingel, Robert. Educational Broadcasting: A Bibliog-
      raphy. Chicago: University of Chicago Press,
      1934.   162 pp.
          Basically a listing of articles, pamphlets and
      booklets, only a few of which have a line or two of
      annotation, this book is divided into two parts: an
      educationally-oriented listing of some 160 categories
      and a supplement on radio law of some 45 pages.
      Both parts are useful guides to the earliest publica-
      tions in radio broadcasting assembled by a key member
      of the New York Public Library's staff. Index.

858   McCoy, Ralph E. Freedom of the Press: An Anno-
      tated Bibliography. Carbondale: Southern Illinois
      University Press, 1968.   508 pp.
          With nearly 8,400 entries in a large (9x12) for-
      mat, this is one of the biggest annotated communica-
      tions bibliographies available. It covers all aspects
      of the subject (including broadcasting) over a 400
      year span with the stress on the last century. At-
      tempt was intended to be comprehensive rather than
      selective with annotations of varied length outlining
      content and point of view of each book, article, or
      document listed. Excludes laws, newspapers and
      popular magazine articles, and propaganda. Index.

859   Marketing Information Guide. Garden City, N. Y. :
      Hoke Communications, Inc.
          Annotated bibliography of about 150 summaries
      of studies, reports, articles, books from some 600

market research studies, giving cost and source of
each. Issued monthly.

860   Mass Communications: A Catalog of Dissertations,
      Theses, Books, and Serials.   Ann Arbor, Mich. :
      Xerox University Microfilms, no date.   73 pp.
         This bibliography lists over 2, 200 dissertations,
      masters theses, books and periodicals that cover as-
      pects of mass communications. Index.

861   Mowlana, Hamid.   International Communication: A Se-
      lected Bibliography.   Dubuque, Iowa: Kendall/Hunt,
      1971.   130 pp.
         A subject-divided unannotated selective listing of
      nearly 1, 500 references divided into the following
      headings: theoretical basis, communication systems
      (by region), international news communication, com-
      munication and foreign policy, propaganda and public
      opinion, cross-cultural communication, communica-
      tion development, communication and the space age,
      regulation and laws, foreign correspondents, and
      bibliographies. Index.

862   National Archives.   Preliminary Inventories.   Washing-
      ton, D. C. : General Services Administration, Na-
      tional Archives and Records Service, 1941-date.
         A series of brief bibliographic guides to the col-
      lections pertaining to government agencies now on
      file for research purposes in the National Archives
      in Washington. Of interest here are: Section 54.
      Records of the Office of Censorship (1953), 16 pp. ;
      Section 56.   Records of the Office of War Informa-
      tion (1953), 149 pp. ; Section 93.   Records of the
      Federal Communications Commission (1956), 21 pp. ;
      Section 115.   Records of the Foreign Broadcast In-
      telligence Service (1959), 53 pp.   Each lists the
      holdings of the Archives with brief annotations as to
      contents and type of material held.   Invaluable for
      research work.

863   National Association of Broadcasters.   Broadcast Pio-
      neers History Project: Historical Inventory and In-
      dustry Reference Library.   Fifth Report.   Washing-
      ton, D. C. : Broadcast Pioneers, 1969.   98 pp.
         Although prepared before the Broadcast Pioneers
      Library moved to its present Washington quarters
      in the NAB building, this listing is a good indication

of the holdings of the project at the time, and suggests the kinds of things available for research use.
Index.

864   Nelson, Marlan.   Free Press--Fair Trial: An Anno-
      tated Bibliography.   Logan: Utah State University
      Department of Journalism, 1971.   89 pp.
         Covering nearly 600 books, periodical articles,
      and theses and dissertations, this reference covers
      the 1950-1969 period and is exhaustive, covering
      legal, scholarly, and trade periodical reports and
      articles.

865   Office of Telecommunications Policy.   Cable Television
      Bibliography.   Springfield, Va.: National Technical
      Information Service, 1972.   27 pp.

866   Owen, Bruce M., et al.   "A Selected Bibliography in
      the Economics of the Mass Media."   Studies in the
      Economics of Mass Communications Memorandum
      No. 99.   Stanford, Calif.: Research Center in Eco-
      nomic Growth, Stanford University, 1970.   83 pp.
         A two-part unannotated listing: the first being
      an alphabetical listing, the second and longest being
      a subject-divided listing with headings such as
      theory and concepts, analysis and description, law
      and regulation, data sources, trade publications,
      technology and development, and general (each fur-
      ther divided).   Emphasis on significant scholarly
      studies.   The two halves are keyed by a number
      code.

867   Paulu, Burton.   A Radio and Television Bibliography:
      Book and Magazine Articles on the Nontechnical As-
      pects of Broadcasting Published Between January 1,
      1949 and June 30, 1952.   Urbana, Ill.: National
      Association of Educational Broadcasters, 1952.
      129 pp.
         Divided into sections on radio and television (and
      then subject-divided further).

868   President's Task Force on Communications Policy.
      Bibliography [on Communications Policy].   Spring-
      field, Va.: National Technical Clearing House,
      U.S. Department of Commerce, 1968.   172 pp.
         Unannotated listing of documents, reports, and
      articles on the problems in and control of telecom-
      munications.

869   Price, Warren C. and Calder M. Pickett. An Anno-
      tated Journalism Bibliography: 1958-1968. Minne-
      apolis: University of Minnesota Press, 1970. 285 pp.
         This volume lists in alphabetical order by author
      name, some 2,200 books each with two to five lines
      of description. Coverage is all items of journalism
      using the term broadly. Index.

870   Radio and Television Bibliography. 5th edition. New
      York: Columbia Broadcasting System, 1942. 89 pp.
         Occasionally annotated listing of books and pamph-
      lets (plus some articles) on all aspects of radio.
      Interesting 15-page listing of pre-1941 CBS publica-
      tions. Nine categories in main listing. Index.

871   Rafi-Zadeh, Hassan. International Mass Communica-
      tions: Computerized Annotated Bibliography [of]
      Articles, Dissertations and Theses. Carbondale,
      Ill. : Honorary Relation-Zone, 1972. 314 pp.
         Annotated listing of articles from Gazette, Jour-
      nalism Quarterly, and Journal of Communication,
      plus theses and dissertations from mid-1950s
      through 1971 presented in alphabetical listing with
      176 subject index. For the limited scope, a valu-
      able research tool, with many references to radio
      and television.

872   Ramey, James W. Television in Medical Teaching and
      Research: A Survey and Annotated Bibliography.
      Washington, D. C. : Government Printing Office
      (Office of Education Publication OE-34040), 1965.
      155 pp.
         A detailed reference to medical uses of television
      since the initial experiments of 1947, this volume
      contains an overview essay and then extended anno-
      tations on journal articles, papers, speeches, and
      books on the topic. The bibliography contains sec-
      tions on basic sciences, endoscopy, eye-ear-nose-
      throat, microscopy, postgraduate education, psychia-
      try, radiology, research and diagnostic instrumenta-
      tion, surgery, and a miscellaneous category. Charts
      and index.

873   Reid, J. Christopher and Donald W. MacLennan, eds.
      Research in Instructional Television and Film.
      Washington, D. C. : Government Printing Office
      (Office of Education Publication 34041), 1967.

216 pp.
This annotated discussion of over 300 studies
covers the 1950-1964 period and deals with all aspects of televised instruction and audience reaction
to same.   There is a brief introductory essay sum-
marizing the period's research, then an alphabetical
listing by author.   Charts, index, and photographs.

874   Rose, Oscar.   Radio Broadcasting and Television: An
      Annotated Bibliography.   New York: H. W. Wilson
      Co. , 1947.   120 pp.
      A direct predecessor in aim and format to the
      present volume, this is a good index to book and
      pamphlet publication in radio up through 1945.   It
      attempts to be all-inclusive (except for technical
      studies), and thus contains a vast number of titles,
      especially of an ephemeral nature which are not de-
      tailed here.   Index.

875   Schramm, Wilbur, ed.   "The Effects of Television on
      Children and Adolescents. "   Reports and Papers on
      Mass Communication No. 43.   Paris: UNESCO,
      1964.   54 pp.
      A fully annotated listing of 165 books, pamphlets,
      and articles in English and other languages dealing
      with topic.   Includes sections on bibliographies, gen-
      eral studies, learning from TV, effects of violence,
      etc.   List of periodicals mentioned and index of au-
      thors and sources.   Index.

876   Seibert, Warren.   Instructional Television: The Best
      of ERIC 1974-1975.   Stanford, Calif. :   Stanford
      University School of Education, 1976.   31 pp.

877   Shiers, George (assisted by May Shiers).   Bibliography
      of the History of Electronics.   Metuchen, N. J. :
      Scarecrow Press, 1972.   323 pp.
      A unique and detailed guide to the technical side
      of broadcasting and related fields, this annotated
      bibliography devotes large sections to telegraphy
      and telephony, radio, television and facsimile, and
      broadcasting, plus other related sections on elec-
      tromagnetic waves, recording and reproduction,
      personal and corporate histories, periodicals, gene-
      ral references, etc.   Over 1, 800 items are dealt
      with, nearly all being annotated in detail, essential-
      ly descriptively rather than evaluatively.   Covered

are books, major periodical articles, some government documents, and serials.   Index.

878   Skolnik, Roger.   A Bibliography of Selected Publications on Foreign and International Broadcasting. East Lansing: Michigan State University, 1966. 62 pp.

A listing of over 700 books and periodical citations under the following headings: foreign broadcast systems (listed by country), international broadcasting (history and propaganda), distributive systems, and current problems.   Index.

879   Smith, Bruce Lannes; Harold D. Lasswell; and Ralph D. Casey.   Propaganda, Communication, and Public Opinion: A Comprehensive Reference Guide. Princeton, N.J.:   Princeton University Press, 1946.   435 pp.

The second in a trio of related books, this volume covers publications of the mid-1934 to mid-1943 period.   Over 2,500 items are covered in a highly organized bibliography with many references to domestic and international broadcasting.   Index.

880   Smith, Bruce Lannes and Chitra M. Smith.   International Communication and Political Opinion: A Guide to the Literature.   Princeton, N.J.:   Princeton University Press, 1956.   325 pp.

The last of a trio of similar bibliographies, this covers material from mid-1943 to 1955 in the same highly structured and annotated format of the earlier books.   Of the three, this is the only volume restricted to international communications and, like the others, it has numerous references to broadcasting among its 2,500 entries.   Index.

881   Smith, Don C.   Selected Bibliography from the Library of Congress Catalog of Books Through September 1963 Classified Under the Subjects of Radio and Television.   Los Angeles: University of Southern California Department of Telecommunications, 1965. 141 pp.

Divided into two parts: the first and longest covers books and pamphlets divided by subjects (general, advertising, education, history, literature, performance, programming, references, regulations, and research-audience), while the second part lists

government documents, periodicals, and dissertations. No annotations.

882 Source Catalog No. 1: Communications.   Chicago:
       Swallow Press, 1971.   119 pp.
       A bibliographic guide to the so-called "under-
ground" view of media, with a large proportion of
the booklet devoted to audio and video media, including broadcasting.   Lists organizations, community
groups, books and pamphlets, etc., all annotated as
to their usefulness to the aware protester.   There
is also coverage of theater, film, periodicals,
printing and publishing, libraries, and community
communications.   Index and photographs.

883 Sparks, Kenneth R.   A Bibliography of Doctoral Dis-
       sertations in Television and Radio.   3rd edition.
       Syracuse, N.Y.: Syracuse University School of
       Journalism, 1971.   119 pp.
       A classified but unannotated listing of over 900
studies in radio and television completed over a
nearly 50-year span.   There are 12 classifications
and an index of authors in this standard list.   Index.

884 Sperry, Robert.   "A Selected Bibliography of Works on
       the Federal Communications Commission." Journal
       of Broadcasting 19: 55-113; Winter 1975.

885 Stroud, William.   Selected Bibliography on Telecom-
       munications (Cable Systems).   Madison: Wisconsin
       Library Association, 1972.   38 pp.
       Emphasis on post-1970 publications on cable tele-
vision with lists of state and federal documents,
books, and periodical articles, divided into research
reports, ordinances, hearings, and bibliographies.
To be revised or supplemented on an annual basis.

886 Taggart, Dorothy T.   A Guide to Sources in Educa-
       tional Media and Technology.   Metuchen, N.J.:
       Scarecrow Press, 1975.   156 pp.
       This book is a guide to books and periodicals.
Excellent source book for individuals interested in
the field of educational media.   Bibliography is annotated.   Index.

887 Television Careers: A Bibliography.   New York:
       Television Information Office, 1966.   44 pp.

Annotated entries under headings of general,
study and training, scholarships, fellowships, in-
ternships, assistantships, occupational specialties,
employment opportunities, placement listings, dissertations and theses, audio-visual aids, publishers'
addresses. Index.

888   Television and Education: A Bibliography.   New York:
      Television Information Office, 1962.   33 pp.
      One of a series of pamphlet bibliographies, this
      contains books and periodical articles under head-
      ings of general, operational ETV reports, research,
      programming, production, and technical, plus a list-
      ing of further reference sources, all of it annotated.

889   Television in Government and Politics: A Bibliography.
      New York: Television Information Office, 1964.
      62 pp.
      Annotated entries of books and articles under
      headings concerning the presidency, candidates and
      national elections, the "Great Debates," Congress,
      state and local politics, regulation, economics,
      practical guides to use of radio-TV, foreign, dis-
      sertations and theses, and bibliography.   Especially
      good for material of late 1950s and early 1960s.

890   Van Bol, Jean-Marie and Abdelfattah Fakhfakh.   The
      Use of Mass Media in the Developing Countries.
      Brussels: International Centre for African Social
      and Economic Documentation, 1971.   751 pp.
      An immense and valuable work with over 2,500
      books and articles in many languages (with annota-
      tions in French and English for each) on all aspects
      of the subject, this work is made more valuable by
      a detailed analytical structure which allows instant
      regional or topical access to the alphabetical listing.
      Coverage is from 1950 to 1969, and the annotations
      are in the form of brief abstracts while the sources
      for the work are international in scope.   Index.

19. ANNUALS

A. Radio

891 Federal Communications Commission. AM-FM Finan-
     cial Data. Washington, D.C. : FCC, 1946-date.

B. Television

See also no. 903.

892 Children's Television Workshop. Annual Report. New
     York: CTW.

893 David, Nina, ed. TV Season. Phoenix, Ariz. : Oryx
     Press.
          A complete guide to television--the programs,
     stars, creators, award winners--for the current
     seasons.

894 Federal Communications Commission. TV Broadcast
     Financial Data. Washington, D.C. : FCC.

895 Federal Communications Commission. Television
     Broadcast Programming Data. Washington, D.C. :
     FCC, 1973-date.

896 Gertner, Richard, ed. International Television Alma-
     nac. New York: Quigley Publishing Co.
          Contains statistics on television usage and TV
     advertising; maps showing location of major net-
     works; Who's Who in motion pictures and television;
     credits for feature films; feature pictures; names
     and addresses of companies, producers, and distrib-
     utors, television stations, advertising agencies, film
     distributors, organizations; as well as sections with

information on the industry in other countries.

897   Jennings, Ralph M. , et al.   Television Station Employ-
      ment Practices: The Status of Minorities and Wom-
      en.   New York: United Church of Christ, 1972-
      date.

898   Nielsen, A. C. , Co.   Nielsen Television.   Northbrook,
      Ill. : Nielsen, 1955-date.

899   Nielsen, A. C. , Co.   The Television Audience.   North-
      brook, Ill. : Nielsen.

900   Perry, Ted, ed.   Performing Arts Resources.   New
      York: Drama Books Specialists/Theater Library
      Association, 1974-date.
            A new series of which each volume contains 15-
      20 articles detailing the contents of various theater
      and media archives.   First volume contains both
      actual video material and documents.

901   Television Factbook.   Washington, D. C. : Television
      Digest, Inc. , 1945-date.
            Issued annually (in two volumes in recent years,
      one for "services," the other for "stations"), this
      is the most exhaustive information source on tele-
      vision in all its aspects.   Extensive information on
      TV audience, many pages of historical statistics,
      data on ownership, sales and transfers, major di-
      rectory of CATV systems and equipment, and (in
      separate volume) coverage map and complete rate
      and audience data for every television station in the
      country, plus directory of foreign television stations.
      Probably the best informed and most accurate in-
      formation on most aspects of the TV industry.

902   TV-Film Filebook.   Ontario, Canada: TV-Film File-
      book.
            Contains everything from sources of advertising
      agencies to unions and guilds.

C.   Cable Television

903   CATV and Station Coverage Atlas.   Washington, D. C. :
      Television Digest, Inc.
            Contains all the FCC rules on cable television

rule-making for CATV systems. It also lists equipment manufacturers, translators, and microwaves
servicing CATV systems and includes two sets of
state maps graphically showing CATV systems,
grade A and B contours of all stations, and 35-mile
zones.

904   Taishoff, Sol, ed. Cable Source Book. Washington,
          D. C. : Broadcasting Publications, Inc.
              Lists cable facts, groups, systems, equipment,
          brokers, consultants, broadcasters, FCC rules,
          Yellow Pages Buyers Guide, program suppliers,
          and CATV associations in the U. S. and Canada.

D.   Public Broadcasting

See also no. 1076.

905   Corporation for Public Broadcasting. Public Television
          Program Content. Washington, D. C. : CPB, 1974-
          date.

906   Corporation for Public Broadcasting. Summary Statis-
          tics of CPB-Qualified Public Radio Stations. Wash-
          ington, D. C. : CPB, 1971-date.

907   Corporation for Public Broadcasting. Summary Statis-
          tics of Public Television Licensees. Washington,
          D. C. : CPB, 1971-date.

908   Henry, Nelson B. , ed. Mass Media and Education.
          53rd Yearbook of the NSSE, Part II. Chicago:
          University of Chicago Press, 1954.
              Concerned with the learning experiences of school
          children and with problems pertaining to the enrich-
          ment of classroom instruction through the introduc-
          tion of and emphasis on audio-visual materials.
          The nature and effects of such materials are also
          considered with respect to their role in the function-
          al operations of society at large.

909   Lee, S. Young and Ronald J. Pedone. Status Report
          on Public Broadcasting. Washington, D. C. : Cor-
          poration for Public Broadcasting.

E. Advertising

910 BBD&O (Batten, Barton, Durstine & Osborn). BBDO
     Audience Coverage and Cost Guide. New York:
     BBD&O, 1962-date.

911 Herdeg, Walter, ed. Graphis Annual: International
     Annual of Advertising and Editorial Graphics. New
     York: Hastings House Publishers.
         Annual which, for more than two decades, has
     richly earned its world-wide reputation as the stan-
     dard work reflecting the latest international trends
     in all design fields.

F. FCC

912 Federal Communications Commission. Annual Report.
     Washington, D. C. : Government Printing Office,
     1934-date (reports for 1934-1955 reprinted by Arno
     Press, 1971).

913 Federal Communications Commission. Telecommunica-
     tions. Washington, D. C. : Government Printing
     Office, Code of Federal Regulations (Title 47).

G. General

914 Barrett, Marvin, ed. Survey of Broadcast Journalism.
     New York: Grosset & Dunlap.
         An annual review of broadcast news coverage of
     the preceding season, the forces that shaped it, and
     the trends most conspicuous within the 12-month
     period.

915 Booth-Clibborn, Edward, ed. European Illustration:
     European Editorial, Book Advertising, Television,
     Cinema and Design Art. New York: Hastings
     House Publishers.
         Drawing its material from the widest range of
     European mass media and from the European pub-
     lishing business this is an unparalleled showcase
     for the versatile talents of the leading artists and
     illustrators at work in Europe today.

916 Broadcasting Yearbook. Washington, D. C. : Broadcasting

Publications, Inc. , 1935-date.
Issued annually (in recent years, in January),
this guide has six major sections: general industry
data, television, radio, equipment and rules, NAB
Codes and program services, and a miscellaneous
section. Highly detailed and accurate information.

917   Brown, James W. , ed. Educational Media Yearbook.
New York: Bowker, 1973-date.
Lengthy section each year of annotated listings
of periodicals, books, and reports dealing with all
aspects of educational media.

918   Canada Radio-Television Commission. Annual Report.
Ottawa: Queen's Printer, 1968-date.

919   Design and Art Direction: British Graphics, Advertising, Television and Editorial Design. New York:
Hastings House Publishers.
The showcase of British creative talent. It provides an essential and indispensable record of the
last year's best work in six related fields: advertising and photography, television and movie advertising, and television and movie graphics.

920   Film/Tape Production Source Book. New York: Television Editorial Corp.
Listing of production services and supply com-
panies.

921   Frost, J. M. , ed. World Radio-TV Handbook. New
York: Billboard Publications, 1947-date.
Contains very detailed listings of frequencies,
power, and times on the air for all the world's stations (mainly shortwave).

922   Hall, William E. , ed. Journalism Abstracts. Columbus: Ohio State University School of Journalism.
Compilation of M. A. theses and doctoral dissertations from schools and departments of journalism
and communication in the United States.

923   Herdeg, Walter, ed. Photographis: The International
Annual of Advertising, Editorial and Television
Photography. New York: Hastings House Publish-
ers.
A valuable yearly graphic arts publication.

924   Kline, F. Gerald and Peter Clarke, co-editors. Sage
      Communication Research Annuals. Ann Arbor:
      University of Michigan Department of Journalism
      and Program in Mass Communication.
           Devoted to a continuing and up-to-date survey of
      current thinking and research in the field of com-
      munications research.

925   Look-Listen Opinion Poll. Madison, Wisc. : American
      Council for Better Broadcasts.
           Annual poll of adults and high school students of
      their opinions of programs; the report is sent to
      networks, national advertisers, the FCC, and inte-
      rested Congressional committees.

926   Montana Journalism Review. Missoula: University of
      Montana School of Journalism.
           Yearly journal of reports, research findings,
      and opinions about the news media, with emphasis
      on Montana newspapers and radio-TV stations. In-
      cludes critical articles on the press. Founded in
      1958 as the first journalism review in the United
      States.

927   Studies of Broadcasting. Tokyo: Radio and TV Cul-
      ture Research Institute of Nippon Hose Kyokai, 1963-
      1969, 1971-date.
           An annual series issued since 1963 under NHK
      auspices.

928   Television/Radio Age: Ten City Directory. New York:
      TV/Radio Age.
           Includes everything from hotels and restaurants
      to agencies and producers in ten major cities in the
      United States.

929   United Nations Educational, Scientific and Cultural Or-
      ganization. Statistical Yearbook. Paris: UNESCO,
      1963-date.

20. PERIODICALS

A. Radio

930   Journal of College Radio.   Edmond, Okla.:   Intercolle-
      giate Broadcasting System, Inc.   (monthly)
         Contains articles of interest to college and uni-
      versity broadcasters.   An annual contains a directory
      of college radio stations.

B. Television

931   Action for Children's Television Newsletter.   Newton-
      ville, Mass. : Action for Children's Television
      (ACT).   (monthly)
         Covers actions related to children's television,
      ranging from FCC hearings to vitamin commercials
      broadcast during children's viewing hours.

932   Children's Television Workshop Newsletter.   New York:
      Children's Television Workshop (CTW).
         Carries information on CTW work and actions
      that affect television for children.

933   Television Age.   New York: Television Editorial
      Corp.   (bi-monthly)
         Provides coverage of the broadcast business for
      buyers and sellers of radio and TV time at the
      agencies and advertisers.   Concentrates on the eco-
      nomics of the broadcasting industry.

934   Television Digest.   Washington, D. C. : Television Di-
      gest, Inc.   (weekly)
         A newsletter for executives in broadcasting, con-
      sumer electronics, and allied fields.   Covers de-
      velopments in the television and consumer electronics

industries, FCC reports, financial reports, cable
television activity, and AM-FM radio. In addition,
complete details of specific activities of the FCC
and the industry, such as applications for new stations and cable systems, sales and engineering data.
In addition, three weekly Addenda (TV, AM-FM,
and CATV) provide complete details of specific activities of the FCC and the industry, such as applications for new stations and cable systems, and
sales and engineering data.

935 TV Guide. Radnor, Pa. : Triangle Publications.
     (weekly)
          Contains news about all aspects of television and
     listings of the week's television programs. There
     are 89 separate regional editions.

936 Television News Index and Abstracts. Nashville:
     Vanderbilt Television News Archive. (monthly)
          Monthly summary of the evening news broadcasts
     of the three major television networks--ABC, CBS,
     and NBC.

937 Television Quarterly. Beverly Hills, Calif. : National
     Academy of Television Arts and Sciences. (quarter-
     ly)
          Contains essays and lengthy reviews of the status
     of television today, with a focus on American TV.
     Coverage of entertainment, serious drama, broad-
     cast journalism, personal reminiscences, political
     broadcasting, etc. , some of the articles being regu-
     lar research pieces. Began 1962; suspended publi-
     cation 1971-72.

938 Televisions. Washington, D. C. : Washington Commu-
     nity Video Center, Inc. (quarterly)
          A newspaper written for individuals involved in
     some sort of media work.

939 Viewers Digest. Palo Alto, Calif. : National Corres-
     pondence Group. (monthly)
          Concerned with violence on television.

C. Audio

940 Audio. Philadelphia: North American Publishing Co.

(monthly)
Discusses audio in general.

D. Video

941 Video Catalog. Boulder, Colo. : Video Catalog. (bi-
      annually)
      An attempt to alleviate the lack of lateral com-
      munications in video and film. Prints lists, arti-
      cles, graphics, ads, components, opinions, services,
      equipment, repairs, news and used, trades, and
      whatever people want video people to know.

942 Video Systems. Overland Park, Kan. : Intertec Pub-
      lishing Corp. (bi-monthly)
      The journal of closed-circuit communication.

943 Videocassette and CATV Newsletter. Beverly Hills,
      Calif. : Martin Roberts Associates. (monthly)
      A newsletter containing the latest developments in
      the fields of videocassettes, CATV, and telecommu-
      nications. Material included from foreign corres-
      pondents giving the latest information and statistics
      on the electronic audio-visual field from major man-
      ufacturing countries in Asia and Europe. Readers
      also receive three-four in-depth Special Reports
      each year.

944 Videography. New York: United Business Publica-
      tions. (monthly)
      Covers all aspects of video from technical to
      production.

E. Educational

See also no. 1019.

945 AV Communication Review. Washington, D. C. : Asso-
      ciation for Educational Communications and Tech-
      nology. (quarterly)
      Contains articles on theory, development, and
      research on communication media and technological
      processes in education, and research abstracts and
      book reviews on communications and technology in
      education.

946 Agency for Instructional Television Newsletter. Bloom-
     ington, Ind. : Agency for Instructional Television
     (AIT). (quarterly)
         AIT, a non-profit American-Canadian agency, was
     established to strengthen education through television
     and other technologies. Its primary function is the
     development of joint program projects involving state
     and provincial agencies. It also acquires, adapts,
     and distributes television, audio-visual, and related
     materials.

947 CPB Report. Washington, D. C. : Corporation for
     Public Broadcasting (CPB). (weekly)
         Newsletter of the CPB, carrying news, features,
     and general information of interest to the public
     broadcasting community.

948 Educational Broadcasting. Los Angeles: Brentwood
     Publishing Corp. (bi-monthly)
         Detailed review of new technological and soft-
     ware developments in educational media.

949 Educational Broadcasting Review (now Public Telecom-
     munications Review). Washington, D. C. : National
     Association of Educational Broadcasters. (bi-
     monthly)
         Reprints speeches and major papers, plus some
     government documents, on all aspects of educational,
     public, and instructional broadcasting with a stress
     on developments in the U. S. Contains three or
     four research articles per issue on a wide variety
     of instructional technology and public policy topics.
     Began in 1967; formerly titled NAEB Journal.

950 JCET News. Washington, D. C. : Joint Council on
     Educational Telecommunications (JCET). (monthly)
         Newsletter which covers all aspects of the elec-
     tronic media, with primary focus on public broad-
     casting. For members only.

951 NAEB Newsletter. Washington, D. C. : National Asso-
     ciation of Educational Broadcasters (NAEB). (bi-
     weekly)
         Newsletter of member and association activities
     in all phases of cable, government regulation, busi-
     ness and professional developments, franchises,
     new systems, personnel changes, etc.

952 Public Telecommunications Review (formerly Education-
     al Broadcasting Review). Washington, D. C. : Na-
     tional Association of Educational Broadcasters
     (NAEB). (bi-monthly)
          Contains research, reporting, and opinion about
     public broadcasting, instructional communications,
     and related fields. Also publishes book reviews.

F.   Advertising

See also no. 859

953 Advertising Age.   Chicago: Crain Communications,
     Inc.   (weekly)
          The main trade newspaper for the industry with
     details of new accounts and agency doings and peri-
     odical statistical summaries.

954 Advertising and Sales Promotion. New York: Crain
     Communications, Inc. (bi-weekly)
          Newspaper for advertising and sales promotion
     management, covering all of the sales promotion
     media and new sales promotion campaigns, person-
     nel changes, case histories, background articles,
     and new product and service coverage.

955 CLIO Magazine. New York: American TV and Radio
     Commercials Festival Group. (quarterly)
          Magazine for the advertising industry.

956 Communication Arts.   Palo Alto, Calif. : Communica-
     tion Arts.   (bi-monthly)
          Contains outstanding work of individuals in the
     design and advertising fields.

957 Daily Variety.   Los Angeles: Daily Variety Ltd.
     (daily)
          Show business newspaper concentrating on Holly-
     wood film, broadcasting, and other show business
     aspects.

958 Direct Marketing.   Garden City, N. Y. : Hoke Commu-
     nications, Inc.   (monthly)
          Directed to national advertisers and their agen-
     cies, with marketing, advertising, and sales man-
     agement news and information.

959   Friday Report.   Garden City, N.Y.:   Hoke Communi-
        cations, Inc.   (weekly)
        Newsletter directed to national advertisers and
        their agencies, with marketing, advertising, and
        sales management news and information.

960   The Gallagher Report.   New York: Gallagher Report,
        Inc.   (weekly)
        Newsletter about advertising, marketing, sales,
        and media with forecasts, news, trends, ideas, and
        latest developments in the advertising, marketing,
        media, and retail management fields.

961   Journal of Advertising Research.   New York: Adver-
        tising Research Foundation.   (bi-monthly)
        Reports findings of field and experimental studies
        related to the effect of advertising on consumers.

962   Journal of Marketing.   Chicago: American Marketing
        Association.   (quarterly)
        Covers new management techniques, ideas,
        trends, views, and solutions to existing problems
        in marketing.

963   Madison Avenue.   New York: Unique Communications,
        Inc.   (monthly)
        The advertising magazine.

964   Marketing.   Montreal: MacLean-Hunter Ltd.   (weekly)
        Canada's weekly newspaper of marketing commu-
        nications.

965   Media Decisions.   New York: Media Decisions.
        (monthly)
        Deals with concepts and trends in the media.
        Non-technical articles about media functions and
        roles in advertising and marketing.

966   Sales and Marketing Management.   New York: Sales
        and Marketing Management.   (January, March, June,
        September, December--monthly; other months bi-
        weekly)
        Published for all executives responsible for the
        profitable sale and marketing of their company's
        products and services.

967   SAM--The Voice of Midwestern Advertising.   Chicago:

SAM Publications, Inc.   (weekly)
Newspaper which deals with advertising agencies
in the midwest.

968   Sponsor.   Duluth, Minn.:   Moore Publishing Co.
      (monthly)

969   Standard Rate & Data.   New York: Standard Rate and
      Data Service, Inc.   (bi-monthly)
         Advertising rate information for newspapers,
      radio, television, magazines, farm publications,
      etc.   Separate publication for each.

970   Television/Radio Age.   New York: Television Editorial
      Corp.   (bi-weekly)
         Trade periodical stressing advertising, with oc-
      casional special issues on news, the FCC, and
      foreign television.

971   Topicator.   Littleton, Colo.:   Thompson Bureau.
      (monthly)
         Monthly classified guide to the advertising-broad-
      casting trade press.   Cumulated quarterly and an-
      nually.   Includes articles from: Advertising Age,
      AV Communication Review, Broadcasting, Education-
      al Broadcasting Review, Journal of Broadcasting,
      Marketing/Communications, Media/Scope, Televi-
      sion Age, Television Digest, Television Quarterly,
      TV Guide, and Variety.

G.   Entertainment

972   AFTRA Magazine.   New York: American Federation
      of Television and Radio Artists (AFTRA).   (quarter-
      ly)
         Sent to 34,000 AFTRA members, with occasional
      articles on future developments in communications,
      and the status of legislation relative to performers
      in its jurisdiction.

973   Back Stage.   New York: Back Stage Publications, Inc.
      (weekly)
         Newspaper with information on the entertainment
      world.

974   Billboard.   New York: Billboard Publications.   (weekly)

The major popular music trade newspaper with
news of records, music in broadcasting, and new
acts and performers.

975   Cash Box.   New York: Cash Box.   (weekly)
        Trade weekly of the popular music industry,
     covering top 100 in music, radio, record sales,
     etc.

976   The Hollywood Reporter.   Hollywood: The Hollywood
        Reporter Corp.   (daily)
        Newspaper with news of tinsel town.

977   National Academy of Television Arts ·& Sciences News-
        letter.   Beverly Hills, Calif.: National Academy of
     Television Arts and Sciences.   (9 times a year)
        Issued to academy members, with information
     about the industry and its members.

978   Screen Actor.   Hollywood: Screen Actors Guild.
        (quarterly)
        Sent to SAG members, with news of the Guild
     and the film and television industries.

979   Variety (Daily).   Hollywood: Daily Variety Ltd.
        (daily)
        Daily newspaper of the entertainment industry.

980   Variety.   New York: Variety, Inc.   (weekly)
        Weekly newspaper of the entertainment industry,
     radio, television, theater, and movies.   Also fol-
     lows cable television and videocassette developments.

H.   Technical

981   Broadcast Engineering.   Overland Park, Kan.: Inter-
        tec Publishing Corp.   (monthly)
        Edited for corporate management, technicians /
     engineers, and other station personnel at commer-
     cial and educational broadcast stations.

982   Communications / Engineering Digest.   Denver: Titsch
        Publishing Co., Inc.   (monthly)
        Reports the technologies of broadband communi-
     cations.

983   Communicator. Washington, D. C. : National Associa-
         tion of Radio-telephone Systems. (monthly)
            Technical journal for radiotelephone systems.

984   EDN (for Designers and Design Managers in Electronics).
         Boston: Cahners Publishing Co. (bi-monthly)
            Technical publication for designers in electronics.

985   Electronics. New York: McGraw-Hill, Inc. (bi-
         weekly)
            Contains articles and information on such topics
         as cable-TV, telecommunications, spectrometers,
         voltage regulators, demodulators, and spectrum
         analyzers.

986   Journal of the SMPTE (Society of Motion Picture and
         Television Engineers). Scarsdale, N.Y. : Society
         of Motion Picture and Television Engineers.
         (monthly)
            For managers, scientists, and engineers in tele-
         vision, motion pictures, and related fields. Covers
         technical aspects of TV and motion picture produc-
         tion. Includes American standards and recommended
         practices related to test films of the SMPTE.

987   Multicast. Rockville Centre, N.Y. : Paul Kagan Asso-
         ciates, Inc. (bi-weekly)
            Newsletter of record for the new Multipoint Dis-
         tribution Service Industry. MDS is the closed-cir-
         cuit common carrier microwave TV and data trans-
         mission field established by the FCC.

I.   Cable Television

988   Blue Sky. Denver: Denver Community Video Center.
         (bi-monthly)
            Newsletter which promotes exchange of informa-
         tion about cable and community television.

989   Broadband Communications Report. New York: Broad-
         band Information Services, Inc. (bi-monthly)
            Newsletter which reports on all aspects of cable
         and other emerging technologies for policymakers,
         franchising authorities, users, and systems manu-
         facturers.

990 Broadcasting--Cable. New York: Broadcasting - Cable.
     (monthly)
          Consumer newsletter aimed at keeping concerned
     citizens abreast of issues involved in regulation and
     litigation.

991 CATJ (Community Antenna Television Journal).   Okla-
     homa City: Community Antenna Television Associa-
     tion, Inc. (monthly)
          Mostly technical information about CATV.

992 CATV Weekly (Newsweekly of Cable Television).
     Englewood, Colo.: Communications Publishing
     Corp. (weekly)
          Weekly news magazine of cable television, pub-
     lished every Monday.   Each issue includes a fran-
     chise summary, a regular column "On Capitol Hill,"
     and a news summary from the Washington bureau.

993 CM/E (Cable Management/Engineering).   New York:
     Broadband Information Services, Inc. (monthly)
          Carries articles of interest to those responsible
     for operating radio/television/cable facilities.   In-
     cludes regular feature interpreting FCC rules and
     regulations.

994 Cable News. Oklahoma City: Cable Communications
     Corp. (weekly)
          For cable television operators and others inte-
     rested in cable.

995 Cable Tech. Englewood, Colo.: C. T. Publishing,
     Inc.
          The technical journal for cable television.

996 Cablecast. Rockville Centre, N.Y.: Paul Kagan Asso-
     ciates, Inc. (bi-weekly)
          Newsletter on cable TV finance.

997 Cablecasting and Cable TV Engineering. Ridgefield,
     Conn.: C. S. Tepfer Publishing Co., Inc. (bi-
     monthly)
          For the owners, operators, and chief technical
     personnel of cable systems.

998 Cablelines. Washington, D.C.: Cable Communications
     Resource Center. (monthly)

Carries articles of interest to minorities in the cable and broadcasting industries.

999   CableVision.   Denver: Titsch Publishing Co. , Inc.
       (bi-weekly)
       Contains articles and ads concerning cable tele-
       vision.

1000 CableVision's Tech Review.   Denver: Titsch Publish-
       ing Co. , Inc.

1001 The I. E. E. E. Transactions on Cable Television.   New
       York: The Institute of Electrical and Electronics
       Engineers, Inc.   (bi-monthly)
       Includes significant technical papers on all as-
       pects of cable television engineering.

1002 Notes From the Center.   Washington, D. C. :   Cable
       Television Information Center.
       Newsletter containing current information con-
       cerning cable television.

1003 The Originator.   Malvern, Pa. :   Broadband Communi-
       cations Networks, Inc.   (monthly)
       Newsletter for cable television operators and
       aspiring user groups on current developments in
       programming and technical innovations in CATV in
       the U. S. and Canada.

1004 Perspective on Cable Television.   Washington, D. C. :
       National Cable Television Association.   (bi-monthly)
       An issue-oriented newsletter concerning major
       developments in the cable television industry.

1005 TVC Communications.   Englewood, Colo. :   Communi-
       cations Publishing Corp.   (monthly)
       The professional journal of cable television.
       Each issue includes feature articles on cable tech-
       nology, local origination, and cable management
       as well as a summary of monthly news events.

1006 Urban Telecommunications Forum.   New York: Ur-
       ban Telecommunications Forum.   (monthly)
       Newsletter concerned with the implications of
       cable communications for urban affairs generally.

J. Financial

1007 Broadcast Investor. Rockville Centre, N. Y. :   Paul
      Kagan Associates, Inc.
          Newsletter containing financial data on buying
      and selling radio-TV stations.

1008 Communications Investor. Rockville Centre, N. Y. :
      Paul Kagan Associates, Inc. (bi-weekly)
          Newsletter on investments in radio-TV, cable
      TV, newspaper publishing, and other communica-
      tions companies, both private and public.

K. International

1009 CTVD. Newberry, S. C. : Hampton Books.   (quarter-
      ly)
          Reviews the serious foreign-language cinema
      and television press, plus original articles.

1010 EBU Review, Geneva edition (Programmes Adminis-
      tration, Law). Geneva: European Broadcasting
      Union (EBU). (bi-monthly)
          Published by the European Broadcasting Union,
      every other issue is devoted to programs, admin-
      istration, and law of European and other foreign
      and international systems; alternating month is a
      technical issue.   Perhaps the best source of
      scholarly analysis and writings by foreign broad-
      casters on comparative systems.

1011 International Radio & Television Society Newsletter.
      New York: International Radio and Television
      Society (IRTS).   (monthly)
          For IRTS members, with information concern-
      ing the organization.

1012 Radio/Television: Review of the International Radio
      & Television Organization. Prague, Czechoslo-
      vakia: U. Mrazovky. (bi-monthly)
          International journal of radio/television with
      articles in various languages.   Articles include
      both production and technical.

1013 Telecommunication Journal. Geneva: International
      Telecommunication Union.   (monthly)

Covers technology, union news, latest equipment, and work in telecommunications. Printed in English, Spanish, and French.

1014 Telecommunications Reports. Washington, D.C. : Telecommunications Publishing Co. (weekly)
Newsletter which covers legislative, regulatory, tax, and business developments affecting the domestic and international telecommunications industry, including satellite communications.

1015 Television International. Hollywood: Television International Publications, Ltd. (bi-monthly)
Coverage of European and American television technology and programming. Contains editorials, book reviews, and interviews. Distributed to 138 countries.

1016 Television/Radio Age International. New York: Television Editorial Corp. (quarterly)
Contains articles concerned with international broadcasting.

L. Industrial

1017 Broadcast News. Camden, N.J. : RCA. (quarterly)
Gives data, specifications, and applications of new company products.

1018 Business Radio/Action. Washington, D.C. : National Association of Business and Education Radio, Inc. (monthly)
Primarily for business radio users.

1019 Educational and Industrial Television. Ridgefield, Conn. : C. S. Tepfer Publishing Co., Inc. (monthly)
Contains technical and practical information related to educational and industrial television. Also contains a section on VTR technology. Periodical directories of TV equipment. Bi-monthly section regarding cartridge cassette formats.

1020 Industrial Photography. New York: Industrial Photography. (monthly)
Magazine for in-house photographers and

communications departments, covering production
and applications of still photography, audio-visuals,
motion picture; trends in visual communications
and relevant new equipment. Incorporates Videography, quarterly supplement on television
techniques and systems for business and industry.

M. FCC

1021 Client. Madison: University of Wisconsin Depart-
      ment of Communication Arts. (tri-annual)
          Mimeographed newsletter with invaluable infor-
      mation on broadcasting and cable regulation.

1022 Federal Communications Bar Journal. Washington,
      D. C. : Federal Communications Bar Association.
      (3 times a year)
          Legal research articles on all aspects of broad-
      cast and telecommunications regulation including
      analysis of FCC and Congressional action (or inac-
      tion). Began in 1947.

1023 Federal Communications Commission Reports. Wash-
      ington, D. C. : U. S. Government Printing Office.
      (weekly)
          Weekly pamphlet of text of decisions, reports,
      public notices, and other documents of the FCC
      and bound volumes of such pamphlets with detailed
      index-digest of contents.

1024 Perry's Broadcasting and the Law. Knoxville, Tenn. :
      Perry Associates, Inc. (bi-weekly)
          Management newsletter on current changes in
      regulation of broadcasting with many question-
      answer overviews of entire areas of regulatory
      controversy.

1025 Radio Regulation--Pike & Fischer. Washington, D. C. :
      Pike & Fischer, Inc. (weekly)
          Newsletter which cites cases and rulings deal-
      ing with broadcasting and cable.

N.   Minorities

1026   AWRT News and Views. Washington, D. C. : American
       Women in Radio and Television (AWRT).   (bi-monthly)
           Newsletter sent to members covering AWRT lo-
       cal, regional, and national meetings and other ac-
       tivities.

1027   The Matrix.   Austin, Tex. :   Women in Communica-
       tion, Inc.   (quarterly)
           Journal of Women in Communication, the pro-
       fessional society for women in journalism and com-
       munications, with professional articles on issues
       concerning women in the fields of communications.

1028   Media Report to Women. Washington, D. C. :   Media
       Report to Women.   (monthly)
           Newsletter on what women are doing and think-
       ing about the communications media.

O.   Journalism

1029   Columbia Journalism Review.   New York: Columbia
       University.   (bi-monthly)
           Critical articles on press, film and television,
       focusing on public service and media responsibility
       issues with about 6 to 8 such articles per issue
       by national figures within and outside the media.
       This is now one of many journalism reviews, but
       most of the more recent ones focus on press and
       usually cover a limited geographic area in content
       and circulation while CJR has a national scope.
       Began in 1962.

1030   The Journalism Educator.   Reno, Nevada: Associa-
       tion for Education in Journalism.   (quarterly)
           Founded by the American Society of Journalism
       School Administrators and published by AEJ to
       promote excellence in teaching to prepare men and
       women for news media careers.

1031   Journalism Quarterly.   Athens, Ohio: Association for
       Education in Journalism.   (quarterly)
           Academic research on all aspects of American
       and foreign media journalism with excellent large
       book and journal review sections and annotated
       bibliographies.

1032 Quill. Chicago: Society of Professional Journalists.
          (monthly)
          For newspaper reporters and editors, photogra-
      phers, radio and television newsmen and newswo-
      men, freelance writers, students and teachers of
      journalism.

P. General

See also no. 837.

1033 Access. Washington, D. C. : National Citizens Com-
          mittee for Broadcasting. (bi-weekly)
          Critical review of broadcasting industry from
      National Citizens Committee on Broadcasting, em-
      phasizing consumer-related policy issues.

1034 Action: World Association for Christian Communica-
          tion Newsletter. London: World Association for
      Christian Communication. (10 times a year)
          Contains news about Christian communication
      from around the world.

1035 BM/E (Broadcast Management/Engineering). New
          York: Broadband Information Services, Inc.
      (monthly)
          Combination management and technical journal
      with good summaries of FCC policies and regula-
      tions; issues a supplement on cable management
      and engineering topics.

1036 Better Broadcasts News. Madison, Wisc. : American
          Council for Better Broadcasts. (5 times a year)
          Newsletter which reports news of radio and tele-
      vision, with an emphasis on efforts by various
      groups to encourage better broadcasts. Evaluates
      programs, publishes articles on trends, and lists
      current reading on broadcasting and future special
      programs.

1037 Better Radio and Television. Topanga, Calif. : Na-
          tional Association for Better Broadcasting. (quar-
      terly)
          Covers programming and responsibilities of
      broadcasters, licensees, and government agencies
      from the viewpoint of the consumer.

1038   Broadcasting. Washington, D. C. : Broadcasting Pub-
              lications, Inc. (weekly)
              The single most important broadcasting trade
       periodical. Although it usually takes a strong pro-
       industry editorial stance, it is indispensable for
       understanding current events, especially those con-
       cerning broadcast management and government re-
       lations. Issues annually the basic reference
       Broadcasting Yearbook (1935) and the similar
       Cable Sourcebook (1971), both of which provide de-
       tails on all stations (or systems), plus overall sta-
       tistical reviews.

1039   Christian Communications. Ottawa, Canada: Christian
              Communications. (quarterly)
              Discusses the fundamental problems as to what
       constitutes the civilized and Christian use of the
       technological power of modern media.

1040   Code News. Washington, D. C. : Code Authority, Na-
              tional Association of Broadcasters. (monthly)
              Newsletter about the Radio and Television Codes
       and other matters related to broadcast self-regula-
       tion.

1041   Communication Research: An International Quarterly.
              Ann Arbor: University of Michigan Department of
       Journalism and Program in Mass Communication.
       (quarterly)
              Deals with communications research in the
       fields of political science, psychology, economics,
       sociology, marketing, speech, and journalism.
       A major concern is unification of common commu-
       nications-research interests.

1042   FOI Digest. Columbia: Freedom of Information
              (FOI) Center, University of Missouri.
              Published periodically to summarize information
       and news about the media and to list recent books
       and articles in periodicals and law reviews.

1043   Freedom of Information Clearinghouse. Washington,
              D. C. : Freedom of Information Clearinghouse.
              The Press Information Center was established
       in 1973 by Ralph Nader's Freedom of Information
       Clearinghouse. Its purpose is to provide legal
       and technical assistance to journalists in obtaining

access to information from the federal government.
A pamphlet entitled "The Freedom of Information
Act: What It Is and How To Use It" is available.

1044   Highlights. Washington, D. C. : National Association
          of Broadcasters (NAB). (weekly)
          Newsletter for executives of NAB-member radio
       and television stations and networks, as well as
       equipment manufacturers, suppliers and film and
       transcription companies which are NAB associate
       members.

1045   Human Communications. Fairfield, Conn. : Fairfield
          University. (3 times a year)
          Published three times a year with articles on
       interpersonal and mass communications.

1046   Impact. Chicago: Impact Publications. (monthly)
          Monthly newsletter on communications trends
       and techniques for editors, public relations execu-
       tives, and communicators.

1047   InformaTIOn. New York: Television Information Of-
          fice (TIO). (quarterly)
          Newsletter on publications and activities of TIO
       and its sponsor stations.

1048   Journal of Broadcasting. Athens: University of
          Georgia. (quarterly)
          A scholarly research journal with coverage of
       broadcast journalism, violence and the media, in-
       ternational and foreign systems of broadcasting,
       cable television, audience research, entertainment
       programming, children and television, political
       broadcasting, broadcast regulation, history of
       radio-TV, etc. Began in 1956.

1049   Journal of Communication. Philadelphia: The Annen-
          berg School Press (in cooperation with the Inter-
          national Communication Association). (quarterly)
          Especially since 1974 editorial revision has
       published heavily in mass communications field,
       with research and opinion material as well as re-
       views.

1050   Journal of Popular Culture. Bowling Green, Ohio:
          Bowling Green University. (quarterly)

Publication of Popular Culture Association, with coverage of advertising, amusements, art, biography, broadcasting and cinema, humor, comics, fiction, and music.

1051   Mass Comm Review.   Philadelphia: Association for Education in Journalism, Mass Comm and Society Division, Temple University.
        Serially published journal of research and opinion relating to mass communication and society.

1052   Mass Media Booknotes.   Philadelphia: Temple University.   (monthly)
        Newsletter with brief descriptive reviews of the latest books on broadcasting and other media. Each August issue reviews the year's media-oriented government documents.

1053   Mass Media Newsletter.   Baltimore, Md.: Mass Media Associates, Inc.   (bi-weekly)
        Devoted to a "responsible encounter between the Church and the Arts." Covers films, movies, television, drama, and filmstrips.

1054   Media Ecology Review.   New York: New York University.   (quarterly)
        Coverage of mass communications as means of communicating environmental data; newsletter of New York University graduate program in this field.

1055   Media Industry Newsletter.   New York: Business Magazines, Inc.   (weekly)
        Reports, analyzes, and evaluates developments in the media industry. Also includes reports of book and magazine industry topics, broadcasting and cable TV, advertising agencies, and Wall Street as it affects media.

1056   Media Information.   New York: Communication Commission, National Council of Churches.   (monthly)
        Newsletter which deals with new trends in media, cable involvement at national and local levels, citizen involvement in media trends, new technologies, and detailed resources. Incorporates former Cable Information.

1057   Media Watch. Washington, D. C. : National Citizens
            Committee for Broadcasting. (monthly)
            Newsletter for the National Citizens Committee
       for Broadcasting.

1058   Motion Picture Product Digest. New York: Motion
            Picture Product Digest. (25 times a year)
            A newsletter and film review service for the
       motion picture and television industries.

1059   Nieman Reports. Cambridge, Mass. : Society of Nie-
            man Fellows. (quarterly)
            Review carrying commentary and criticism of
       the mass media.

1060   The Pay TV Newsletter. Rockville Centre, N. Y. :
            Paul Kagan Associates, Inc. (bi-weekly)
            On industrial and regulatory developments in
       pay television.

1061   Political Communication Bulletin. Washington, D. C. :
            American Institute for Political Communication.
            (monthly)
            Newsletter which highlights the findings from
       analyses of current media and governmental activi-
       ties. Also summarizes major opinion polls and
       arguments for/against proposed publicities.

1062   Public Opinion Quarterly. New York: Columbia Uni-
            versity. (quarterly)
            Journal of research in polling, the mass media,
       and communications processes. Articles relating
       to public opinion polls, mass media, survey me-
       thods, and communications effects.

1063   RTNDA Communicator. Washington, D. C. : Radio
            Television News Directors Association. (monthly)
            Newsletter for radio-television news directors.
       Devoted particularly to matters of government reg-
       ulation and freedom of information, but also con-
       taining news about the Association and the field of
       news broadcasting.

1064   Signal. Falls Church, Va. : Armed Forces Communi-
            cations and Electronics Association. (monthly)
            Technical and non-technical information concern-
       ing communications and the armed forces.

1065 <u>WACC Journal</u>. Federal Republic of Germany: World
      Association for Christian Communication. (quar-
      terly)
         News of broadcasting in the Christian world.

21. REFERENCES

A. Radio

1066 Buxton, Frank and Bill Owen. The Big Broadcast:
      1920-1950. New York: Viking Press, 1972.
      301 pp.
         Compendium of casts, backstage talent, program
      themes, stars, stock lines, theme songs, and more
      from music, drama, and sports programs, quiz
      shows, and variety hours. Good reference to early
      radio. Bibliography, index, and photographs.

1067 Dunning, John. Tune in Yesterday: The Ultimate En-
      cyclopedia of Old-Time Radio, 1925-1976. Engle-
      wood Cliffs, N.J.: Prentice-Hall, 1976. 703 pp.
         Provides an alphabetical listing of all network
      drama, comedy, and variety programs.

1068 Pitts, Michael R. Radio Soundtracks: A Reference
      Guide. Metuchen, N.J.: Scarecrow Press, 1976.
      169 pp.
         Describes what is available on records and tapes
      of network programs from 1926 to the 1950s,
      covering drama, variety, and other entertainment
      formats.

1069 Terman, Frederick Emmons. Radio Engineers' Hand-
      book. New York: McGraw-Hill, 1943. 1019 pp.
         A reference book summarizing the body of en-
      gineering knowledge that is the basis of radio and
      electronics. Charts, illustrations, and index.

1070 Variety Radio Directory. New York: Variety, Inc.,
      1937-1938 through 1940-1941.
         Issued for only four years, the Variety Radio
      Directory is of limited value today as most of the

211

data in it are obtainable in the annuals which lasted
over a longer period of time. Still, while offering
the massive station and other data typical with such
large books, it is of interest today especially for
its data on program favorites and preferences each
year, plus financial information on the industry.
Index.

B. Television

1071 Comstock, George and Marilyn Fisher. Television
      and Human Behavior: A Guide to the Pertinent
      Scientific Literature. Volume I. Santa Monica,
      Calif.: Rand Corp., 1975. 344 pp.
          First in a series of three studies, this offers
      2,300 reference with brief annotations, including
      research still in progress in 1974-1975. In addi-
      tion, offers 11 specialized bibliographies.

1072 Comstock, George, et al. Television and Human Be-
      havior: The Key Studies. Volume II. Santa
      Monica, Calif.: Rand Corp., 1975. 251 pp.
          More detailed coverage of some 450 journal
      articles, books, and other studies thought particu-
      larly important.

1073 Comstock, George and Eli Rubinstein. Television and
      Social Behavior: Media Content and Control, 5
      volumes. Washington, D.C.: U.S. Department of
      Health, Education, and Welfare, 1972. 546 pp.
          A technical report to the Surgeon General's Sci-
      entific Advisory Committee on Television and So-
      cial Behavior. The major emphasis is on an ex-
      amination of the relationship between televised vio-
      lence and the attitudes and behavior of children.
      Charts.

1074 Kempner, Stanley. Television Encyclopedia. New
      York: Fairchild, 1948. 415 pp.
          A useful three-part reference work: the first
      40 pages offers a chronology of TV history, the
      next 90 pages is a collection of short biographies
      of key TV pioneers and then contemporaries, and
      the last and longest portion is a non-technical dic-
      tionary of TV's technical terms. There is a brief
      concluding discussion on the likely urban TV

market of the late 1940s.   Throughout, the emphasis is on the background and development of the
medium.   Bibliography, illustrations, and photographs.

1075 Parish, James Robert.   Actors' Television Credits
      (1950-1972).   Metuchen, N. J. : Scarecrow Press,
      1973.   869 pp.
      Provides the first authoritative single source
and documentation for the spectrum of entertainment performances of a wide range of video players, from stars to character players.

C.   Public Television

1076 National Association of Educational Broadcasters.
      Public Telecommunications Directory.   Washington,
      D. C. :   NAEB.
      Lists both individual NAEB members and public
radio and television stations in the United States.

D.   Programming

1077 Terrace, Vincent.   The Complete Encyclopedia of
      Television Programs, 1947-1976, 2 volumes.
      South Brunswick, N. J. : A. S. Barnes, 1976.
      900 pp.
      A collection of data listed alphabetically giving
lines of what the show does, cast, length of epi-
sodes, network, and dates of start and stop, and
an indication of whether the show was syndicated.

E.   Advertising

1078 Macdonald, Jack.   Handbook of Radio Publicity &
      Promotion.   Blue Ridge Summit, Pa. : TAB
      Books, 1970.   372 pp.
      This handbook is a virtual promotion encyclo-
pedia--includes over 250,000 words, over 1,500
on-air promo themes adaptable to any format, and
over 350 contests, stunts, station and personality
promos.   One idea alone of the hundreds offered
can be worth many times the small cost of this indispensable sourcebook.

1079   Vigrolio, Tom and Jack Zahler.   Marketing and Com-
          munications Media Dictionary.   Norfolk, Mass. :
          NBS Publishing Co. , 1969.   423 pp.
             An illustrated dictionary with strong reference
          value.   Illustrations.

F.   Technical

1080   Marsh, Ken.   Independent Video: A Complete Guide
          to the Physics, Operation, and Application of the
          New Television for the Student, the Artist and for
          Community TV.   San Francisco: Straight Arrow
          Books, 1974.   212 pp.
             The sub-title tells it all.

1081   Matlon, Ronald J. and Irene R. Matlon.   Index to
          Journals in Communication Studies Through 1974.
          Falls Church, Va. :   Speech Communication Asso-
          ciation, 1976.   365 pp.
             This book, of considerable value to authors,
          editors, and researchers, is an issue-by-issue
          table of contents, an index of subjects, and an in-
          dex of contributors for 13 journals.   One of the
          major topics is mass communication, which makes
          this a handy bibliographic reference, even if most
          of it refers to other than mass communication
          matters.   Index.

G.   General

1082   American Women in Radio and Television, Inc.   The
          World of A. W. R. T.   Washington, D. C. :   Ameri-
          can Women in Radio and Television, Inc. , 1974.
          16 pp.
             A compilation of information on women employed
          in executive, administrative, creative and on-air
          positions in the broadcast industry, broadcast ad-
          vertising, and closely allied fields.   It contains
          the results of a recent membership survey with
          statistics on such areas as the types of jobs held,
          income and responsibilities, education, discrimina-
          tion, advancement, and the private lives of A. W.
          R. T. members.

1083   BM/E Magazine Editors.   Interpreting FCC Broadcast

Rules & Regulations, Volumes 1-3. Blue Ridge
Summit, Pa. : TAB Books, 1968-1972.
These reference-guidebooks discuss the most
important FCC rulings, with hints on how these
rulings apply in actual station operation. Volume
3 includes cable rules.

1084 Diamant, Lincoln, ed. _The Broadcast Communications Dictionary_. New York: Hastings House
Publishers, 1974. 128 pp.
Defines broadcasting terms from A to Z. Good
reference for the student of broadcasting.

1085 Herling, Michele, ed. _The American Film Institute
Guide to College Courses in Film and Television_.
Washington, D. C. : Acropolis Books, 1973.
308 pp.
Provides data on program aims, specific
courses offered, faculty, facilities, etc.

1086 Jacobson, Howard Boone, ed. _A Mass Communications Dictionary_. New York: Philosophical Library, 1961. 377 pp.
A heavily printed technology oriented dictionary.

1087 Kahn, Frank J. , ed. _Documents of American Broad-
casting_. 2nd edition. Englewood Cliffs, N. J. :
Prentice-Hall, 1973. 684 pp.
A basic historical reference providing a valuable reference and text of legal documents on
broadcasting from 1910 to the early 1970s. Bibliography and illustrations.

1088 Kirschner, Allen and Linda Kirschner, eds. _Radio
and Television: Readings in the Mass Media_.
New York: Odyssey, 1971. 301 pp.
Contains sections on form and technique, audience and effect, and critics and criticism. Bibliography.

1089 Levitan, Eli L. _An Alphabetical Guide to Motion Pic-
ture, Television, and Videotape Production_. New
York: McGraw-Hill, 1970. 797 pp.
A very useful dictionary with clear explanations
of the major production equipment and procedures.
Illustrations.

1090   Lichty, Lawrence W. and Malachi C. Topping, eds.
       American Broadcasting: A Source Book on the
       History of Radio and Television. New York:
       Hastings House Publishers, 1975. 745 pp.
       Combining a skillfully edited anthology of over
       90 selections from the literature of broadcasting
       with text and supplementary commentaries, this is
       a unique source book. Bibliography, charts, and
       photographs.

1091   Newsfilm Standards Conference. A Guidebook and
       Working Manual for Students and Professionals.
       New York: Time-Life Broadcasting, Inc., 1964.
       90 pp.
       A brief conference symposium issued by the
       Radio Television News Directors' Association and
       Time-Life Broadcast, this book is a useful film
       standards manual.

1092   Rivers, William L. and William Slater, eds. Aspen
       Handbook on the Media: Research, Publications,
       Organizations. 2nd edition. Palo Alto, Calif.:
       Aspen Program on Communications and Society,
       1975. 195 pp.
       Good reference for funding sources, publica-
       tions, government bodies, etc. This guide is to
       be revised regularly. Bibliography.

1093   Rose, Ernest D. World Film and Television Study
       Resources: A Reference Guide to Major Training
       Centers and Archives. Bonn, Germany: Fried-
       rich-Ebert-Stiftung, 1974. 421 pp.
       The first such international guide since a 1950
       UNESCO effort, this reviews both schools and ar-
       chives of film and TV material in all areas of the
       world with addresses and other details.

1094   Seligman, Norman, ed. The Working Press of the
       Nation (Volume III): Radio and Television Direc-
       tory. Chicago: National Research Bureau, 1964.
       Includes names and descriptions of local pro-
       grams with personnel involved, complete data
       about all major radio and TV stations, including
       power, news service, and executive personnel.

1095   Sharp, Harold S. and Marjorie Z. Sharp, compilers.
       Index to Characters in the Performing Arts. Part

IV: <u>Radio and Television</u>. Metuchen, N.J.: Scarecrow Press, 1973. 697 pp.
Like other books in the series, the object of this one is to identify characters with the productions in which they appear. It also gives a little information concerning each character and designates the type of each program.

1096 Smith, Bruce Lannes; Harold D. Lasswell; and Ralph D. Casey. <u>Propaganda, Communication, and Public Opinion: A Comprehensive Reference Guide.</u> Princeton, N.J.: Princeton University Press, 1946. 435 pp.
This volume consists of four introductory essays and an expansive annotated bibliography which covers pages 119-392. Bibliography, charts, and index.

1097 Spottiswoode, Raymond; Bernard Happe; and Eric Vast, eds. <u>The Focal Encyclopedia of Film and Television Techniques.</u> New York: Hastings House Publishers, 1969. 1,124 pp.
Consult this volume for the answer to any questions concerning film and television techniques-- whether it involves the technique itself, its application, or its production process, or whether you want detailed information on acoustics or zoom lens. Illustrations and index.

1098 Sterling, Christopher H. <u>The Media Sourcebook: Comparative Reviews and Listings of Textbooks in Mass Communication.</u> Washington, D.C.: National Association of Educational Broadcasters, 1974. 53 pp.
Reprint of six articles from NAEB journals providing comparative evaluations of some 350 volumes suitable for text use in mass communications generally, and broadcasting specifically. All published in the 1960-1973 period. Bibliography.

1099 Weber, Olga S. <u>North American Film and Video Directory: A Guide to Media Collections and Services.</u> New York: R. R. Bowker, 1976. 284 pp.
Information on some 2,000 college, public, and special libraries and media centers listed alphabetically by state, with a separate 25-page section covering Canada. Index.

1100   Zelmer, A. C. Lynn. Community Media Handbook.
       Metuchen, N.J. : Scarecrow Press, 1973. 241 pp.
       This handbook provides the basic data common-
       ly encountered by community groups. It is pri-
       marily designed to be a reference and training tool
       for community and volunteer groups. Bibliography,
       charts, glossary, illustrations, index, and photo-
       graphs.

AUTHOR INDEX

This index also includes magazines, journals, societies and organizations.